HOME FRONT
SOLDIER

HOME FRONT SOLDIER

The Story of a GI and His Italian American Family During World War II

RICHARD AQUILA

State University
of New York
Press

The publication of this book was supported by a grant from Ball State University's Publications and Intellectual Properties Committee.

Photo reproductions by John Huffer, Ball State University Photo Services.

Published by
State University of New York Press, Albany

D811
.A646
1999

Production by Susan Geraghty
Marketing by Dana Yanulavich

Printed in the United States of America

For information, address State University of New York
Press, State University Plaza, Albany, N.Y., 12246

Library of Congress Cataloging-in-Publication Data

Aquila, Philip L., d. 1994.
    Home front soldier : the story of a GI and his Italian American family during World War II / Richard Aquila.
       p.   cm.
    Letters written by Philip L. Aquila to his family, addressed to his sister, Mary.
    Includes bibliographical references and index.
    ISBN 0-7914-4075-3 (hc : alk. paper). — ISBN 0-7914-4076-1 (pb : alk. paper)
    1. Aquila, Philip L., d. 1994—Correspondence. 2. World War, 1939–1945—Personal narratives, American. 3. United States. Army-
-Biography. 4. Soldiers—United States—Correspondence. 5. Italian Americans—Correspondence. 6. Family life. 7. Buffalo (N.Y.)-
-Social life and customs. I. Aquila, Mary. II. Aquila, Richard. III. Title.
D811.A646 1999
940.54'8173—dc21
                                   98-4321
                                   CIP

10 9 8 7 6 5 4 3 2 1

Dedicated to:

Philip L. Aquila,
who wrote in 1945 that he wanted to be
"the grandest Dad any boy ever had."
He succeeded.

CONTENTS

ILLUSTRATIONS

ACKNOWLEDGMENTS

This book would not have been possible without the help of four extremely important people. Philip L. Aquila cared enough for his family and posterity to write letters home every single day that he was in the Army Air Force during World War II. His sister, Mary (Aquila) Pardi, had the wherewithal to save the letters for over fifty years. His brother, Frank Aquila, understood the personal and historical importance of the letters and made sure they were returned to Phil's widow and sons. Finally, Phil's wife of fifty years, Mary (Cavarella) Aquila, provided additional pieces of correspondence and answers to many questions that made this project both possible and worthwhile.

Other individuals contributed to this project in a variety of ways of which they sometimes were not even aware. During World War II, Phil received the love and support of his entire family—his mother, Calogera; father, Francesco; six brothers, Joe, Tony, Sam (Shadow), Frankie, Carmen, and Carlo; and two sisters, Mary and Francie. After the war, he took great pride and comfort in his "new" family—his wife, Mary, and two sons, Phil Jr. and Dick. He later welcomed into the family two daughters-in-law, Phil Jr.'s wife, Sandy, and Dick's wife, Marie. In his later years, Phil became the proud, loving grandfather of Stephen and Valerie Aquila.

In short, all acknowledgments must begin and end with Phil Aquila and his family, because that is what this book is all about—family.

PART 1

Introduction: "What Did You Do in the War, Pop?"

My father, Philip L. Aquila, died on December 2, 1994. A few weeks later, I was talking long-distance to my mother when she dropped a bombshell right in the middle of the conversation: "Your Uncle Frank called the other day. He said Aunt Mary told him that she had some letters Dad had written to his family during World War II and that we could have them if we wanted them."

Naturally, I said we should jump at the chance, but I was curious how many letters there were. "Uncle Frank just said there were lots," came the reply.

All sorts of possibilities rushed into my head. For personal reasons I was anxious to read about what my Dad had to say. He, my older brother, and I always used to talk about politics and other things, and in a way, it would be like Dad was still around. But I also hoped that these letters could be more than just one last visit with my Dad. Perhaps they could be published as a book. My Dad would have loved that. Although he earned his living as a bricklayer with the Bethlehem Steel Company, his real interests were always history, politics, and geography. His enthusiasm for history rubbed off on me, and he was extremely proud when I later became a professional historian and writer. He always insisted that someday he, too, would write a history book.

That is why when I first heard about the letters I thought how ironic it would be if Dad had already written his book, but none of us had ever realized it. Given my Dad's interests, I suspected that his letters could be a treasure trove of information about World War II.

My biggest concern, though, was whether there would be enough letters to make a book. Exactly how many letters were "lots?" Were we talking ten letters? Twenty letters? Fifty? Since I had barely seen or talked to my father's sister or brother since I had moved away from

Fig. 1.1. Portrait of Philip L. Aquila taken in May 1943, at McChord Field in Washington State. (Philip L. Aquila Collection)

Buffalo to become a history professor almost twenty-five years ago, I didn't feel comfortable enough to ask them directly. So I decided to just wait patiently until the letters arrived. Well, almost patiently. I did nag my mother every week to get my Uncle Frank to drop off the letters, before he forgot or before something happened to the letters.

Eventually the persistence paid off. Several weeks later my mother told me over the phone, "Well, Uncle Frank finally gave me the letters."

"Great," I replied, "how many are there?"

"Lots," she said, "a really big pile."

Not only was I no closer to knowing how many letters "lots" was, but now I also found myself wondering about how big "a really big pile" was. The answers came a few months later when I visited my mother in Buffalo, New York. She handed me a large shopping bag with handles. Inside were approximately five hundred letters that my Dad had written to his family between 1944 and 1946. Included were a few letters that he had received during the war from his brothers who were also in the service. In addition my mother gave me eleven other letters, as well as several poems, that my father had written during the war and then saved in his locked tool chest down in the basement.

Given my father's love of politics and history, I expected detailed accounts of the war effort. But, as I quickly skimmed through the pile, I found very few in-depth descriptions of the war. At first my heart sank with disappointment, because I knew that although I would certainly get personal satisfaction from reading the letters, the correspondence probably did not have enough historical significance to be published as a book. It was not until several weeks later, after I got the letters back to my office and began arranging them chronologically, that I realized what I actually had.

The collection of letters turned out to be very different from what I had expected, but, nonetheless, just as important. Rather than a first-hand account of the war itself, the letters offered a revealing look at a soldier and his family during the war.

THE CORRESPONDENCE OF SGT. PHILIP L. AQUILA

The first thing I noticed about the letters was their vastness and completeness. Hardly a day passed without Phil Aquila writing at least one letter to his family back home in Buffalo. Although he was drafted in February 1943, the letters he wrote throughout 1943 and early 1944 were either destroyed or are missing. The surviving letters cover approximately the last two years of World War II. The first entry is dated August 7, 1944, the last February 4, 1946.

Fig. 1.2. Collage of envelopes containing letters mailed by Philip L. Aquila to his family. (Philip L. Aquila Collection)

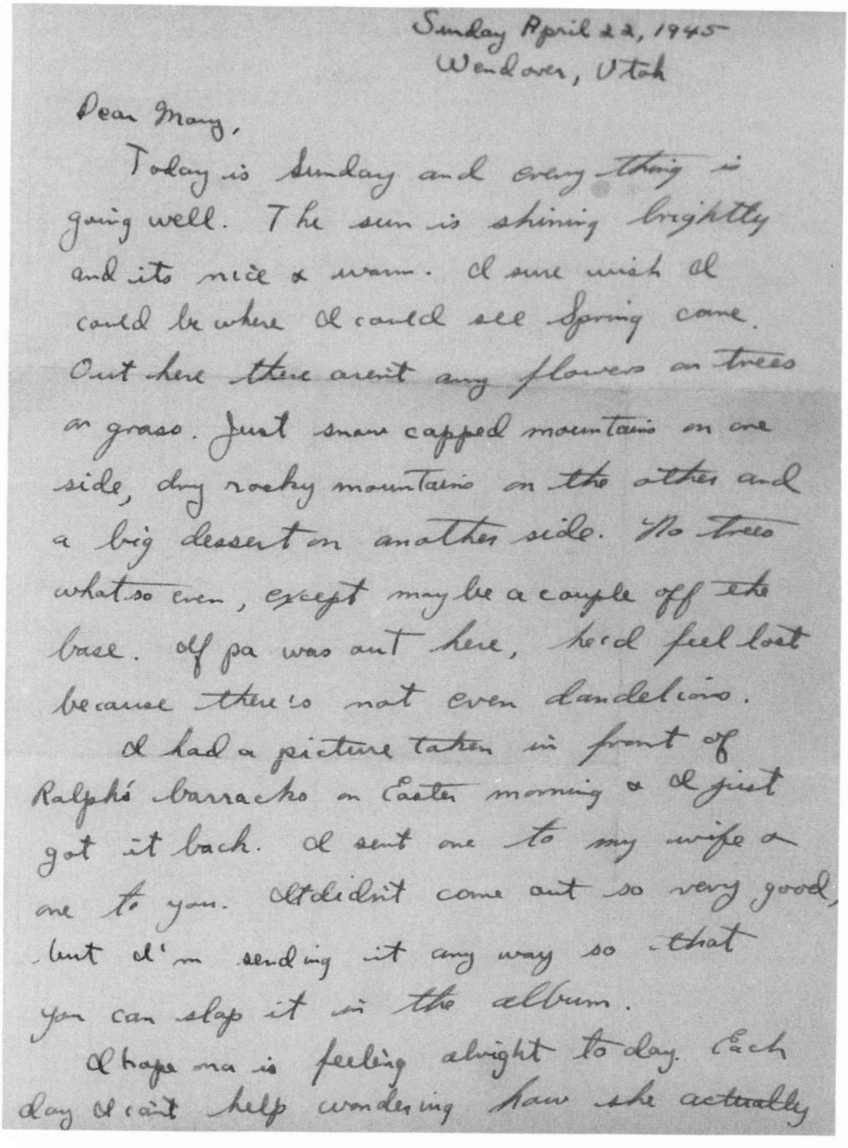

Sunday April 22, 1945
Wendover, Utah

Dear Mary,

Today is Sunday and everything is going well. The sun is shining brightly and its nice & warm. I sure wish I could be where I could see Spring come. Out here there aren't any flowers or trees or grass. Just snow capped mountains on one side, dry rocky mountains on the other and a big dessert on another side. No trees whatsoever, except may be a couple off the base. If pa was out here, he'd feel lost because there is not even dandelions.

I had a picture taken in front of Ralph's barracks on Easter morning & I just got it back. I sent one to my wife & one to you. It didn't come out so very good, but I'm sending it any way so that you can slap it in the album.

I hope ma is feeling alright to day. Each day I can't help wondering how she actually

Fig. 1.3. First page of a letter that Phil Aquila wrote to his sister Mary, on April 22, 1945. (Philip L. Aquila Collection)

Most of the letters are addressed to his older sister, Mary, but they were really being written to his entire family. "The reason he was writing to me was actually very simple," explained his sister in a recent interview, "neither Ma nor Pa could read or write, so Phil would write to me, and I would read the letters to everybody. Then I would place his letters on the table, with any other letters we got from my other brothers in the service, and they would stay there for a few days. Anybody who came into the house could read them."[1]

Even though Mary had two older brothers at home, she was the one who was responsible for maintaining communications with the boys in the service. The Aquilas, like most Italian American families, assumed that the oldest daughter should be in charge of all domestic matters, including the family's correspondence. Occasionally Phil sent personal letters to his older brother, Tony, who was still living at home, or to a younger sibling. But over 95 percent of the letters were sent to Mary, and, therefore, meant to be shared by the entire family.

In addition to the letters home, Phil Aquila was also writing to other people. He wrote regularly to his three brothers, two cousins, and several neighborhood friends who were in the service. Those letters, however, did not survive the war. Most of Phil's correspondence was with his wife, the former Mary Cavarella. Sometimes he wrote her up to seven letters a day, frequently including love poems or poems he wrote for special occasions. It was in these very personal letters that Phil revealed his deepest thoughts and emotions. With the exception of one letter and several poems (some of which are included in this book), none of the letters to his wife now exist. After the war the couple decided to destroy them because the letters were too personal.

Obviously, Phil Aquila was a dedicated letter writer. Usually every evening after dinner (and sometimes during the day), he would settle into his bunk, pen and paper in hand, and begin writing anywhere from two to ten letters a day. During his three years in the Army Air Force, he probably wrote at least 2,500 letters, of which over 500 still survive.

Why did he write so much? The most obvious answer is because he wanted his family and friends to know that he was doing fine. He explained the reason for his numerous, but brief, letters to his sister on November 3, 1944: "Just another little letter short and snappy and to the point as usual. I never make my letters long because I have hardly nothing to say. Just so you hear from me, right?"[2] Six days later, he began another letter as follows: "Just my daily letter again. You see as I told you when I was there [home on furlough], I hardly have nothing at all to say except that everything out here is going along okay, and that I hope it's the same out there. But I figure a letter each day helps Ma stay a little happy."[3]

There were also more complicated reasons why Phil was writing so often. For one thing, he was a very private man who would rather spend his free time with his family than socializing with strangers. Writing letters everyday during the war also may have given him a sense of security, making him think that he was in control of his life and his family's destiny. He believed that his constant letters would help the morale of his family and friends. In addition, the frequent correspondence enabled him to have a continuing say in family matters, and it guaranteed that loved ones would not forget him. The daily letters might also be the result of Phil's sense of history: he was determined to leave a record of where he was and what he was doing during the war.

Sgt. Aquila's letters are written in an informal, conversational style. The basic form and structure of the letters follow the accepted style of the day, which Phil had learned in school just like millions of other working-class students.[4] His strict adherence to the format reveals a deliberate attention to detail and a need to follow established rules.

The similar structure and repetitive phrases of the letters served as literary devices. The sameness of the daily mail undoubtedly assured readers that Phil was doing fine and that nothing had changed. The top of each letter records the exact date and place where Phil was stationed. The salutation follows. Although usually addressed to his sister, Mary, the letter was actually being written for the entire family, especially his mother, Calogera.

The first paragraph of each letter gets right to the point. Frequently he uses a sentence such as this: "October 7 [1944] and all is well out here, and I hope it stays that way." Or, like this one he wrote three days later: "Everything is going okay out here and I hope it's the same out there."[5]

The body of each letter then discusses particular concerns or news of the day. Most often, Phil ends the text with some variation of the phrase, "So long and God bless you all" (e.g. see letter of September 22, 1944).

Every letter uses the same closing: "Love to: Ma, Pa, Mary, Tony, Francie, and Carlo. X X X X X X [i.e. kisses]. Phil." Significantly, his mother, to whom he was devoted, is always mentioned first. Out of respect, his father is mentioned second; then comes his sister Mary, to whom he is writing the letter; next is Tony (who was one year older than Mary); followed by Francie (who was in high school); and last in the pecking order is Carlo, who was still in elementary school.

Though the letters are usually brief, their form, frequency, and sheer numbers imbue them with power. The repetition in the letters' structure and content provides order in a world surrounded by chaos, and the astonishing regularity of the correspondence results in a vast collection of primary-source materials relating to daily life in America during World War II.

THE SIGNIFICANCE OF THE LETTERS

As I began reading the letters one after another in the order in which they were written, I was drawn into Philip Aquila's world of 1944–45. It is a world at war, yet still a world of hope for the future. Like a daily soap opera, fascinating characters appear and disappear, with their story lines always going forward but never quite ending. The main plot revolves around Sgt. Aquila, stationed at Army Air Force bases in Kansas and Utah, and his concern for his family back home. But numerous subplots also unfold in the daily drama: concerns about his new wife, aging parents, brothers, sisters, birth, death, illness, family problems, neighborhood friends, as well as occasional commentary about the war effort and military life.

The narrative's major and minor plots illustrate many of the important issues and themes in American social history of the World War II era. These letters offer valuable insights about family history of the late 1930s and early '40s. They demonstrate that soldiers, especially those stationed at home, often retained close contacts with family and friends. By 1943, the average GI was receiving fourteen letters a week. Sgt. Aquila's correspondence underscores how important this communication with loved ones was to a soldier.[6]

Writing letters back and forth within the United States was relatively easy and inexpensive (free for the soldiers). Mail delivery normally took two to four days from the moment it was mailed to the time it arrived. So soldiers not only could stay in touch with friends and family back home, but they could remain an integral part of the family's daily activities. Phil Aquila, for example, was able to give family members advice about the family car, furniture, finances, health concerns, and personal matters. Rapid mail delivery also enabled him to share other things with his family: he often sent them gum, cigarettes, birthday cards, gifts, and even palms for Palm Sunday. In effect, the rapid and efficient postal service enabled soldiers to play continuing roles in daily family matters even though they were thousands of miles away from home.

Sgt. Aquila's letters constitute an excellent case study of how one American family—with four sons in the war—struggled for its very survival. The correspondence allows us to experience first-hand the rhythms of family life during World War II. We share the family's joy in new marriages, reunions, and births, as well as their sorrow when faced with disappointment, death, and serious illness.

By recording the early years of marriage between Phil and Mary (Cavarella) Aquila, these letters offer fascinating glimpses of GI marriages during World War II. By the spring of 1943, approximately 30 percent of all American soldiers were married.[7] Sgt. Aquila's letters help us understand why so many young couples decided to get married and have babies even though the world was at war. They reflect the hopes and fears, successes and failures of young couples who were trying to establish marriages and new lives during wartime.

The letters capture the sense of helplessness and despair that resulted from soldiers being away from their wives and babies back home. They also demonstrate vividly how in-law problems, misunderstandings, and other marital stresses were exacerbated by both the war and the great distances that separated husbands and wives. The letters illustrate, for example, the concerns—whether warranted or not—that many young soldiers had about unfaithful wives and girlfriends. "Even in the normal person there appears to be considerable apprehension about the fidelity of the soldier's wife or sweetheart," explains one psychiatrist. "Most often in the 'normal' the entire conflict is repressed. But if the question is ever raised, as during a 'bull session,' the conversation becomes charged with considerable feeling."[8]

Since the Aquilas were Italian Americans, their story provides us with details about immigrants and ethnic history. The letters reveal the inner dynamics of an Italian American family. Scholars have written extensively about the "familistic" loyalties of southern Italian peasants, maintaining that the nuclear or extended family took precedence over the individual or even the community.[9] The letters of Philip L. Aquila demonstrate that familism was still important to Italian Americans of the 1940s. The letters show repeatedly that each of the Aquilas viewed his or her primary social role within the context of the family. For example, when Phil's mother becomes ill, his sister Mary willingly forsakes her job in a box factory to care for her mother and keep the family and household functioning. In numerous other cases, Phil and his brothers make it clear that even though they are married and in the military they still want to do their part in helping out the family at home.[10]

The letters provide solid evidence that the Aquila family—like Italian Americans in general—believed in the traditional notion of "onore di famiglia" (family honor). In one letter, Phil strongly encourages his sister to confront a farmer who apparently has cheated the family out of some of their earnings. We can almost see Phil shake his head in frustration as he writes: "Maybe that [farmer] thinks that just because most of us [boys] are in the army, there's no one to take an interest out there."

Perhaps the best example of Phil's dedication to preserving family honor is his response to an individual who threatened not only his life, but also his wife's reputation and safety. Writing to a police officer investigating the case, Sgt. Aquila comes right to the point: "Frankly, Sir, I'd just as soon put a bullet through this person as I would a Nazi or Jap soldier, but fortunately my mind isn't as stupid as this person's. . . . [But] I'll never rest until this [guilty] person is apprehended."[11]

Sgt. Aquila's letters offer insights into the role of women in Italian American families. Contrary to popular myth, many Italian American women were not passive or dependent upon males. Although marriages in the old country supposedly were patriarchal, women often dominated their husbands. "Such a wife would rarely contradict her husband in the presence of strangers," explain historians Jere Mangione and Ben Morreale, "but once left alone with her eldest children, she would drop the mask of docile wife and 'speak her mind openly and eloquently.'" Sociologist Constance Cronin insists that such Italian American women became, in effect, family managers.[12]

The women spotlighted in Sgt. Aquila's letters are clearly independent and dominant personalities. Phil's mother, Calogera, assumes center stage, while the father, Francesco, remains in the shadows. Unlike those Italian American families where the male was dominant, the mother emerged as the honored and cherished head of the Aquila household. The father, though loved, lacked authority. While Phil's letters only occasionally inquire about "Pa," they provide numerous examples of his devotion to "Ma."

Significantly, Calogera was not the only strong-willed woman in Phil Aquila's life. His sister, Mary Aquila, and his wife, Mary (Cavarella) Aquila, also had strong opinions and considerable influence in family discussions. The Aquila letters offer solid evidence that Italian American women frequently played important and active leadership roles in family matters.

Sgt. Aquila's letters provide a detailed account of how one Italian American family responded to the social and cultural crises stemming from the Great Depression and World War II. By demonstrating the stability of the Aquila family, as well as its ability to cope with social change, the letters call into question the work of scholars who stress the disorganization of immigrant families, the importance of cultural continuity for immigrant families, or new family functions that emerged in industrial America. The letters support historian Virginia Yans-McLaughlin's belief that there was "a dynamic process of give and take between new conditions and old social forms as the immigrant families made their transition from Europe to America."[13] Detailed evidence found in these letters suggests that the stability of Italian American families actually facilitated their members' adjustments to social change.

The letters transport us back in time to an Italian American neighborhood in Buffalo, New York, where we are introduced to renters, friends, uncles, aunts, cousins, *compari*, and *paesani*.[14] We observe how this immigrant family works, plays, and lives. We read about the father doing blue-collar work, while the mother takes in day work and leads the children out to the farms where they pick beans and fruits during the summer and early fall.

We can almost smell the salami, sausage, fried peppers, and other foods that are described as we come to understand the cultural importance of food in Italian families. We also come to realize the importance of religion in the Italian American family's daily activities, not necessarily the organized Catholic Church variety, but a more basic everyday faith that God will get them through hard times and crises. We learn about Italian American superstitions and the southern Italians' traditional suspicion of authority figures and institutions. In the Aquilas' case in the 1940s, this included mistrust of doctors, hospitals, and, of course, army officers and politicians.

Phil Aquila's letters demonstrate the impact that public education had on immigrant families. Although their mother and father could not read or write, the Aquila children became fluent in English and were schooled enough in grammar and sentence structure to write legible, coherent letters. At the same time, the letters offer evidence that at least some Italian American and working-class expressions survived Phil's success in learning to write clear, standard English. His letter of May 30, 1945, for example, combined the two: "I didn't go no place, though, just stood on the base and loafed around." That double negative is typical of working-class speech, while the use of the verb "to stand" instead of "to stay" is a literal translation into English of Italian American idiom.[15]

The letters reveal that the Aquila children also acquired a practical education: the boys had the ability to tackle jobs involving mechanical and physical skills, while sister Mary was able to cook, clean, and keep the house functioning.

Some of the brothers demonstrated an interest in reading and world events. Phil, in particular, thoroughly absorbed the lessons and values taught at school. He believed in America as a land of freedom and opportunity, and was convinced that he—a common man—was equal, if not superior, to anybody regardless of their wealth, power, or position in life. A firm believer in the American dream, Phil was determined to accomplish his goals.

Phil's love of education often caused him to try and improve other family members. For example, in one letter he encourages his brother Tony to brief their mother about the war and politics: "You'd be surprised how interested Ma is in geography, history, and world events." In another, he tells his sister, "As for reading, we should've taught [Ma] long ago. It's never too late to learn, you know." In still other letters, he admonishes the two youngest children to attend school and do their homework.[16]

The Aquila letters demonstrate the primary importance of family loyalties and obligations among Italian Americans. The sons were expected to protect family members, take care of home repairs, and contribute money to the household, while the daughters, particularly the eldest, Mary, were supposed to handle domestic chores and provide support for other family members. The close-knit family supported one another as much as possible throughout the war. A network of letters kept family members in constant contact, enabling them to reassure one another and solve any family problems that might arise.

Despite the family's attempts to hold together, World War II still had a devastating impact. Having four sons in the armed forces altered patterns of daily life. Everything seemed to revolve around the boys' safety and whereabouts. Family members at home even stopped celebrating Christmas and other holidays while the boys were at war. The constant worrying eventually drained the mother's strength, endurance, and vitality. Very likely this stress contributed to her illness, a crisis that eventually threatened the family's very existence. Yet, through it all, this Italian American family remained loyal to the United States, even though it was fighting against enemies that included Italy, the Aquilas' original homeland.

While the correspondence of Sgt. Philip L. Aquila teaches us about Italian American families, it also provides us with fascinating glimpses of everyday life in the United States during World War II. Historians frequently write about the upsurge in American patriotism during the war. These letters qualify that interpretation. They show that the Aquila family strongly supported their nation's fight against the Axis powers, but they were not overzealous patriots eager to give their lives for the cause. None of the sons rushed out to enlist; none volunteered for combat; and all retained a strong sense of skepticism about the army and politicians in general. The Aquilas were probably no better or worse than most families of the day. They were willing to contribute their fair share to the war effort, but reluctant to follow their nation blindly.

The letters enable us to experience the rhythms of everyday life. We see people learning to live with war-related shortages of gas, cigarettes, gum, food, and other desirable items. We catch glimpses of life going on as usual in cities and towns across the country. And we learn about Americans' expectations for the future: their faith that the United States would triumph, their hope that the future would be better, and their fear that the Depression might return.

All too often, the story of World War II is told through the lives and actions of famous people, politicians, and military commanders. Sgt. Aquila's correspondence provides us with snapshots of the war from the vantage point of "ordinary soldiers." We learn about GIs' attitudes toward the war. We see how they respond to news about the death of President Roosevelt, the rise of Harry Truman, and other important events. And we see firsthand what daily life was like on military bases in the United States. Phil describes the friendly citizens of Pratt, Kansas, who invited GIs into their homes to share holiday dinners. He also gives us a fascinating insider's view of Wendover Field, the isolated base in Utah where the crew of the Enola Gay trained secretly.

Sgt. Aquila fills in gaps in our knowledge about soldiers stationed in the United States. He captures the daily monotony of military life. He explains what GIs did in their spare time: popular activities included movies, gambling, drinking, carousing, socializing at service clubs, reading newspapers and books, writing letters back home, and worrying about the future and loved ones. He explains how wonderful, but also how difficult and expensive it was, to place long-distance phone calls to people back home. He also helps us understand the highs and lows of furloughs. Soldiers were desperate for leaves that would enable them to go home. Yet getting there and back was often time consuming and expensive. Travel by train was extremely difficult, and parting was indeed sweet sorrow for soldiers and loved ones alike. Sometimes the great expectations that soldiers and family members had for furloughs resulted in disappointment.

The letters are full of surprises. For example, Sgt. Aquila often praises both the quality and quantity of army meals, particularly on holidays. "It just burns me up," he complains to his sister, "when people squawk about the army food."[17] Phil's fondness for military cooking probably says more about his family's particular circumstances than the excellence of army cuisine. Very likely his family, which included two parents and nine children, had difficulty putting enough food, especially meat, on the table during the Depression. *Pasta fagioli*—macaroni and beans—was a common dinner in the Aquila household.

At the same time, there were numerous other soldiers stationed at U.S. bases who, like Phil, appreciated the quantity, if not quality, of army food. American GIs were the best-fed soldiers in the world. "The Army's standard garrison ration, the one found in stateside training camps, provided about 4,300 calories daily," writes historian Lee Kennett. That would explain why the average soldier gained six to nine pounds during his first few months in the military.[18]

Other interesting tidbits about soldiers on the home front abound. For instance, Sgt. Aquila explains that soldiers often had their own cars:

"At every base I've been at there's hundreds of guys with cars from every state. They drive all over with them."[19] Phil also describes the emotional letdown that many Americans felt following Japan's surrender. "Now that the war is over," he writes, "I really don't see any reason to continue writing as much as I have. I'm really pretty tired of it after 2½ years of doing it." Other soldiers felt the same way, as evidenced by Phil's brother, Frankie, who was stationed in the South Pacific and was "just plain tired of writing letters."[20] The end of the war affected family relationships in other ways. Once the euphoria of peace wore off, reality reasserted itself. Like many families, the Aquilas found that mundane matters involving marriages, babies, in-laws, and other domestic concerns, which had been relegated to a back burner during the war, boiled over in the weeks following V-J Day.

Aquila's descriptive letters reveal additional insights about GIs on the home front. Most soldiers, he explains, did not want to be in the army; few wanted to go into battle; but all were prepared to fight if necessary. He also expresses the soldiers' ambivalence about being stationed at home. They felt guilty about not going overseas and believed they were not doing enough to defeat the Axis powers. At the same time, though, they knew they were doing their best in important support roles, and they resented anyone who questioned their bravery or contributions to the war effort.

Sgt. Aquila's letters enable us to understand more clearly the unique problems of soldiers stationed at home. We feel the monotony of Phil's everyday existence; we wonder with him whether he will be shipped into battle; we hold our breath alongside him as he waits anxiously for furloughs; we share his daily worries about births, deaths, illnesses, and family problems; we feel his despair when he cannot be with his ailing mother; we understand his longing for his new wife; and we share his regret that he cannot experience his baby growing up.

This collection of letters contains fascinating glimpses of marriage and family history, information about ethnic and immigration history, and a look at the home front "from the bottom up." But, significantly, the letters are not just a mere reflection of the times. They provide fresh evidence about everyday life in World War II America, demonstrating the daily heroism of both soldiers and private citizens on the home front. They offer first-hand accounts of daily tensions, hopes, and fears. They provide insights into how immigrant families coped with adversity and poverty in the midst of world war. And they contribute to our understanding of the role played by GIs on the home front by revealing the soldiers' dreams, anxieties, nightmares, guilt, and frustrations.

Obviously, it is possible to argue that the correspondence could have been more valuable if it contained additional details about the war itself. But that was not Phil Aquila's purpose in writing. He wrote for private reasons, for family reasons. That was his main concern. And he succeeded brilliantly.

The letters of Sgt. Aquila offer a richly textured story that operates on numerous levels. This collection constitutes an extremely important and unique source for studying American society and culture during World War II. Its unrelenting dailiness gives it drama, continuity, and significance. As Philip L. Aquila writes home, he reveals not only himself, but also everyday life and ordinary people of another time and another place.

THE AQUILA FAMILY HISTORY

Since Sgt. Phil Aquila's story is primarily a family history of World War II, it is important to understand the background of his parents— Francesco and Calogera Aquila—as well as that of Phil and his six brothers and two sisters.[21]

Francesco was born in 1881 to peasant parents in Naso, Sicily, a tiny mountain village in Messina Province. In late 1907 or early 1908, his parents arranged for him to marry a local girl. When the girl backed out of the wedding at the last minute, her younger, nineteen-year-old sister, Calogera Ferraoto, agreed to marry Francesco, perhaps because he had plans to emigrate to the United States. Their eight-year age difference was nearly perfect for marriage, according to a Sicilian proverb: "L'uomo di ventotto; la donna diciotto" ("The man at twenty-eight, the woman at eighteen").[22] Following the wedding, Francesco said goodbye to his new bride and set out for *LaMerica*. Like many other Italian immigrants, he planned to find work in the United States before sending for his wife.

Francesco Aquila was twenty-seven years old when he left Sicily for the United States in 1908. Given the location of his hometown, he probably embarked from either Palermo or Naples. Like other poor, southern Italian emigrants, Francesco had little money to finance his trip to *LaMerica*. So, he probably purchased a steam ship ticket for "steerage class," the least expensive way to travel. Steerage provided emigrants with cramped quarters down in the bowels of the ship right next to the steering equipment. Sometimes up to three hundred people were packed into tiny berths and were allowed up on deck only in shifts. Down below, steerage passengers had to cope with overcrowded conditions, sea-sickness, storms, and stale air that reeked with body odors and human waste, mixed in with the smells of salami, cheeses, wine, and other provisions carried by travelers.[23]

Fig. 1.4. The "boat" that Francesco Aquila came to America on probably looked like this vessel that brought European immigrants to America in 1906. (Library of Congress)

When Francesco's ship finally arrived in New York harbor, he may have missed seeing the Statue of Liberty if he, like other immigrants, was more intent on viewing the debarkation point, Ellis Island. The closer they got to America, the more they worried about Ellis Island immigration officials. Immigrants had heard terrifying rumors about hostile government inspectors who would treat them like animals; they feared questions they would have to answer about their backgrounds and plans; and they cringed in anticipation of the medical exams awaiting them. One wrong response or physical ailment could result in deportation back to Italy.[24]

Francesco and his fellow Italians probably feared the worst by the time they arrived at the castlelike federal building on Ellis Island. They were herded into a large "Registry Room," which, according to one American observer, looked like the Chicago stockyards. There they were given medical examinations, which usually took one to four hours to complete. Inspectors also asked a series of questions, including name, sex, last residence, and destination, as well as whether they were planning to stay in the United States, whether they had jobs already lined up, and how much money were they bringing into the country.[25]

Undoubtedly, Francesco was relieved when the officials granted him admission into the United States. Possibly he was even grateful to the inspector who anglicized his first name to "Frank."

Stepping off the Ellis Island ferry at Battery Park in Manhattan, Frank Aquila soon realized that he was indeed embarking on a new life in a new world. The peasant immigrant was astounded at every turn by the sights and sounds of New York City: buildings that scraped the sky, crowded and bustling city streets, and, of course, the ever-present automobiles and streetcars.

In all likelihood, Frank Aquila was greeted in New York by *paesani* (acquaintances from his small town of Naso). These friends or relatives probably had been the ones who encouraged him to join them in *LaMerica*. Frank followed his *paesani* to Johnstown, Pennsylvania, where he found work as a laborer.

Six years passed before Frank sent for his wife. The long separation was fairly typical of Italian immigrants in the early 1900s. A local reporter in Buffalo in 1905 found that it took Italian immigrants five to ten years to save enough money to send for their wives and families. Historians suggest that the average Italian American family probably took three and a half to four years to reunite.[26]

In 1914, Calogera made the passage to *LaMerica* and joined Frank in Johnstown, where the immigrant couple settled into their new lives. Less than a year later, Calogera gave birth to their first child. The baby boy was named Joseph, in keeping with the Italian tradition of naming the first son in honor of the paternal grandfather. In 1916, the couple had another boy, Anthony, who, if the Aquilas continued to follow tradition, was named after his mother's father.

In late 1916 or early 1917, the immigrant couple and their two sons moved northward to Buffalo, New York, in search of better employment opportunities. Like most Italian immigrants, Frank Aquila was a "general laborer." Although he occasionally found work in factories, he was usually employed in various seasonal jobs involving railroads, construction projects, or other outdoor employment. The lyrics to a popular folk song in the Aquilas' neighborhood not only poke fun at the immigrants' broken English, but they suggest that many Buffalo Italians found unskilled jobs working for the local Lackawanna railroad: "Where de you worka John?/ On the Delaware Lackawan/ And whatta you do-a, John?/ I poosh, I poosh, I poosh."[27]

Immigrants such as Frank Aquila sometimes worked only five or six months a year. One Italian American immigrant vividly recalls how difficult it was to find employment in Buffalo in the early 1900s: "I helped build roads. To find work you carried your shovel around and went from one place to another seeking work. I would work for a month or two. World War I made it possible for me to obtain more steady work. The steel mills needed workers. After the war, the Italians got fired first."[28]

The Aquila family settled into their rented home in Buffalo and quickly grew in size if not wealth. Over the next several years, while Frank worked hard at manual labor, Calogera gave birth to seven more children: Mary (1917), Sam (1919), Philip (1922), Frank (1924), Carmen (1925), Francie (1928), and Carlo (1935). The large size of their family was not unusual. Statistics show that back in the old country typical southern Italian families had six to ten children. Buffalo newspaper accounts from the early 1900s note that the average Italian mother over forty-five years of age had eleven children.[29]

Given Buffalo's cost of living and the low wages paid to general laborers, Italian immigrant families often lived close to what one social worker called "the ragged edge."[30] When economic times were good in the 1920s, the Aquila family struggled to make ends meet. When the Great Depression hit, their life became even harder. Pa worked at a series of low-paying, menial jobs, while Ma took in laundry and other day work to supplement the family income. The two oldest boys, Joe and Tony, found work as soon as they could. The younger Aquilas played equally important roles earning money for the family. Every summer, Calogera and her children were employed as migrant workers, picking beans and fruits on farms in western New York.

By the 1920s, Italian immigrants in the Buffalo area had become a

Fig. 1.5. Portrait of Aquila family taken in 1931. *Bottom row, left to right*: Carmen, Calogera (mother), Francie, Mary, Frankie. *Top row, left to right*: Phil, Joe, Francesco (*father is standing on two pillows*), Tony, Sam. The only person missing from the photo is Carlo, who was born in 1935. (Philip L. Aquila Collection)

valuable source of labor for local farmers. For example, farmers from North Collins, an agricultural community about forty miles south of Buffalo, would dispatch their trucks to the city's Italian neighborhoods to pick up families and transport them to the farms, where they would spend the summer and early fall tending and harvesting crops.[31]

The Cavarella family was one of the Italian American families that the Aquilas knew from the farms in North Collins. Mary Cavarella, who later became the wife of Phil Aquila, was seven or eight years old when her family first went out to the farm. She still remembers the annual routine:

> We usually left one or two weeks before school let out in June, and stayed all summer until about the second week in September. That meant we would always miss the first week of school. Everybody in my family except my father was out there. But that wasn't unusual. There were hardly any adult males there, because they would stay in the city where they had jobs. My father usually came out on weekends to see us and bring us food for the week.[32]

Although the farmer provided living quarters, each family had to bring along whatever furnishings they wanted, including a table, chairs, and mattresses, as well as eating utensils, pots, pans, and food.

The ride out to the farm took about an hour. As the truck approached the farm on a bumpy, unpaved road, the migrant workers would peer out the sides at the rural countryside. When they reached the farm, they got a good look at their summer home. Four wooden buildings resembling barracks had been constructed for the migrant workers. The buildings (which Mary Cavarella and Phil Aquila always called "the shacks") were arranged in a large square, facing inward, with a community well and cookhouse in the center.

Each building contained five or six units. Each one-room unit had one window and housed one family. Until the late 1930s, the shacks lacked electricity and gas, so the families had to use kerosene lamps for light and woodburning stoves to cook on. Although most of the cooking was done in individual shacks, the residents could also use the ovens in the central cookhouse to prepare big meals or bake bread in large quantities. The units did not have running water or indoor plumbing, so the twenty families shared a community well and outhouses.

Mary Cavarella vividly recalls what it was like to live in the shacks:

> Our shack had only one room, about twelve feet by sixteen feet. We would hang up a clothesline for privacy. I would sleep with my mother, while my three brothers [Mike was three years older than Mary, Nickie was a year younger, and Jimmie, two years younger] would sleep in another double bed. We always tried to avoid using the outhouse in the middle of the night, because of the spiders and snakes.[33]

She describes her life on the farm:

> The farmer would come every morning between 4:30 and 5:00 A.M. and wake us up by pounding on the door. After a quick breakfast, a truck would take us out to the fields. The dew was terrible in the morning and would soak us up to our knees. We'd work until lunch, then break for thirty to sixty minutes depending on the weather. Then we'd continue working the fields until 6:00 P.M., although there were times that we'd keep going until nightfall. The truck would then bring us back to the shacks. We'd eat a quick supper, clean up, and collapse exhausted into our beds.
>
> Most of us worked six days a week. Saturday was an off day for the children, because the older workers would have to hoe in the fields. We picked strawberries in June; red and purple raspberries in early July; then we'd spend about a week trimming the fields and covering the berries; and then we would pick green beans from early August through early September. Each family had a "card" to keep track of how much they picked, and the family would be paid at the end of the year. [*For a detailed description of the varieties and quantities of crops picked and how much money a family earned in one season, see Phil Aquila's letter of September 24, 1944.*][34]

Despite the hardships of farm life, Calogera Aquila jumped at the chance to get her family out to the farm. Not only was it an opportunity to make money for the family, but it enabled her to raise her children in a rural, farming environment like the one she had been accustomed to back in Sicily. Her daughter Mary recently explained, "Ma thought it was a great chance to get out of the city during the summer, and keep us kids out of trouble."[35]

If Calogera thought going out to the farm would keep her children out of trouble, she was mistaken. The boys, in particular, soon discovered that North Collins offered plenty of opportunities for mischief. Phil liked to tell the story about getting lost out there when he was ten years old. It happened one evening when he, his older brother Sam, and some friends were cutting across a neighboring farm. Seeing ripe grapes on the vines, they stopped for a refreshing snack. All at once the farmer came rushing into the field, shotgun in hand. He shouted at them to come toward him with their hands up. All the boys obeyed, except Phil who dashed away and hid in the bushes. After nightfall, Phil crept out of his hiding place and made his way home through nearby woods. Unfortunately, the ten-year-old got lost. When he finally found his way back hours later, he learned that the farmer had turned Sam and the other boys over to the local sheriff. Though no one received serious punishment, Phil never forgot the incident.

Years later when he was a sophomore in high school, Phil used the "grapes" incident as the basis for an English class writing assignment. Significantly, he made two changes: first, he described the boys as going off for a swim rather than stealing grapes on the farmer's land; secondly, he wrote that the incident occurred while his family was vacationing in the country. Evidently, Phil was too embarrassed to admit to his teacher that his family picked beans during the summer, so his theme, entitled "How I Was Lost," refers matter-of-factly to "our vacation on the outskirts of North Collins":

> One summer during the year 1932, some friends and I spent our vacation on the outskirts of North Collins. One day the boys wanted to go swimming, and although I liked swimming very much I excused myself and told them I was going for a little walk. As this was my first time in this lonely region, I did not know the roads so well. I walked about two miles and then cut through a forest where I began to wander further and further away.
>
> As it was getting dark, and I was seeing strange farms before me, I began to search for the path I had made. After a while I began to realize I was lost. It was now pitch dark and I was groping my way through the woods over stumps and ditches. I soon began to hear strange noises and being small, I got frightened and started to run, which caused me to fall bodily into a creek. Drenched as I was, I began climbing the tallest tree, because I realized that it was the only opportunity I had to see a light. From atop the tree I got a bird's eye view of the region and soon noticed a road where automobiles were going by. I quickly climbed down from the tree and headed in the direction of the road. After many hardships, I finally came to the road, which I noticed was quite near to my guest host's house. When I reached home, I was very grateful that I was safe and sound, although I was thoroughly wet.[36]

Although Calogera certainly welcomed the opportunity to get her children out of the city during the summer, her son Frankie insists that "money was the main reason our family went out to the farms during the 1930s."[37]

Historical evidence supports Frankie's contention. For example, the annual report of a Buffalo settlement house in 1916 complained that when poor Italian immigrants refused charity, they had to either "beg, borrow, [or] steal," or they had to live in "miserable rooms," take in boarders, or send their wives and children to work.[38] Economic conditions became even worse for Buffalo's Italians in the late 1920s and '30s. Since most Italian Americans were too proud to accept welfare and too honest to steal, their only remaining option was to put the entire family to work, including women and small children.[39]

The farms on the outskirts of Buffalo offered the Aquilas and other

Italian American families an efficient way to employ every member of the family. Child labor laws or legislation regulating the number of hours women and children could work were difficult if not impossible to enforce out on the farms. As a result, Calogera Aquila and other immigrant parents could control the amount of work their children did. As a bonus, the adults were able to work longer hours without having to worry about their children's whereabouts.

Each family usually earned enough money during the summer to carry them through the lean winter months when the husband lost his seasonal outside jobs in the city. For example, Calogera and her children made a total of $556.42 picking beans and fruit during the summer and early fall of 1944. That was roughly the same amount of money that her husband earned for the entire year.[40]

Working on the farms was an acceptable—if not ideal—way to make money for Italian American immigrants like the Aquilas. Very likely both Calogera and Francesco had done similar work back in Sicily when they were young. As late as the early 1900s, the vast majority of Sicily's workforce was involved in farming. Perhaps two thirds of those workers were landless peasants who were hired to work on nearby farms. Because the majority of Buffalo's Italian immigrants came from this type of background, they were familiar with migrant farmwork and accustomed to having women working out in the fields at harvest time.[41]

The division of labor and type of work required on the farms fit perfectly into Italian traditions. Even Calogera's supervision of her children's work on the farm replicated the domestic role of peasant wives and mothers in Sicily. A federal government report in 1911 noted how immigrant workers in agriculture organized themselves along traditional family lines: "since the women and children can work efficiently, the laborers, particularly the south Italians, make the family the working unit. This means that the whole family engages in farm labor or berry picking and the earnings all go into the family fund."[42]

Not only did the farms provide immigrants with the means to make money in familiar ways, but they allowed the migrants to socialize and retain traditional customs and lifestyles. The rural setting, with its small village and fields that were reminiscent of the old country, enabled Calogera to work and chat alongside *paesani, compari,* and friends. They could talk about the good old days in Italy or discuss current affairs or problems in their new world.

Not surprisingly, even after Calogera Aquila was older and too ill to work in the fields, she still wanted desperately to go out to the farm every summer. Her son Phil understood his mother's need to socialize out there. During the war, he wrote home to his sister: "You said that now that summer is coming Ma feels pretty bad about not being able to go out to the farm. . . . It'll be a good idea . . . to take Ma for a nice drive on Sundays to the farm and get some fresh air."[43]

Life on the farm recalled the traditional seasonal rhythms to which Italian immigrants were accustomed. In the old country, peasant families frequently undertook seasonal migrations following harvests throughout the Mezzogiorno, the area south of Rome that produced over 80 percent of America's Italian immigrants. Even the temporary disruption of the family that occurred when the father stayed in Buffalo while his wife and children went out to the farm had roots in old country traditions. In Italy, peasant families were often separated for weeks at a time when the men were off harvesting crops in neighboring areas. Even longer periods of family separation occurred when Italian males came to America on their own in search of employment.[44]

Calogera no doubt felt very much at ease on the farms. There she could watch her children grow up in a familiar, rural, agricultural setting, playing with and later courting other young Italians from similar backgrounds. In effect, Calogera Aquila and her fellow migrant workers used the farms to recreate in America the peasant villages they had left behind in Italy. The familiar setting and lifestyles eased their transition from the old country to the New World. The farms offered familiar ways to earn a living, as well as the means to retain traditional Italian social and cultural customs.

The Aquila family spent every summer between 1929 and 1944 on the farms in North Collins. Ma and the kids picked beans and fruits, while Pa stayed at home working in the city. On Saturday mornings, he would go to Buffalo's outdoor market and hitch a ride on a truck heading to the farms. He would bring weekly provisions to his family, then return to the city in time to begin his weekday job. After the fall harvest, Ma and the kids returned to their Buffalo home, and the kids would begin school, usually a week or two later than their fellow students. The Aquila children stuck to this routine until they were old enough to leave school and get their own full-time jobs.[45]

The older children were just coming of age when World War II erupted in 1941. Joe, the oldest at twenty-six, had recently gotten married, had a baby, and was working at Allegheny-Ludlum Steel Company, where one of his wife's relatives was a foreman. Because of this connection, Joe managed to get jobs at Allegheny-Ludlum for his father and one of his brothers, Tony, who was one year younger.

The other Aquilas worked elsewhere. Twenty-four-year-old Mary assembled cosmetic boxes at F. N. Burt's. Twenty-two-year-old Sam (who was nicknamed "Shadow" because of the way he always tagged around with friends) worked at Bell Aircraft, as did Phil, who was nineteen. Frankie, seventeen, was employed at Eagle Office Equipment,

AFTER MILLET'
GLEANER.—Mrs.
Calogera Aquila o
Buffalo picking bear.
at Eden, N. Y.

Fig. 1.6. Picture of Calogera Aquila modeled after Jean-François Millet's painting of *The Gleaners* (1857). The picture appeared in the *Buffalo Courier-Express*, October 1, 1933. (Courtesy of Mary Aquila Pardi)

while sixteen-year-old Carmen had just dropped out of school to find work. The only kids still in school were Francie, thirteen, and Carlo, six.

The entrance of the United States into World War II had an immediate impact on the Aquila household. The two oldest sons received deferments because they were in their mid-twenties and worked in a defense plant. The younger ones, however, soon received induction notices. Phil was the first to get drafted. He entered the Army Air Force in February 1943. Later that year Frankie was inducted into the Army Transportation Corps. Next, Shadow, who had managed to defer things for a while because he was married and had a baby on the way, was drafted into the Navy. Carmen was also drafted into the Navy in 1943.

Historians have demonstrated that ethnic groups were often drafted in greater numbers than their proportion of the population warranted.[46] Whether this was true in the case of the Aquilas is unknown. All we know for sure is that the local draft board inducted four of the Aquilas' six eligible sons into the armed forces during World War II. A fifth, Tony, lost his deferment and was about to be drafted when the war ended in 1945.

SGT. PHILIP L. AQUILA'S BACKGROUND

Phil was twenty-one years old when he received his draft notice in the mail in early 1943: "Greetings. You are hereby ordered for induction into the Armed Forces of the United States. . . ."[47] He reported to Local Draft Board Number 595 on February 1 and was transported to a reception center at Fort Niagara, New York. After passing preliminary exams, he was allowed to return home to get things in order.

On February 8, he and other local draftees boarded a train for another "reception center," this one at Fort Dix, New Jersey. They spent the next week to ten days being processed by the army: they were given uniforms and supplies, vaccinations for smallpox and typhoid, and a complete physical examination. They also took various aptitude tests, as well as the Army General Classification Test (AGCT).

The AGCT was perhaps the most important test new soldiers had to take, because it helped determine their placement in the armed services. The exam consisted of 150 multiple choice questions covering math, vocabulary, and basic logic. According to the Army, the exam measured "usable intelligence" or "trainability." The men's scores on the AGCT placed them in one of five classes: Class I included those who scored over 130 points; Class II, 110 to 130 points; Class III, which was considered average, included those with 90 to 109 points; Class IV, 70 to 89 points; and Class V, below 70 points.[48]

The inductees tried to do as well as they could on the AGCT, knowing a high score could mean a better and perhaps even a safer position in the military. High test scores could keep a draftee out of the infantry, since a "skimming policy" was in effect that allowed the Army Air Force to select the cream of the crop of inductees. A soldier who scored at least 110 might also qualify for the Army Air Force's Air Cadet Program or the Army's Officer Candidate School.[49]

Philip L. Aquila attracted the military's attention with extremely high scores on his induction exams. After the Army Air Force selected him, he was dispatched to Jefferson Barracks near St. Louis for basic training.

Anyone familiar with Phil Aquila's school record was not surprised by his impressive performance on the AGCT. When it came to academics, Phil had always been a star. In fact, he valued school and learning so much that he saved all his report cards, school records, and even daily homework assignments dating back to elementary school. (Not only does this tell us something about the importance he placed on education, but it also reflects his sense of "history." Throughout his life he continued to save newspaper clippings, papers, and anything else he thought might be important in the future. In every case, he made sure the item was well documented, explaining its date and its contents.)

Because he saved all his schoolwork, we can easily reconstruct his years as a student. We know that he got almost straight As in elementary school and high school and had almost perfect attendance, remarkable achievements considering that he came from an immigrant family where his parents placed no pressure on him to succeed in school and older siblings never served as academic role models. Phil's love of and aptitude for history, geography, literature, and other subjects impressed his fellow students. He was elected president of his graduating class at Public School No. 6 in Buffalo, New York. As class president, he gave the Superintendent's Address at graduation. In the graduation booklet, his fellow students named him "Most Likely to Become Secretary of State."

Given Phil's impressive grades and honors, he should have been assigned to the college preparation curriculum in high school, but instead, his guidance counselor at School 6 either convinced him to sign up for or consigned him to the vocational program offered at Buffalo's Technical High School. By the mid-1930s, the Buffalo School System adhered closely to a strict "tracking" system, in part to prevent "undesirable" student populations (such as blacks and immigrants) from mixing with traditional middle-class groups. "By not mixing 'trade' and 'academic' students," explains historian William Graebner, "the 'atmosphere' in each school remained 'homogeneous.'"[50] Very likely, young Phil Aquila, despite his

Fig. 1.7. Picture of Phil Aquila, president of his eighth grade class, with Theresa Guarnieri, the vice president. Photo appeared in *The Buffalo Times*, June 1936. (Philip L. Aquila Collection)

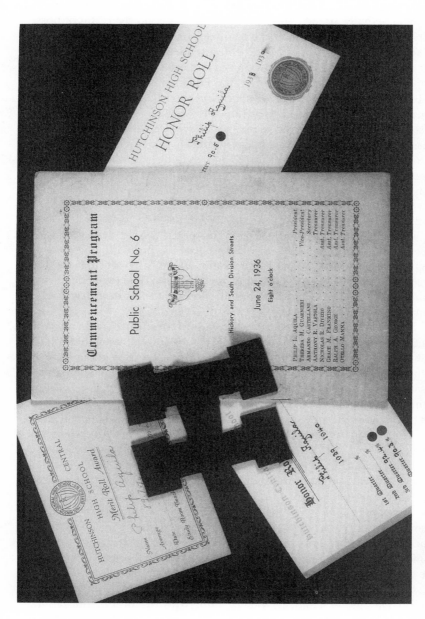

Fig. 1.8. Collage of Phil Aquila's memorabilia from grades 8–12. (Philip L. Aquila Collection)

excellent grades, was shunted off to the technical school, because he came from a poor Italian American family with nine children. The notion that he might actually attend college was probably beyond the realm of possibility as far as either his guidance counselor or even Phil was concerned.

Throughout 1937 and 1938, Phil attended Technical High School and dutifully applied himself to courses in mechanical drafting, machine shop, and technical math. But by the end of his sophomore year he decided he wanted more out of education than just job training, so he transferred to Hutchinson Central, the "regular" high school that offered the courses he loved in the social sciences and humanities. He blossomed in the new academic environment, taking classes in French, history, citizenship, and literature, and making the honor roll every semester. When Phil graduated from "Hutch" in 1940 he became the first one in his family to earn a high school diploma—an achievement that must have seemed truly astounding to the poorly educated immigrant family of Francesco and Calogera Aquila.

Despite Phil's academic success and potential, he never seriously considered going to college. As a high school junior he did complete an English assignment, "What I Am Going to Be," by writing about a career in forestry. "To be a good trained forester," he explained, "one would have to be well-educated and in physical fitness in order to meet many dangerous emergencies."[51]

Perhaps Phil's summer experiences on the farms help explain why this Italian American boy from an urban neighborhood wanted to be a forester. But while he may have dreamed and even written about a career in forestry, Phil never acted on it. He knew in his heart that such a profession, which required a college degree, was beyond his grasp. To begin with, the very notion of college was alien to his family and background. His parents were totally illiterate, while his four older brothers and sister had dropped out of high school to work. Like most Italian Americans, the Aquilas believed that higher education was not as important as earning a living and acquiring property for the family. Furthermore, Phil knew that the country was still in the midst of the Great Depression and that his family desperately needed money to survive. He also knew that now that he was out of school he was obligated to help his family financially. Had he been born twenty years later, Phil probably would have gone on to higher education, but the times and circumstances were against him. Coming from a large, poor immigrant family during the Depression, Phil had only one choice: he had to find employment to help his family.

Phil Aquila took great pride in the important role he played in his family. The middle child, he viewed himself as the hub of the family. When his father proved either unwilling or unable to provide a leadership role, Phil stepped in and assumed authority. By the time he was in his teens, he was giving advice to his three older brothers and one older sister, and issuing orders to his four younger siblings. After the oldest son, Joe, got married and moved out of the house, the next oldest, Tony, frequently locked horns with the upstart Phil, who was six years his junior. "Those two used to always go at it," recalled Frankie in a recent interview, "Phil and Tony would try to outdo each other, using big words and arguing about politics and other things."[52]

The younger children had an even more difficult time trying to resist Phil's control. Assuming parental authority, Phil forced them to do their homework and to go to school every day. He also made sure they didn't swear, drink, or get into any kind of trouble. Carmen and Frankie both referred to him as "the Warden," because of the tight control he maintained.

Even when Phil was away in the Army Air Force, he continued to lecture his younger brothers. For example, on June 14, 1943, he wrote the following letter to his youngest brother, hoping to improve the eleven-year-old's behavior and writing skills:

My Little Brother, Carlo,
   I liked your letter very much, but how come it took you three days to write one? Heck, all the time I thought you were smart enough to write me a letter in about two hours, and here it took you three days. You spent all that time on your letter and still, your sentences were pretty bad. Carlo, you've got to know where to put your period and commas, or didn't your teacher tell you about them, yet?
   Another thing, Carlo, when you tell me about something and then you finish, don't start telling me the same thing all over again later in the letter. It doesn't take much to write a good letter, just a little thinking! When [brother] Tony writes me a letter, you just watch him and you can see him stop writing, he thinks for awhile and then he starts writing again. Carlo, I am writing you a letter just as if you are a big boy [now]. Now show me you can answer me that way. . . . I'm happy to hear that you finished your work quicker than all the rest of the children [in school]. Make sure it's right, though. Well, Carlo, I'll write you another letter when I get paid again, so I can give you a quarter, okay? But don't forget, you have to be a good boy, eat everything Ma gives you, and don't swear. God bless you,

Love, Phil[53]

Phil knew he was being hard on his brothers, but he was convinced that he was doing the right thing. "Make Carlo go to school everyday," he advised his sister, while admitting, "I sure pity my son, having a father like me. I've always tried to boss Frankie, Carmen, Francie, and Carlo. I used to be rough with them, but I tried to tell them right from wrong. I'd take an interest in everything they'd do."[54]

As the household's self-appointed leader, he firmly believed that the family would function properly only if everyone listened to him. He was confident of his ability and the rightness of his decisions. His intelligence and determination were matched and reinforced by his physical ability. Although not physically big (he was five feet six inches, and about 155 pounds by the time he graduated from high school), Phil had unusual strength and agility. By the time he was in his mid-teens, he had earned the reputation as the toughest fighter on the streets of his Buffalo neighborhood, as well as out on the farms of North Collins.

Phil viewed himself as a "good guy," very much like his favorite B Western cowboy, Buck Jones, or the superhero Tarzan, as played in the movies by Johnny Weissmuller. Patterning himself after his heroes, he was straightlaced, extremely moral, and religious. He refused to drink alcohol or compromise his beliefs in any way. Phil was convinced that he had the brains and brawn to set the world right. He also believed that a person should never quit. Later in life Phil liked to tell about the time he went out for football in his senior year in high school. As a newcomer, he usually rode the bench. But just prior to the last game, he got a chance to play as a running back in practice. He insisted that it took almost the entire team to stop him, but even then they could not tackle him to the ground. "Go down, Aquila, go down," the coach allegedly pleaded, "so we can get on with practice." According to Phil, the coach was so impressed that he even tried to get him to return to school the following year just so he could play football.

Whether or not the story is true is debatable. But it certainly speaks volumes about Phil's self-image. He was not a quitter, no matter what the odds were against him. He was always proud that he completed every task he set his mind to. In one of his letters to his sister, he even boasted that he never quit a job simply because he didn't like it. He always insisted that people, like successful boxers, had to learn how to take life's setbacks "on the chin." If they were knocked down, they had to get back up and continue fighting until victory was assured. But under no circumstances should a person ever quit.[55]

Phil's belief in truth, justice, and the American way is evidenced by the following letter to the editor that he wrote and *The Buffalo Evening News* published in 1940:

> About 9 o'clock last Tuesday evening I was watching a group of boys play "beef trust" on Spring Street near Eagle. As this sport is interesting to watch, many passing pedestrians showed their satisfaction. I confess the game is a bit noisy, but who minds a little extra noise when there are loud conversations, laughter, and skating going on?
>
> However, suddenly a police car appeared, which resulted in the game being stopped and the boys sent home. Without any saucy lan-

guage against the officers, these lads, who average 16 years of age, obediently separated.

The point I wish to emphasize is this: Where is the principle of democracy in Buffalo if the boys can't be left to themselves? These boys weren't hindering traffic or making excess racket. The police should be grateful that these boys are not taking part in crimes.[56]

While Phil Aquila believed in helping out his fellow citizens, he typified many Italian Americans in that his first loyalty was always to his family. Throughout the Great Depression, the Aquilas struggled to make ends meet. As he was growing up in the 1920s and '30s, Phil repeatedly witnessed his mother's never-ending effort to take care of her family: she took in laundry, did chores around the house, and then went out to the farms each summer to pick beans in the hot sun. Through it all she received little support from her husband.

The sight of his mother working hard every minute of the day to make ends meet was always wrenching for Phil. Perhaps his close ties to his mother reflected his Sicilian upbringing. Southern Italians traditionally idealized women and motherhood. For example, in 1907, an editorial writer in one of Buffalo's Italian language newspapers admonished young boys to treat their mothers properly: "respect her, venerate her, adore her."[57]

Some scholars insist that the devotion of Italian males to their mothers might be attributed to a psychological dependency called the "madonna complex," which caused them to identify strongly with their mothers. Others trace the attachment to the Italian peasants' understanding that females were the source of all life.[58]

Of course there may be simpler explanations for the special relationship between Calogera and her son. Perhaps she doted on him because she recognized his special talents. Or maybe she appreciated him because he always went out of his way to be with her. As he was growing up Phil spent considerable time talking to his mother and helping her with chores. When he was handed a high school assignment to write a letter to someone who had gone away, he chose his mother as the subject. Though the formal letter maintained that she had gone away on vacation, "Ma" was probably either at home or away at the farm. The opening paragraph, though stilted, clearly expressed Phil's feelings: "Dear Mother, It is approximately two weeks since you left, but to me it seems as if two centuries have gone by. The reason why I am sometimes lonely is because I miss you so much. Another reason why I'm lonely at your being absent is because I'm anxious to know when you will return."[59]

Devoted to his mother, Phil was determined to help her every way he could. By the time he reached high school, he was contributing as

Fig. 1.9. Portrait of Phil's mother, Calogera. She is wearing the cross that Phil sent her in 1943. See letter of January 5, 1945. This picture was mailed to Phil shortly after Easter, 1944. (Philip L. Aquila Collection)

much money as he could earn to the family and was taking care of all their financial affairs. After graduation, his solid academic record helped him land a job at Possinger's Tool and Die Company, where he made $18 per week. In late 1941 he got an even better job as a turret lathe operator at Bell Aircraft. By the end of 1942, the twenty-year-old was promoted to head machinist at a salary of $52 a week. Although his older brothers told him he was crazy, he gave all but five dollars of his weekly paycheck to his mother. He desperately wanted to make her life easier, and offered her most of his earnings so she could buy her own house. That way, no matter how bad things got, she would always have a roof over her head. Little by little the money grew into a nest egg. Finally, in 1943, the family was able to purchase its first house, with over half of the money contributed by Phil.[60]

Phil's willingness to contribute almost all of his earnings in order to support his family and buy them a house says a great deal about his personal values, as well as his adherence to the Italian American belief that the family should always come first. "Neither the immigrant generation nor its children conformed to the American ideal of occupational success," explains Virginia Yans-McLaughlin, "but they had their own standard of achievement, namely, the acquisition of family property, usually a home."[61]

Phil's mother was not the only female to whom he was devoted. In 1940, Phil met the other love of his life—Mary Cavarella, the woman who would become his wife of fifty years. The Cavarella family, like the Aquilas, were Italian American immigrants from Buffalo who spent their summers working on the farms near North Collins. During the 1930s, the Cavarellas and the Aquilas worked on different farms. But, in the summer of 1940, the Aquila family switched farms, and took up residence in one of the shacks near the Cavarellas.

Mary Cavarella was fifteen years old that summer. She had known two of the Aquila boys from school—Frankie was one year older than her, while Carmen had been in her class since grammar school. Although she had never met their older brother Phil, who was eighteen, she knew him by reputation. Carmen would frequently complain to her that he couldn't skip school like the other boys or not do his homework because "Phil the Warden" would beat him up.

Mary was totally surprised when the Aquilas showed up at her farm in 1940:

> I had gone out to get a bucket of water for my mother when all of a sudden I heard someone yell, "Hello, Mary!" I turned around and there was Carmen. We talked for awhile, and he said, "Why don't you come over to the cookhouse and you can finally meet the guy I've been telling you about, you know, the Warden?"

Fig. 1.10. Picture of Phil's wife, Mary, taken in 1943 before they were married. (Philip L. Aquila Collection)

At first, I hesitated, but he said, "Don't worry, he won't beat you up. He only forces me and Frankie to do things." So we walked around the corner and I met his brother.

Phil was nothing like what Carmen had described. He was real handsome, all the girls chased him around. He was also real shy and nice.

We flirted all summer. Finally, in August, on August 6th, he asked me to go to a Lawn Fete at the Church in North Collins. My mother wouldn't let me go with him, but I went with a friend, and Phil was there. He bought me a coke, a really big deal since none of us had any money. Later that night, we went for a walk, and he kissed me. The rest of August we went out for walks almost every night.[62]

After Mary and Phil returned to their homes in Buffalo they continued to see each other a couple of times a week. Usually they went to the movies on a weeknight and then to church on Sunday. Phil and Mary dated for two years. They got engaged in 1942, shortly after Mary turned seventeen. They did not set a date for their marriage, however, because of the uncertainty that resulted from World War II.

When the twenty-one-year-old Phil was drafted in February, 1943, he said farewell to his fianceé and his family and left for basic training at Jefferson Barracks outside St. Louis. In his wallet he carried pictures of Mary Cavarella and his mother, as well as a Longfellow poem that he had clipped out of the Buffalo newspaper:

> Our lives are rivers gliding free
> To that unfathom'd, boundless sea
> The silent grave!
> Thither all earthly pomp and boast
> Roll, to be swallow'd up and lost
> In one dark wave.[63]

The U.S. military, according to historians, did an excellent job of using inductees' skills. "The GI generally got his army assignment on the basis of what he had done in civilian life," writes Lee Kennett.[64] Phil was clearly an exception to the rule. The military recorded this description of Private Aquila's previous job: "[He] set up and operated turret lathes to shape internal and external surfaces of metal parts for airplanes. Followed blueprints and written orders. Worked to .001 of an inch. Used calipers, micrometer, veneer gauge." Disregarding his skills and experience working on airplane parts, the Army Air Force decided to use him as a specialist in chemical warfare. Aquila went through a rigorous program that taught him how to identify the various gases used in warfare, how to defend against them, and what types of first aid should be applied to gas victims.[65]

Fig. 1.11. Phil Aquila says a gallant goodbye to Mary Cavarella just before he leaves to be inducted into the army. January 1943. (Philip L. Aquila Collection)

In May 1945, Private Aquila was sent to McChord Air Base near Tacoma, Washington, where he was to instruct enlisted personnel in chemical warfare. Hand-written notes in his copy of *The Basic Field Manual and Soldier's Handbook* outline the first lecture he gave to the troops:

Lecture I

I.   The Subject Today (includes Gas Mask Drill)
II. Gas Discipline
III. Nomenclature of Gas Mask
IV. Operation of Gas Mask
V.   Care of Gas Mask
VI. Demonstration of Proper Method of Putting On Mask and Testing for Gas
VII. Gas Mask Drill
     A. By Numbers Describing
     B. By Numbers Only
     C. Without the Numbers[66]

Phil took great pride in his job as a chemical warfare instructor. Applying the same diligence and skills that had made him an honor student in high school, he became thoroughly versed in the various types of gases used in warfare. Within a month, his expertise and teaching ability helped get him promoted to corporal. His dedication and determination to get information across to enlisted personnel also almost got him into trouble.

The problem began when Corporal Aquila became convinced that one of his classes had not been paying attention to his lectures on identifying gases and using the gas mask. He decided to teach them a lesson when he took them out for a field demonstration. As the troops joked with each other and ignored his instructions, Aquila released some harmless gas. Unable to get their masks on properly, the soldiers and their lieutenant panicked and ran from the area.

The lieutenant was furious that he and his men had been gassed, and demanded that the commanding officer take disciplinary action. The C.O. sided with his instructor, however, explaining that the corporal was not only doing his job, but he was doing it in an exemplary manner. Instead of being disciplined, Aquila was promoted to sergeant.[67]

After only nine weeks at McChord Field, Phil Aquila had impressed his superiors so much that they recommended him for the Army Air Force's Air Cadets Program. The officer in charge wrote: "I have known

Fig. 1.12. Gas mask poster from World War II. Part of Phil Aquila's military job was training soldiers how to use and care for gas masks. (Government poster/Ball State University Photo Services)

Sgt. Aquila for the past two months. In that time he has displayed qualities that should fit him for the position [in the Air Cadets]. . . . He applies himself diligently to the task at hand. He has the ability to make quick and correct decisions, possesses good physical and mental coordination, and displays courage, initiative, and loyalty."[68]

Sgt. Aquila was accepted for the Air Cadets Program in August and given a brief furlough. He immediately went back to Buffalo to see his girl and family. On September 27, 1943, he reported to the Air Cadets training site at Utah State Agricultural College in Logan, Utah. If Phil was excited that he finally had the opportunity to prove himself on a college campus, his relatives were equally impressed that an Aquila was doing so well. His younger brother Frankie wrote from his post in New Guinea to congratulate him: "Well, I see that you got your sergeant's stripes already. Well, that's nice going. I also see you're still not satisfied. I think you'll make a pretty good pilot when you become a Cadet. Of course, it's a tough grind but I don't see any reason for you to fail. Then too, it'll be nice to have a lieutenant in the family."[69]

A week later Frankie wrote another letter, this time teasing his older brother about the Air Cadets: "I see you did it again [i.e., Phil chalked up another accomplishment]. So you're going to be a pilot, eh? Well, congratulations again. No kidding, I think it's swell." At the same time, Frankie couldn't resist the chance to taunt his former "Warden": "The only thing is you'll probably get to be a stuffed shirt lieutenant who thinks he knows it all. If they ever send you to wherever I'm at, I'll just have to beat you up, bars or no bars. I'm only kidding, because I don't think I could do it more than once."[70]

Phil needed all the comic relief and moral support he could get from family and friends, because the Air Cadets Program proved to be a real challenge. For three and a half months, Aquila experienced what it was like to be a college student on the Utah State campus. He went to classes daily and studied as hard as he could, focusing all his energies and attention on the rigorous Air Cadet Training Program. The hard work paid off. At the end of the semester, he received the following grades: "A" in History; "A" in Physics; "A" in Military Customs and Courtesies; "B+" in Mathematics; "C" in Civil Air Regulations; "B+" in Medical Aid; "B" in Flying (Pilot Training); and "B" in Physical Training. On January 8, 1944, Cadet Aquila received his diploma from Utah State Agricultural College. It read: "This will certify that Philip L. Aquila has completed three months of the United States Army Air Forces College Training Program with the 318th College Training Detachment (Aircrew)."[71]

Following graduation, the Air Cadets were immediately dispatched to the Army Air Force West Coast Training Center in Santa Ana, California. Three weeks later after a brief interview, Cadet Aquila received official word that he was not being recommended for the next phase of pilot training. The exact reason for his "washing out" of the program is not known. The most obvious answer is that by early 1944, the Air Force could afford to be highly selective, because they simply did not need as many pilots. Not only was the war winding down, but the Air Force had a surplus of pilot trainees already in the pipeline. Months earlier, Phil's brother Frankie had warned him about this situation: "Between me and you, I don't think you'll ever get to be a pilot. Now that Italy is out of the war it can't last too long. We're not doing so bad in the Southwest Pacific, either."[72]

At the same time, Phil suspected that his Italian American background might have contributed to the decision. He recalled that during the interview he was asked whether his ethnic heritage would prevent him from dropping bombs on Italy or any of Italy's allies. He replied, perhaps too strenuously, that his total loyalty was with the United States of America, and, if necessary, he would fight against any enemy, including Italy.[73] Though there is no way of proving that ethnic discrimination played a part in Cadet Aquila's dismissal, it certainly is possible given attitudes of the day. Not only did middle-class Americans commonly use ethnic slurs such as "dago" or "wop" to describe "swarthy" Italians, but they also discriminated against them when it came to jobs and housing. During World War II, the U.S. military, not trusting the loyalty of Italian American GIs, usually assigned them to the Pacific arena.[74]

When Army Air Force officials informed Sgt. Aquila that he would not be given further pilot training, they offered him three options: he could become a navigator, apply for Officer Candidate School, or return to his former position as a chemical warfare instructor. Phil decided that the last alternative was probably the best, and perhaps the safest.[75]

In February 1944, Sgt. Aquila reported for duty to the Army Air Force Base in Pratt, Kansas. Along with teaching enlisted men about chemical warfare, he was placed in charge of the base's chemical supplies. Official papers described his job as follows:

> CHEMICAL NCO [i.e., Noncommissioned Officer]: Shipped and received chemical supplies. Filled out requisitions, shipping documents, and typed up forms. Kept stock records and took inventories. Instructed enlisted personnel in various toxic and non-toxic gases used in warfare and defenses against them. Described first aid for gas casualties.[76]

Believing that his assignment at Pratt Air Force Base would last at least several months, Phil and Mary decided to get married as soon as he could get a furlough. To everyone's surprise, Phil made it back to Buffalo in late March, and the marriage took place on March 25, 1944.

Mary Cavarella's younger brother, Nickie, was best man, while Phil's older sister, Mary, was maid of honor. The happy couple dashed off for an afternoon in nearby Niagara Falls, then spent the rest of Phil's furlough (and their honeymoon) at an apartment temporarily vacated by June Aquila, the wife of Phil's older brother Shadow. She had left recently to visit her husband at his naval base in Memphis.

On April 9, Phil Aquila and his nineteen-year-old bride boarded a train for Pratt, Kansas. Mary still recalls how homesick she was being away from Buffalo for the first time. She also has vivid memories of Pratt, Kansas:

> My heart sank when I first saw Pratt. It was so small. It looked like one of those old Western towns that you see in the movies. When we pulled into the tiny train station, the man working there was playing a guitar and singing cowboy songs. Phil turned to me and said, "See, I told you this was just a one-horse town."
>
> Pratt was in the middle of nowhere. The isolation scared me. Whenever there was a rain storm, the thunder would just roll on forever across the flat prairies.
>
> The main street had two restaurants, a Woolworth's, and a J.C. Penney's with wood plank floors. There was a U.S.O. there, where we spent a lot of time. We went there every night for dancing, entertainment, and free food. The U.S.O. was the only place in town where you could hear big band music. Everywhere else—in stores, in restaurants, everywhere—all you could hear was cowboy music.[77]

When Phil and Mary first arrived in Pratt, they got a room at the only hotel in town, the Roberts. Phil would go off every day to his job on the base, and Mary would check the town's small newspaper hoping to locate an apartment for rent. But the town was small and the demand on the part of servicemen so great that the young couple eventually had to settle for a room in a nearby house.

The elderly couple who owned the house, Mr. and Mrs. Moon, initially stipulated numerous regulations for their new boarders. Mary and Phil had a pretty room with two windows overlooking a big porch, so the sun came pouring in. Another couple, a young captain and his wife, rented a smaller spare room down the hall. The two couples were not allowed to smoke in the home, nor did they have cooking privileges. The Moons also insisted that the wives could not remain in the home during the day while their husbands were on the base. As a result, Mary and Phil had to eat out every night, and every day Mary had to find something outside the house to occupy her time. She recalls her daily schedule:

> Every morning after Phil left for the base, I would walk about eight blocks to Main Street and go to Woolworth's for breakfast. Even at 8 in the morning, the heat coming up from the sidewalk felt like a

Fig. 1.13. Wedding portrait, March 25, 1944. *From left*: Nickie Cavarella (Phil's brother-in-law); Mary (Cavarella) Aquila; Phil Aquila; Mary Aquila (Phil's sister). (Philip L. Aquila Collection)

furnace. Sometimes I felt so nauseous that I was afraid I'd pass out before getting to Woolworth's. In the afternoons, I'd go shopping or to a matinee. Often, I'd just hang out at the U.S.O. with other wives, or a group of us would go on a picnic.[78]

Mrs. Moon, who was in her early eighties, soon took a liking to the young Mrs. Aquila, and began inviting her into the kitchen for tea after the captain's wife had left the house for the day. Mrs. Moon frequently told Mary about how peaceful and quiet Pratt was before the air base was built. "But now," she complained, "you can't even go to a restaurant without waiting in line for an hour." Mrs. Moon liked to talk about her family. One day she and her husband even drove Mary and Phil out into the country to show them their honeymoon cottage and farm.[79]

Mary was just beginning to adjust to her new lifestyle when she became pregnant. Pratt's hot and humid weather, combined with a steady diet of restaurant food and what seemed like never-ending morning sickness, spelled disaster. When Mary's normal weight of 112 pounds dropped down to 94, she went to see a doctor, who recommended that she return to Buffalo where she could eat home cooking and rest comfortably. Otherwise she might lose the baby. Shortly thereafter, Phil escorted her on the train to Chicago, where they were met by Mary's mother, Alice Cavarella, who then took her back to Buffalo while Phil returned to Pratt.

As summer faded into autumn, Phil found himself alone once more. Sitting on his bunk he worried not just about his young pregnant wife, but also about his next military assignment. He realized that the Army Air Force would probably be transferring him in the very near future. The question was where?

Knowing that there was a very good possibility he would be sent overseas, Phil decided to apply for Officer Candidate School. He figured that if he had to go into combat, he might as well do it as an officer. Phil was confident he would be accepted, because of his high scores on his induction exams, his superb performance in the Air Cadet Training Program, and his impressive military record. His commanding officers at Pratt agreed, and they recommended him highly.[80]

Fate intervened once more, however, to derail his promising military career. In early March, Sgt. Aquila received a new assignment: the Army Air Force was transferring him to Wendover Field, Utah. Realizing that his new position would most likely prevent him from going overseas for at least several months, he immediately withdrew his application to Officer Candidate School. Phil knew that if he completed officer training he would be sent into battle within weeks. Like most soldiers, Aquila was willing but certainly not eager to go into combat.

What Sgt. Aquila did not know at the time was how important the new assignment was. Wendover Field was a top secret base located just outside Wendover, Utah (population 100). One observer described its location in the salt flats on the Utah-Nevada border as "the end of nowhere." Bob Hope cracked that the tiny town should be called "Leftover." Not to be outdone, Bing Crosby joked that the village looked like "Tobacco Road with slot machines." Yet it was at Wendover Field that the U.S. military made preparations for the most secret and important mission of the war, the atomic bombing of Hiroshima and Nagasaki.[81] Sgt. Aquila, as Wendover Field's Chemical Warfare NCO, got to play a supporting role in one of the war's most significant dramas: the training of the crew of the *Enola Gay*.

By the end of 1943, Wendover Field had over 2,000 civilian and 17,500 military employees. For most of the war, the base's main purpose was to train the crews of B-17, B-24, and B-29 bombers.[82] But in 1945, the base had a special mission. Historians Leonard J. Arrington and Thomas G. Alexander explain:

> Easily the most spectacular unit to assemble and train at Wendover was the 509th Composite Group, officially activated on December 17, 1944, under the command of Colonel Paul W. Tibbets, Jr. While the services which its various component parts performed were similar to those performed by other units which trained at the [Wendover] base, its overall mission proved to be without precedent. The arrival of its first B-29 Superfortress marked the beginning of training to drop bombs over Japan.[83]

When Sgt. Aquila reported to Wendover Field on March 6, 1945, he soon learned that the base was cloaked in secrecy. "This camp handles mighty secret work," he wrote cryptically to his sister, "so I can't tell you too much about it."[84]

Phil Aquila spent the last twelve months of his military career at Wendover Field. Initially, he had a difficult time adjusting to his new assignment. His letters home complained repeatedly about the base's isolation and desert location, as well as his predecessor's incompetence. But eventually he settled in and managed to get everything in order. As the NCO in charge of chemical supplies, Sgt. Aquila supervised his office, ordered necessary supplies, filled out required forms, made sure soldiers were well equipped, and trained officers and enlisted personnel in chemical warfare.

After the atomic bomb was dropped on Hiroshima, Phil wrote home proudly to his family:

> I just sent my wife a clipping about Wendover Field, which I found in the Salt Lake paper. I'd like you to read it. You see, I haven't said any-

thing about this field, but I knew way back in May or June that as soon as one of these Wendover [bomber] outfits went across [the Pacific] the war would end real quickly. In other words, I'm talking about the Atomic Bomb, and this is the field that trained the men who dropped it on Japan twice. I can't say I did much except keep the field going and help these outfits as much as possible. . . . In other words, this field is or was the most important in the world, and did the most to win the war.[85]

In early February 1946, Sgt. Aquila was notified that he was being discharged from the Army Air Force. A few weeks later he reported to the Separation Center at Fort Dix, New Jersey, the same base where he had been inducted into active service three years before.

The official military record shows that Philip L. Aquila was awarded the Good Conduct Medal, the American Service Medal, the World War II Victory Medal, the American Campaign Medal, and, of course, the ubiquitous discharge gold lapel pin with the American eagle on it. He also qualified as a "sharpshooter." More important to him, during his three years in the military he received 103 days furlough and ultimately he got out of the Army in one piece. Like other veterans, he received the following form letter from President Truman thanking him for his service:

To you who answered the call of your country and served in its Armed Forces to bring about the total defeat of the enemy, I extend the heart-felt thanks of a grateful nation. As one of the Nation's finest, you undertook the most severe task one can be called upon to perform. Because you demonstrated the fortitude, resourcefulness and calm judgement necessary to carry out that task, we now look to you for leadership and example in further exalting our country in peace.[86]

"WHAT DID YOU DO IN THE WAR, POP?"

After the war, Phil Aquila always insisted—only partly in jest—that the Army Air Force had collected all its top personnel at Wendover to guarantee the success of the atomic bomb mission. As I was going through his papers shortly after his death, I came across a George Will column about Colonel Tibbets and the *Enola Gay* crew that my father had clipped out of *The Buffalo Evening News* in 1994. In the margin, he had written: "What did you do in the Big One, Pop? I trained this outfit in chemical warfare in 1945 at Wendover Field."[87]

The question posed in his note brought back a vivid childhood memory. In the early 1950s, my father loved to recite a poem to me and my brother that was called "What Did You Do in the War, Pop?" The whimsical poem featured an excited little boy asking his daddy about

World War II. He wanted all the details about his pop's heroic deeds and war stories. But the former GI, who had never been overseas, could only shrug and admit that the only fighting he ever did was with a broom.

No doubt many World War II veterans could relate to the poem, because, like my father, they too had spent their entire military careers on the home front. Yet every soldier, including those who never went overseas, played a role in America's victory in World War II.

The letters of Sgt. Philip L. Aquila not only provide an answer to what he did in the war, but they enable us to better understand the role played by all GIs on the home front. Along with showing what Phil Aquila did as a soldier, they demonstrate what he did as a man. They reveal a patriotic young American whose family came first, a reluctant warrior not eager to volunteer but certainly willing to do whatever his nation demanded. His determination echoed the nation's. His story demonstrates the daily heroism of ordinary people on the home front during World War II.

So sit back and prepare to enter the world of 1944. Pretend you have just walked into the Aquila household at 507 Eagle Street in Buffalo, New York. Phil's sister Mary invites you to sit down, enjoy some spaghetti, and read the daily letters that were kept in a large 20 lb. macaroni box on the dining room table for everyone to see. You will get to know the entire Italian immigrant family through the letters. You will see the war and the home front through Phil's eyes. You'll be introduced to his wife, the former Mary Cavarella, as well as to aunts, uncles, cousins, friends, and in-laws. Every once in a while, his brothers will drop into the conversation. You'll hear about Frankie in the South Pacific, Carmen aboard the *U.S.S. Vicksburg* in the Pacific, Shadow at a naval base in Memphis, and Tony, still in Buffalo hoping not to get drafted. You will experience World War II, family history, and immigrant history firsthand—as recorded in the correspondence of Sgt. Philip L. Aquila.

PART 2

Letters from a GI on the Home Front, 1944–1946

[All letters are addressed to Phil's older sister, Mary, unless otherwise noted. In a few minor instances names have been changed to avoid embarrassment. In no case, however, has a name change altered the historical significance or meaning of an event. Due to space limitations extraneous statements have been removed as indicated by ellipses. Repetitive phrases that Phil commonly uses to begin a letter, such as "I'm feeling fine out here and I hope you are all feeling the same out there," have been deleted, along with general comments about the weather or other superfluous statements that add nothing to the narrative.]

Monday, August 7, 1944/Pratt, Kansas

Dear Mary,

Tonight as I sit and write to you, my heart is filled with something desperate. I'm about to do something that may change my very future. I can't as yet explain the details to you, because I've just begun. I assure you though, if everything turns out okay I'll be the happiest man in the world, and if it doesn't, well, it's just too bad for all the happy dreams I have had for many long years.

Outside of the plans I'm working on, everything out here is okay with me. Don't worry, about what I just said because I'll explain completely in a week or two. You see, I'm trying to punish some guy in Buffalo from here and so far it looks as if I'm going to succeed.

Please don't ask my wife for any information concerning what I've just written. Sort of a mystery story to you isn't it? Well, it'll prove interesting the way I'm going to work things. So-long now and God bless you all. Not a word to Ma about this.

Love to: Ma, Pa, Mary, Tony, Francie, & Carlo

X X X — Phil ("The Fighting Sarge")

P.S. I know I hardly mention any body's [sic] name in my letters, but, Mary, you always tell Pa for me that I'm always asking about him. The old man is getting old regardless of how he is. I know in his heart he feels that four of his sons are off to war. So long.

[Phil is twenty-two years old, and his father is sixty-three. Phil wrote this letter to his sister Mary a few weeks after his pregnant wife had moved back to Buffalo for health reasons. He was concerned about his pregnant wife's safety, because of a series of events that had begun several months earlier. On the eve of their wedding, Phil received an anonymous letter, allegedly written by a man who claimed to be in love with Phil's fiancée. The writer threatened to kill Phil if he showed up for the marriage ceremony.

Mary Cavarella was as shocked as Phil. She assured him that she had never dated anyone else, and she was just as puzzled as he was about who had written the letter. Although nothing happened at the wedding, both Phil and Mary were quite shaken by the entire incident.

Shortly after Mary returned to Buffalo because of health problems related to a difficult pregnancy, Phil received another letter. This time it was signed, allegedly by a man who had worked at a candy store with Mary. The furious letter writer insisted that he was the baby's real father, and he threatened both Mary and Phil.

Not only was Phil Aquila not the type of person to simply sit back passively when threatened, but his sense of Italian family honor required him to strike back at the offender. Phil approached his superior officer for help, and the two decided that the best course of action would be to ask the Buffalo police to find and arrest the letter writer. That's why Phil signs the letter to his sister, "The Fighting Sarge." He has decided to fight back against the vindictive letter writer.

Although he trusted and believed his new wife, Phil realized that there was always the possibility that the police investigation could reveal that Mary was lying to him. That's why he tells his sister that if things don't turn out, all his "happy dreams" will be ruined.

A few weeks after Phil's commanding officer contacted the Buffalo police on his behalf, Phil received the following letter from the District Attorney's Office:]

Buffalo, New York/September 6, 1944

Friend Philip,

As a lieutenant of police in the Buffalo Police Department and assigned to the District Attorney's Office, I received the letter written by your 2nd lieutenant, Harold J. Erlandson, to investigate. Now I interviewed Jason B. [the man who allegedly had signed the hate letter] and after talking to him for a half an hour I will assure you that you have nothing to worry about. Now I [am] the father of a soldier boy now in the third army in France [and] he has a wife and a baby back home in Buffalo, [so] you can rest assured that I will do everything possible to take care of a soldier boy.

Now when I started to interview Jason B. I told him who I was and that I had a letter to investigate. I will assure you that he sure played the part of a gentleman. He told me that he would answer any question that I asked him. He informed me that he knew your wife when they worked together at the Emerick Candy Company and he also knew her mother who worked with them. He felt awful bad to think that he should be accused of writing any letters to you. He told me that he knew that you had married Mary around the first of April and that he has never seen her since. Jason B. also said for me to get the letters that were written and he would pay to have a handwriting expert examine them. As far as I am concerned I think Jason B. is sure a gentleman. I also informed him that the F.B.I. would take charge of the case if any more letters were written.

Now, I also visited the home of your mother-in-law and had a long talk with your wife and mother-in-law. I learned that your wife, Mary, was at camp with you for three months and then she returned to Buffalo. The mother-in-law informs me that Mary has never left the home unless she was with her. I also learned the condition your wife is in [due to the pregnancy], and I talked to her accordingly so not to excite her. You sure have a wonderful little wife and as I am the father of four, I surely know when I see a good girl.

Now, friend, send me the letters that you have received and I will get the sender which after all my talks, I think you will find that it is a girl that is trying to cause you and your wife trouble. I will again assure you that you have nothing to worry about and if there is anything that I can do to help you just drop me a line. Now keep that chin of yours up and just keep praying and I know it will soon be over. I wish you the best of luck.

William E. Downey, District Attorney's Office

[Phil was relieved when he received the letter from the police officer, assuring him that his wife had not been having an affair. He replied immediately to Mr. Downey, sending him the hate letters he requested, as well as the following letter:]

Section D: 246th Base Unit/Army Air Field/Pratt, Kansas
Dear Sir:

I received your letter, reassuring me that Mr. Jason B. was completely innocent of writing these letters which I am enclosing at this time.

I was surprised to hear that it may be a woman who is causing all this trouble. Sir, I trust my wife with my very life, and the moment anybody insults her, I lose all my control. The person who wrote these letters to me has committed several crimes. She has attempted to undermine the morale of a member of the armed forces, which does place her on the side of Germany and Japan. She has attempted to destroy a family, and families are the one great symbol of the backbone of this nation. She has undoubtedly committed a crime which would banish her from any religion of this country. Furthermore, Sir, if anything should happen to my wife and coming baby, as a result of all this worrying and excitement, this person who has written these letters would have committed nothing less than attempted murder. Literally speaking, she has stabbed me in the back, at the time she thought I was helpless to act. Fortunately our great army has methods to deal with such criminals who are the equivalent of saboteurs. Sir, I place everything in your hands in the hope that you will put a stop to this great outrage and serve justice if possible. It is a terrible disgrace that this person is even an American citizen. Beside me, I have three other brothers in the forces, both here and overseas, also one close cousin of 19 years of age who has already been killed in France. Sir, my brothers and my cousin have fought and died so that we could have this so-called Freedom of Fear and the right to live in happiness. Frankly, Sir, I'd just as soon put a bullet through this person as I would a Nazi or Jap soldier, but fortunately my mind isn't as stupid as this person's.

In closing I wish to thank you very much for all that you are doing and will do for me, and Sir, if we succeed in tracking down this person you may destroy these letters. But if we don't, please hang on to them, because I'll never rest until this person is apprehended. Thank you very much.

Yours truly, Philip L. Aquila, Sgt., Air Corps

P.S. If you look very closely at these letters, you will notice that the person tried to change her handwriting each time, but the letter "D" at the end of a word proves it's the same person.

[*The entire hate mail incident was resolved to Phil's satisfaction. Both Phil and Mary were stunned when they learned who wrote the letters and why. When Lt. Downey first went to the Cavarellas' house, he asked Mary and her mother if the family was having any problems with any persons who might have a motive for such letters. Mary's mother told him about a recent problem she had had with a former friend named Sophia. Shortly before Phil had married Mary Cavarella on March 25, 1944, Mary's mother discovered that her sixteen-year-old*] *nephew was having an affair with thirty–year-old Sophia, who was a close friend of the Cavarellas. When Mary's mother told her sister about the entire affair, Sophia vowed vengeance.*

Suspecting that Sophia was behind both letters, the detective then asked Phil to send him the hate mail. After he received the letters, he took them to Sophia's home to confront her directly. A few hours later he returned to the Cavarellas and told them not to worry because the matter had been resolved. Just to be sure, though, he told them to let him know if Mary or Phil received any more letters. No other letters ever arrived.

Sophia later married a soldier, and repeatedly told friends she hoped he died so she could receive the allotment. One night she went out on the town and was never heard from again.

Though Phil's worries about his wife turned out to be unfounded, the question of fidelity was one that most couples were concerned about during World War II. After all, soldiers who left wives or girlfriends behind could never really be certain that their loved ones were being faithful. Frequent newspaper accounts about "Allotment Annies" who married soldiers hoping to cash in on the government's promise of a $10,000 life insurance policy should the husband die during the war, along with the era's ubiquitous "Dear John" letters, fed the insecurities of many soldiers. Phil's letters demonstrate that even though he loved and trusted his wife, he was not immune to the fears felt by soldiers stationed at home or abroad.]

Thursday, September 21, 1944/Pratt, Kansas

Dear Mary,

I just got another letter from you and thanks a lot. Glad to hear that everything there is fine, because out here it is too. Yes, I'd sure like to see a picture of Frankie, as he looks now.

In this letter you sent me [there are] some corrections to make on the list you sent of Ma's earnings. Don't worry. I'll check over everything and you'll get the amount by Thursday the 27th of September. . . . Well, I guess I have nothing to say for today, so I'll close. So-long and God bless you all.

Love to: Ma, Pa, Mary, Tony, Francie, and Carlo.
X X X X X X X X X X X X — Phil

[The earnings refer to the amount of money that Phil's family earned picking beans and other crops on farms near Buffalo, New York. The fact that Phil is still keeping the books indicates that even though he's in the army, he is still very much involved in family activities and concerns.]

Friday September 22, 1944/Pratt, Kansas

Dear Mary,

I'm writing this letter, during my working hours, so, I don't have too much to say. Right now I'm about to go to lunch.

The weather is just right out here, not too warm and not too cold. It's just a little windy though. Everything out here is going along pretty good so far today. I hope it's the same out there too.

I think I told you that my furlough was delayed a little while longer. If everything goes along okay each day, I believe I'll be home sometime in October next month. I know the date already but there's no use in telling you about it, because they change it every so often.

Sunday night I'm on Charge of Quarters and I'll figure up Ma's earnings on the adding machine in the office. Well, that's all for now, so until tomorrow night, so-long and God bless you all.

Love To: Ma, Pa, Mary, Tony, Francie, & Carlo

X X X X X X X X X — Phil

[Phil almost always closes with "so-long and God Bless you all," even though he doesn't go to church very often. Interestingly, later letters demonstrate that his brother Frankie also used a similar closing. Perhaps they learned this in school, or it could simply be the Catholic/Italian love of ritual. The closing reads like the benediction at the end of the mass. Also, note the order in which Phil lists his family. His mother, to whom he was devoted comes first; his father, with whom he really doesn't have much contact, comes second out of respect; then comes Mary, to whom he is writing; then Tony, the older brother; and then the two youngest, Francie and Carlo. The fact that he used this closing letter after letter suggests that Phil instinctively understood the importance of repetition and ritual in letter writing. The sameness assured the reader that Phil was doing fine and that nothing had changed.]

Saturday, September 23, 1944/Pratt, Kansas

Dear Mary,

. . . I've got all the corrections you've been sending me about Ma's earnings. You said she made $533.82 cents all season. That's pretty good, in fact that's real good. Tomorrow night, I'll see if that's all figured out right. If you sent me the right figures, I'll give you the most accurate amount and I hope it checks with the $533.82.

I was glad to hear that Carmen arrived there even if it was for only two days. You said he got thinner. Don't say that no more, it reminds me of Aunt Josephine always complaining about Joe getting thinner. *[Cousin Joe was later killed in battle shortly after D-Day.]* You and Ma just think the kid got thinner. Just ask him how much he weighed before he was inducted and how much he weighs now. Then, if he lost weight, then say he got thinner. I see too many healthy guys to believe they get thin. Even myself, I think of home, my wife, and everything and a lot of other problems, and I haven't lost or gained a pound since I was inducted. I'm 153 lbs. and I'll stay that way. Carmen's okay, Frankie's okay, Shadow's okay, and I'm okay. Don't anybody lose faith in us, because when faith is lost, all is lost. We are coming back, every one of us, don't you ever forget that.

Thanks a lot for you and Ma going over to my wife's house and bringing her the eggs, tomatoes, grape, and melon. She always tells me that she does appreciate Ma's kindness. Yep, I'll prove to her yet that you all are the best family in the world and also I'll prove to you that my wife will be the best in-law to our family. Well, so-long for now and God bless you all.

Love To: Ma, Pa, Mary, Tony, Francie, & Carlo
X X X X X X — Phil

Sunday, September 24, 1944/Army Air Field/Pratt, Kansas
Dear Mary,

It's Sunday afternoon out here and I feel rather lazy as usual. I'll write you this letter for now, and tonight I'm on Charge of Quarters. I will write again because I want to figure up Ma's earnings.

In this letter I want to enclose the letter Frankie sent me, so that you too can read it. . . . I got up at 8:30 A.M. this morning and read a book in bed until 11 A.M. It's kind of cold and cloudy outside and I doubt if we'll get any real warm days any more out here for this year.

Each day that passes brings me a day closer to my furlough. But, as usual, some thing might come up to prevent my getting it. It's just my luck, I guess. Some guys out here get their furloughs real easy while I have to sweat it out a couple months before hand.

My watch is on the blink. It just won't run so I gave it up. When I come home I'll bring it with me and I'll see which one I'll have fixed, okay?

Well, I hope each of you is doing okay in your jobs. How does Pa get along with his job [at Allegheny-Ludlum Steel] now that Tony doesn't work there anymore? *[Tony has just gotten a new job at Bell Aircraft, where Phil worked before getting drafted.]* So-long for now and God bless you all.

Love To: Ma, Pa, Mary, Tony, Francie & Carlo
X X X X X X — Phil

Sunday September 24, 1944/Army Air Field/Pratt, Kansas
Dear Mary,

Here I am again for the second time today. I'm on Charge of Quarters right now. I just got through figuring up Ma's earnings. I did it by machine and I also checked it by my own head, so the amount is correct and as far as I'm concerned Ma was robbed out of $22.60. Now wait a minute, I figured $556.42 according to all those amounts you gave me. I have them all down on the machine paper here, so you can check them over. $533.82 is the amount you said Mr. M. [the farmer who is the boss] checked, and that's including Monday September 18th work that you didn't endorse. My amount is up to <u>September 17th only</u>. Now, whether you made a mistake in the red berries, I don't know. You said to figure up at 6 cents a quart and there's 616 quarts. I always thought it was figured in pints. And another thing, did Mr. M. deduct the money from the tomatoes & leave $533.82 or is $533.82 the completed amount? If you are right in letting me figure the red berries (which includes 6 full tickets & 16 quarts at 6 cents a quart) & if Mr. M. didn't deduct the tomato money thus leaving $533.82, then Ma should've gotten $556.42 and also, plus the money that she made Monday September 18th if she worked on that day. My amount is perfect according to the amounts you gave me & I think Ma's getting gypped of $22.60 plus the money of September 18th if she worked that day. So-long & God bless you all. And let me know how you make out in this, okay?

Love To: Ma, Pa, Mary, Tony, Francie, & Carlo

X X X X X X X X — Phil

[Enclosed in this letter was an adding machine printout that detailed the amount of work done and money owed. It is reprinted below verbatim, including Phil's handwritten note on the back of it]

Ma's Earnings for 1944

1. <u>GREEN BEANS</u>

August	21 ——	186 lbs.
	22 ——	129
	29 ——	209
	30 ——	288
	31 ——	152
September	1 ——	316
	2 ——	240
	3 ——	714
	5 ——	522
	6 ——	230
	7 ——	142
	8 ——	273
	9 ——	334
	10 ——	868
	11 ——	222
	12 ——	111

13 —— 239
14 —— 263
15 —— 210
16 —— 297
17 —— 135
6080 total lbs.
x.03 cents per lb.
$182.40 money for green beans

2. YELLOW BEANS

July   18 —— 350
            19 —— 162
            22 —— 401
            23 —— 198
            24 —— 386
            25 —— 64
August   1 —— 97
            6 —— 464
            22 —— 117
            25 —— 398
September   2 —— 435
            6 —— 120
            7 —— 171
            9 —— 66
            15 —— 56
            17 —— 339
3824 lbs.
x.03 cents per lb.
$114.72 money for yellow beans

3. DAY WORK:

152 hours
x.50 cents per hour
$76.00 money for Day Work

4. STRAWBERRIES:

2,088 quarts
x.05 cents per quart
$104.40 money for Strawberries

5. BLACKBERRIES:

699 quarts
x.06 cents per quart
$41.94 money for Blackberries

6. <u>REDBERRIES:</u>

    616 quarts
    <u>x.06</u> per quart
    $36.96 money for Redberries

7. <u>TOTALS:</u> $556.42 is the correct and complete amount of Ma's
        Earnings.

    Greenbeans —— $182.40
    Yellow Wax —— 114.72
    Day Work   ——   76.00
    Strawberries —— 104.40
    Blackberries ——   41.94
    Redberries ——   <u>36.96</u>
       Total Earnings $556.42

[The following was written on the back of the adding machine slip totals.]

To $556.42 add the money Ma made on September 18th if she worked and that will give you the complete amount, and then subtract $533.82 and that will give you the amount missing.

    $556.42 — up to Sept. 17th
    <u>–533.82</u> — Mr. M's [the farmer's] amount
    $ 22.60 plus Sept. 18th is missing

Monday September 25, 1944/Pratt, Kansas

Dear Mary,

Another week is starting out here and I hope it goes as good as last week did. I feel a lot of changes about to be made here and I'm sure keeping my fingers crossed.

Well, I hope by now that you got the figuring I did on Ma's earnings. For your information, I don't want you to think that I just sat by the machine & figured it easily in 5 minutes. Nope, I started on all of it at 5:30 p.m. and I finished at exactly 8:45. Yes, it took me over 3 hours, because I kept checking & rechecking. You see, I too couldn't believe Ma was $22.60 short, but at the end I had to because both the machine and me were checking each time. It's up to you, what you'll do about it, but one thing I hate is being cheated. Anybody that goes out to help a farmer during these times when they don't have to, and then gets cheated out of money, is getting a raw deal. I'd hate to think Ma worked for nothing out there. Let Francie and especially Tony go over the amounts carefully and see if they don't check with mine. . . . I'll close now so take it easy. So-long & God bless you all.

        Love To: Ma, Pa, Mary, Tony, Francie, & Carlo
            X X X X X X X X — Phil

P.S. Maybe that Mr. M. [the farmer] thinks that just because most of us are in the army, there's no one to take an interest out there. So-long.

Tuesday September 26, 1944/Pratt, Kansas

Dear Mary,

Today is one of the few days that I didn't get any mail from any-body. Once in every two or three weeks that happens to me. That's o.k., because tomorrow I know I'll get a little pile of them.

Well, here I am, still keeping my fingers crossed and hoping that nothing happens to prevent my furlough. The weather out here is still o.k. It's cold in the mornings and nights. Right now we are still wearing our summer uniforms, but after September 30th we have to change to winter uniforms again, and that's what I'll wear when I come home. I was hoping to come there with my summer outfit, but I can't no more.

Well, everything out here is going along o.k., and I hope everything there is o.k., too. So long and God bless you all.

Love To: Ma, Pa, Mary, Tony, Francie, & Carlo
X X X X X X X — Phil

Wednesday September 27, 1944/Pratt, Kansas

Dear Mary,

Today I received the letters you wrote Saturday and Monday. You sure gave me all the family details in Saturday's letter & thanks a lot. It's been raining all day long without stopping.

It sure was too bad about Carmen almost missing the train back to his camp. He would have been doing a lot of wrong though if he had missed the train & stayed in Buffalo all week long. He thinks they'd have given him the same amount of punishment, but they'd have given him more. So, if anything ever happens like that again & he misses the train, make sure he catches the very next train.

I was glad to hear that you heard from Frankie again. The only rea-son I can see why he doesn't write is because he doesn't get the right chance to write. He probably works all kinds of shifts.

I'm glad the car runs good again & I hope it stays that way. I'll use it if I come home, but not too much, because I'd prefer to make my wife do a lot of walking, it's good for her at this time. *[She's four months pregnant.]*

About cousin Johnny. I don't hear from him. I wrote him the last letter before he got a furlough and he hasn't answered me. Well, when he answers me I'll write him, anyway I don't know his address. Well, so-long for now & God bless you all.

Love To: Ma, Pa, Mary, Tony, & Francie & Carlo
X X X X X X X — Phil

Thursday September 28, 1944/Pratt, Kansas

Dear Mary,

Everything is going okay out here and I hope it keeps that way just a little while longer. I hope it's likewise out there too. The weather out here is rather cold and we've got the fires going full blast.

I'm glad you were able to see the Bell Ringer that Tony brought from work [at Bell Aircraft]. He'll get it every month. My Ordnance Department isn't there any more. It moved to Vermont you know.

Well, the war seems to be going slow again. The Germans are putting up a tough fight. According to the papers, our casualty list is pretty high and it'll get higher yet. We've got to keep hoping, that's all. *[Phil is probably referring to a fierce German counterattack that occurred in late September in response to the Allies' attempt to capture the Arnhem Bridge in Holland, which would have enabled the Allies to cross the Rhine. The Allies failed to take the bridge, and suffered well over 10,000 casualties.]*

Well so-long for tonight, so God bless you all.

Love To: Ma, Pa, Mary, Tony, Francie & Carlo

X X X X X X — Phil

Friday September 29, 1944/Pratt, Kansas

Dear Mary,

Today I received the letter you wrote last Tuesday the 26th of September. You said 3 days between letters are okay. That's nothing, sometimes I receive one of your letters in two days. Like the letter you wrote Monday, I got it on a Wednesday.

I was glad to hear that Ma & Pa are getting along fine with each other. There's no reason ever why they can't stay peaceful all the time. I was also glad to hear that you are putting eggplants and peppers in oil and vinegar. You know there's nothing better I like than eggplants and peppers to eat. The only thing though I never did like them with vinegar.

You said Tony works in Department 76 [at Bell Aircraft]. Yes, it sounds familiar, but I don't exactly know what type of work they do in that department. What type of work does he do and what shift does he work on?

Out here things are getting tougher and tougher. I guess God just wouldn't grant me this furlough. It's sure real tough to be robbed out of a furlough just by a very few days. What ever they are doing had to happen just when I'm about to get a furlough. Nothing happened yet, but I'm completely discouraged about getting a furlough. It's just my damn luck I guess. Well, I'll get to come home one of these days, you can bet on that, so don't worry, wherever I am in the U.S. I'll get a furlough if I should ever go overseas.

Well, so-long for now & God bless you all.

Love To: Ma, Pa, Mary, Tony, Francie & Carlo

X X X X X X X — Phil

Saturday September 30, 1944/Pratt, Kansas

Dear Mary,

Everything out here is going along pretty good so far and I hope it continues to be that way. . . .

Tomorrow is Sunday and I should go to church, but I guess I won't. . . . It just doesn't seem like church out here. When I think of going to church, I picture my wife & I all dressed up together and going. Well, I hope those days will come around soon. By the looks of things, though, peace may come real quick, and then again it may still take a long time.

Today I got paid again. From $78, insurance, allotment, and bond are taken out, and I got $42 as my pay.

Well, so-long for now and God bless you all.

Love To: Ma, Pa, Mary, Tony, Francie & Carlo

X X X X X X X — Phil

Sunday October 1, 1944/Pratt, Kansas

Dear Mary,

Today is Sunday and the 1st of October. Slowly, time is going by. I hope I have better luck in coming home this month, than I had last month. We'll just have to see, I guess.

The weather here is cold and cloudy and there's a very light drizzling rain coming down to make it all the more miserable. I slept till 10:00 a.m. this morning, but I stayed in bed until 12 reading a book.

Today a fellow named Bob Hope will be here to crack some of his jokes. I have no ambition to see him though. But if he'll come and see me in my barracks it'll be okay, otherwise I won't see him.

Everything is going along as fast as possible out here. I had stewed chicken this afternoon. It's a shame to waste all those good chickens that way. They could've fried them and made everybody happy, but no, they had to make a stew out of them. Well at times like that, I eat just enough to keep me well and going.

Now that the car springs are all fixed, does Tony still run it up the curb into our yard to park it at night? Has he got any riders that he takes to work at Bell [Aircraft] yet? Yep, as Tony goes to work each day, he follows the same routes that Shadow took. He can be sure that every landmark he passes some time or other Shadow and I always got stuck there when his car broke down. We pushed Shadow's cars to work more than we rode them. If Tony drives the car to work, he can use the same short cut we used to use.

Well that's all for now, so take it easy and God bless you all.

Love To: Ma, Pa, Mary, Tony, Francie & Carlo

X X X X X X X — Phil

Figure 2.1: Phil Aquila with family car ready to go on a date with Mary Cavarella, 1941. (Philip L. Aquila Collection)

Monday October 2, 1944/Pratt, Kansas

Dear Mary,

. . . The weather out here has been cold, rainy, and very cloudy, and it's made this camp pretty muddy. I don't dress up to go nowhere so it doesn't bother me. All I do some nights is put on some clean clothes and take in a movie. Tonight, I got back from work, ate, bought a newspaper, and laid on my bunk reading it for about an hour. I do exactly what Tony does at night after work there, only he does more to win the war than I do and that's an honest to goodness fact, but don't say nothing.

I hope by now Ma's finished canning although she still can buy a lot of stuff at the market of Bailey & Clinton Streets to can if she feels she needs more food for this winter. Yep, people in this country are sure lucky, to be able to stock up as much food as they want. That's what us guys are fighting for, so tell Ma to stock up. So long and God bless you all.

Love To: Ma, Pa, Mary, Tony, Francie & Carlo
X X X X X X X — Phil

Tuesday October 3, 1944/Pratt, Kansas

Dear Mary,

Everything is going okay out there and according to schedule, and I hope it keeps up that way because if it does I don't see why I shouldn't get a furlough, maybe soon.

Today I didn't get no mail from nobody. Something wrong with the mail I guess. My wife writes every day, there's hardly a day when I don't get a letter from her, so on these days that I don't I know it was delayed along the line some place. . . .

I'm glad to hear that Tony has some riders going to Bell with him. You still didn't tell me if he works the day shift or 2nd shift? Well, that's all for tonight. I hope Ma and all of you are all feeling fine and I hope now Ma will start to put on the weight she lost out on the farm. So-long and God bless you all.

Love To: Ma, Pa, Mary, Tony, Francie & Carlo
X X X X X Phil X X X X X

Wednesday, October 4, 1944/Pratt, Kansas

Dear Mary,

I just got your letter of last Sunday. That's okay if you haven't got time to write so much. I understand, so don't worry.

Thanks for going to see my wife again. Anything you do to help her out in any way, I'll always appreciate it. . . .

As for my furlough, I'll get one only if nothing happens. As I said before I could give you the date I'll be home, but because they keep changing it and because I want to do a little surprising, I won't tell you or my wife.

Glad to hear that Carmen called up from Boston and said he might come home on a long weekend leave. Who knows, I may see him yet? . . . So-long for now, and God bless you all.

Love To: Ma, Pa, Mary, Tony, Francie & Carlo
X X X X X X X — Phil

Thursday October 5, 1944/Pratt, Kansas

Dear Mary,

. . . I got the pictures you sent me of Frankie. Honest, he came out okay. He's just the same. He didn't look no huskier and no thinner, although he may have grown taller. I'm sending you the small set back as you asked and I'll keep the ones you had enlarged. Thanks a lot. It was nice to see Frankie's pictures.

As for Shadow and me not wanting any packages or anything, we just can't help it. It's okay for Frankie and Carmen. They are of the younger type and they are out to have a good time and get what they want, but Shadow and I, we don't need anything. If we need clothes or anything we buy them ourselves. Thanks a lot for asking to send something anyway.

So long for now and God bless you all.

Love To: Ma, Pa, Mary, Tony, Francie & Carlo
X X X X X Phil X X X X X

Friday October 6, 1944/Pratt, Kansas

Dear Mary,

. . . I'm still holding out for a furlough. Right now, it wouldn't surprise me if I got it, and it wouldn't surprise me if I didn't. If Ma wants to though, she can sort of keep an eye open, because when I do come I'll sneak through the yard so she won't see me. So, just in case Ma is allergic to being startled, just tell her not to be too surprised if she hears a knock and opens the door to find me there. I guess I'm talking as if I'll be there for sure but don't count on it. When Carmen, Shadow, and Frankie say they are coming home, they usually know for sure. But I'm in a different situation out here. From day to day I'm on call, because I'm physically fit for overseas and at this time especially, there's a lot going on out here, so you see what I mean. . . . So-long and God bless you all.

Love To: Ma, Pa, Mary, Tony, Francie & Carlo
X X X X Phil X X X X

Saturday October 7, 1944/Pratt, Kansas

Dear Mary,

. . . I received the letter you wrote last Thursday. It came quickly, just like air mail. You probably mailed it Thursday night, and I received it Saturday evening at 5:00 p.m. . . . I was glad to hear that you picked up my wife and took her to the beauty parlor and then to our house and I'm glad you walked her home.

I'm sorry to hear that the people upstairs are moving. Don't let no [bad] people in. Leave it empty, if necessary. If any [bad] people inquire, don't tell them you don't want them [for that reason]. Ask them if they've got children. If they say yes, tell them you aren't giving the flat to anybody with children, and if they say they haven't got children, tell them you want a family with children. Catch on? And for Pete's sake, don't act as if you are willing to take anybody that asks. See if the people are polite first. If a man comes in and fails to take off his hat even at our doorway when he asks, why heck refuse him. Better to lose $24 or so for a month than have the wrong type of tenants who get drunk and cause a lot of trouble, noise and damage. That's one of the reasons why I wanted Ma to get her own house so nobody could bother her. So take your time in renting that house, and make sure you get the right people.

Why heck, when my wife and I looked for a room out here you should see what we had to go through and it was only for a room. Before the landlady would tell my wife we could have the room, she made my wife promise that we'd go out on Sunday and that my wife couldn't stay in all day and that I wasn't supposed to smoke in the house. So before you take in people, tell them what you expect of them. Don't be afraid and if they promise, let them have it, if not tell them you're sorry. If somebody inquires when Ma's alone, tell Ma to tell them to come back at night so you and Tony will be there. People are easy to get and there's all types so don't worry, and judge the people as if you were going to give them a job. You don't have to do any work to that upper flat no more, just sweep and maybe mop the rooms clean and dust off the shelves and clean the bathroom. That monkeying around each time people move in is unnecessary. Don't forget what I've said now.

I was glad to hear that Tony works the first shift. He's mighty lucky, because at Bell they usually hand out the second or third shifts. As for the assembly job he's got, well I think it's okay. Maybe at first it may not be interesting, but later on as he gets used to it, it will be and he can learn a lot about airplanes if he keeps his eyes open.

Well, so-long for now and God bless you all and I hope I'll be able to see you all soon.

Love To: Ma, Pa, Mary, Tony, Francie & Carlo

X X X X X X X — Phil

Sunday October 8, 1944/Pratt, Kansas

Dear Mary,

Sunday out here and all is well so far. I should've gone to church, but I didn't. I'm too lazy, I guess. . . .

I was glad to hear that you received two letters from Frankie and I was happy to hear that he told you quite a lot about himself. Yep, still the same old kid. They don't change. It's just the guys who don't care that change.

About people buying houses at this time, yes, it's true a lot of them will lose them. But not Ma. That's why I wanted her to be able to pay cash for her house. That way she'll have no worries except for taxes and if worse ever came to worse a few dollars from all the brothers will always pay for taxes and upkeep. *[Shortly before going into the army, Phil gave his mother cash he had saved from his job so the family could buy their own house, rather than renting like they had always done. He contributed most of the house's cost.]*

Well that's all for today. . . . So-long and God bless you all.

Love To: Ma, Pa, Mary, Tony, Francie & Carlo
X X X X X Phil X X X

Monday October 9, 1944/Pratt, Kansas

Dear Mary,

Everything is okay as usual. Now the time is getting closer to my furlough and each day seems pretty long and the nights are tough too because my mind stays wide awake thinking and even worrying. Well, I hope nothing happens.

Today I'm sending you a birthday card. Today should be October 12th and the 13th is your birthday, right? I sent it a day earlier and I hope you like it. Yep, I'm familiar pretty good with everybody in our family's birthday.

The weather out here is once again cold and cloudy. That's okay, though, it could be worse. I hope everything out there is going along fine with all of you. So-long for now and God bless you all.

Love To: Ma, Pa, Mary, Tony, Francie & Carlo
X X X X Phil X X X X

Tuesday October 10, 1944/Pratt, Kansas

Dear Mary,

. . . Well, I'm still sweating out this furlough and I believe I'm on my last lap. I hope nothing comes up and I know you are hoping the same thing. Yes, you can tell Ma to keep on the look out for me if you want.

One thing I'm positive that I'll move from here. The only thing that'll keep me from getting a furlough is shipping orders. One way or the other, I'll be traveling again.

Well so-long for now and take it easy.

Love To: Ma, Pa, Mary, Tony, Francie & Carlo

X X X X X X X — Phil

[His furlough came through, and he doesn't write again until October 31.]

Tuesday October 31, 1944/Pratt, Kansas

Dear Mary,

Here I am back at camp again. I just got back a few hours ago at 5:30 p.m. I made pretty good connections all the way back. I feel just how you'd expect me to feel. I'll have to get used to it all over again. It'll be kind of tough, but there's nothing anybody can do about it.

As yet I don't know what the score is out here. *[Phil is worried that he may be shipped overseas, since many of the GIs at his base have already been shipped out.]* I hope for my wife's sake that I can keep staying out here. Well, we'll have to hope for the best I guess.

I hope you are all feeling okay. Tell Ma not to worry about me because I'll always be alright. Incidently let me know if I left enough gas in the car so that Tony was able to go to work with it last Monday and Tuesday. Well, that's about all for now so take it easy and God bless you all.

Love To: Ma, Pa, Mary, Tony, Francie & Carlo

X X X X X X — Phil

Wednesday November 1, 1944/Pratt, Kansas

Dear Mary,

Today I received about 15 letters that were sent to me by everybody before I came home on furlough. Everything out here is going along the same as usual. I got settled down today.

You know, when we visited Aunt Josephine last Sunday, she seemed to think that I did everything on purpose to stay in the U.S. so long. She's so very wrong. I guess some people think I'm afraid to go out and fight, well they're wrong. I'm still out here waiting for any assignment or order. I'm just taking things as they come along. I ask for no privileges and I get none and I don't intend to volunteer for anything, so don't worry. Whatever happens to me happens because it had to. *[Aunt Josephine is Phil's mother's sister. Her son, Joe, was killed in battle shortly after D-Day. The aunt's criticism suggests that at least some Americans on the home front resented those soldiers who did not go overseas.]*

I got a letter from Frankie also today. He wrote it October 11, 1944. I'll send it to you as soon as I answer him.

Well, so-long for now and God bless you all.

Love To: Ma, Pa, Mary, Tony, Francie & Carlo
X X X X X X X — Phil

Thursday November 2, 1944/Pratt, Kansas

Dear Mary,

Just another day out here. . . . [A]nd I can't kick. . . . I was surprised at how warm it has been the last couple days. It was much colder when I left for my furlough, but I guess it won't be long now and it'll be very cold.

I hope things are going along alright for all of you out there. Mary, any time you can help my wife out, do so. Call her up once in awhile and ask her if she needs anything that she wants you to get. Well I guess there's hardly nothing left for me to say so take it easy and God bless you all.

Love To: Ma, Pa, Mary, Tony, Francie & Carlo
X X X X X X X — Phil

Friday November 3, 1944/Pratt, Kansas

Dear Mary,

Just another little letter short and snappy and to the point as usual. I never make my letters long because I have hardly nothing to say, just so you hear from me, right?

Well, what did you think of my furlough? Do you realize I spent 19 nights and 18 days home? See if you can find another soldier who can get a furlough like that one. Did I make Ma happy enough? I really tried to do my best to please everybody. I'm sorry about *Capare* [i.e., Godfather] Joe, however. Well next time I'll see him alright. One of these days I'll write him a letter and try to cheer him up a little that way. If I did anything wrong though beside that, let me know about it.

Yesterday I sent Carmen a birthday card because November 4th is his birthday. See, I didn't forget. I wonder if you out there forgot? Well, that finishes me up for tonight. Right now I'm on Charge of Quarters again. It's not so bad, so I really don't mind it. So-long for now and God bless you all.

Love To: Ma, Pa, Mary, Tony, Francie & Carlo
X X X X X X X — Phil

P.S. I forgot to tell Francie. I'm not against her going steady with this Tony. She could if she wants to. Find out what kind of a guy he is. All I want to put in Francie's head about boys is to first make sure they won't leave her flat, and second to make sure they always treat her like a gentleman. So-long (a little bit of Mr. Anthony *[Phil was joking that his lecture about boys sounds like one that the famous advice columnist, Mr. Anthony, might give]*).

Saturday November 4, 1944/Pratt, Kansas

Dear Mary,

Just another day out here. . . . Tonight I listened to both Dewey and Roosevelt. I'll still pick Dewey. I already voted for Dewey you know. He's got a pretty fair chance to win. But regardless which guy wins, it'll make little difference. . . . Well, that's all for now so take it easy and God bless you all.

Love To: Ma, Pa, Mary, Tony, Francie & Carlo
X X X X X X X — Phil

Sunday November 5, 1944/Pratt, Kansas

Dear Mary,

Today is Sunday out here. . . . I got up at 11:00 a.m. this morning. I did want to go to church, but I just didn't wake up. I guess you know how it is to be able to sleep until late when you are off duty.

The weather is pretty nice out here today. It was very cloudy but the sun broke through and it's a pretty good day after all. I hope everything there is going along okay. And I wish Carmen can keep coming home every once in a while, like he's been doing.

Yep, I sure miss all the food I used to eat out there. I'd be over my mother-in-law's house and I'd eat, then I'd come home and I'd eat, but I didn't gain any weight. The food here is pretty darn good though. Three good meals a day is good enough for me. Well that's all for now so so-long and God bless you all.

Love To: Ma, Pa, Mary, Tony, Francie & Carlo
X X X X X X X — Phil

Monday November 6, 1944/Pratt, Kansas

Dear Mary,

Today I received the letter you wrote last Saturday. It was the first letter from you since I left Buffalo.

About the money my wife wants you to deposit, you know where to go don't you? I called up the Liberty Bank on William Street and I asked them if it would be okay to deposit money in the same account in the Liberty Bank main branch on Main Street and they said it would be okay. So, Mary, instead of going on William Street [in the bad neighborhood], go on Main Street. It's up to you, though. I was just figuring that while you were shopping on Main some time and the banks were open you could deposit down there.

Don't worry, I didn't let Aunt [Josephine] bother me by what she said about me using my head to stay here [in the States]. I just went where they told me and did what they told me. A lot of guys are being transferred into the infantry from here, so don't be surprised at anything. (Don't worry my wife though. Don't tell her).

I was real glad to hear that Tony has another deferment. That's fine. Well so-long and don't worry. God bless you all.

Love To: Ma, Pa, Mary, Tony, Francie & Carlo
X X X X X X X X — Phil

Tuesday November 7, 1944/Pratt, Kansas

Dear Mary,

Today is election day and I suppose everything in Buffalo is in an uproar just like here in Kansas and every place else. It's 9:45 p.m. right now and according to reports on the radio, Roosevelt is ahead. I voted for Dewey, but if Roosevelt wins it's okay with me. Regardless of who won, the war would still go on and everybody would still be in the army. Right?

Everything out here has been going along okay, and I hope you can say the same for out there. . . . So-long for now, I guess, and God bless you all.

Love To: Ma, Pa, Mary, Tony, Francie & Carlo
X X X X X X X X — Phil

Wednesday November 8, 1944/Pratt, Kansas

Dear Mary,

Everything out here is going along okey dokey and I can't kick. I hope you are all in the best of health also.

I received a letter from Carmen today, which he mailed from Paterson, New Jersey. So by the looks of it, the kid keeps traveling around the coast. He sure visits a lot of different cities in his short voyages.

Well, elections are over with and Roosevelt won again. He'll spend 16 years in office. That's a longer time than most kings, dictators or Emperors spend, but if the people want him, it's okay. Well so-long for now and God bless you all.

Love To: Ma, Pa, Mary, Tony, Francie & Carlo
X X X X X X X — Phil

Thursday November 9, 1944/Pratt, Kansas

Dear Mary,

Just my daily letter again. You see, as I told you when I was there, I hardly have nothing at all to say except that everything out here is going along okay and that I hope it's the same out there, but I figure a letter each day helps Ma stay a little happy.

The weather out here was swell today. This morning was real cold, but this afternoon was like summer.

Well, just about 2 months from now, I'll have a son or a daughter. Heck, sure I wish it was a son, but if it's a daughter, it won't make much difference. I just hope Mary will be alright afterwards.

Well, so-long for now and God bless you all.

> Love To: Ma, Pa, Mary, Tony, Francie & Carlo
> X X X X X X X X X — Phil

Friday November 10, 1944/Pratt, Kansas

Dear Mary,

I received the swell letter you wrote last Tuesday while you were working. I was glad to hear that you get a lot of mail once in a while from all of us guys. Also, thanks a lot for going down to see my wife and doing her some favors every so often. I tell her to ask you if she wants anything done.

So the gasoline gauge is fixed. I was glad to hear that Tony had winter oil and alcohol put in the car. It was in November one time that the car froze on me and the block cracked because I didn't have no alcohol in it. You can say it again that I had trouble with the car when I was home. After that trip to North Collins though I broke the car in for myself again, and I never had a bit of trouble with it. Well that's all for now. . . . So-long and God bless you all.

> Love To: Ma, Pa, Mary, Tony, Francie & Carlo
> X X X X X X X — Phil

Saturday November 11, 1944/Pratt, Kansas

Dear Mary,

. . . Well, today was Armistice Day. It's like a laugh now. Yes, we celebrated it by having a parade. By the time this war ends we'll have two other armistices. One for Germany and one for Japan. So unless they do something about it we'll have to celebrate 3 Armistice Days and that'll mean the schools will close down for 3 days in one year and that's too much, don't you think?

All kidding aside I'm disgusted with all the monkeying around. They should get down to business and fight this war to a finish. Well, so-long for now and God bless you all.

> Love To: Ma, Pa, Mary, Tony, Francie & Carlo
> X X X X X X X — Phil —

[The next letter is written to his older brother Tony.]

Saturday November 11, 1944/Pratt, Kansas

Hello Tony,

You can tell I think of you once in a while because I write a letter now and then. I just got through writing a letter to our sister Mary to sort of help Ma's morale, and a letter to our sister Francie to see what I could do in ways of advice and now a little letter to you with the reason that I just want to write you.

It was good of you to come along that night to the Aloha Cafe. I had a nice time and so did my wife. The reason why I don't let myself go and have a good time the way you see it is because I just don't like to drink. I can probably take liquor as good as you, but I have no taste for it.

I was real glad to hear that you were deferred again. Grab all you can. There's about 12,000,000 men in the service and there's about 11,999,990 screaming for discharges, the other 10 found a home in the army and hate to leave. So, there's no sense in you ever wanting to be a private. All kidding aside, you can't get nowhere in the army no matter how good you are, because all the positions are taken up. They are drafting [i.e. transferring] us guys out of the air corps into the infantry, so figure it out for yourself. You'll be a private in the infantry under some kid who thinks he knows it all because he's been across 8 or 9 months. So-long and God bless you.

Love, your brother and pal, Phil

[Phil was right when he told Tony that ability was no longer a consideration in the induction process. Beginning in late 1943, the Army Air Force was no longer allowed to skim off the best inductees. In addition, by 1944, the Army was filling its combat needs in part by transferring soldiers from the Army Air Force into the infantry. That change in policy helps explain why Phil believed that he might soon be shipped overseas.]

Sunday November 12, 1944/Pratt, Kansas

Dear Mary,

. . . Well, I got up at 11:00 a.m. this morning. Not bad, is it? The weather is swell. I had two big chunks of chicken to eat this afternoon. I don't do much on Sundays. I usually write letters all day then at night I go to the show.

Everything is okay out here and I hope the same is out there. By the way how are those potatoes I bought for Ma getting along? I hope they don't get rotten. Well, that's all I have to say for today, so until tomorrow, so-long and God bless you all.

Love To: Ma, Pa, Mary, Tony, Francie & Carlo

X X X X X X X — Phil —

Monday November 13, 1944/Pratt, Kansas

Dear Mary,

There's not too much to report about from this corner of the world. Things are going along okay out here and I hope you can say the same out there. The weather today was really beautiful. Nice and warm. This morning especially, it was just like a Spring day. It's Indian Summer, I guess.

Well, the mail system out here seems to be okay. I manage to hear from everybody. Everybody that I'm interested to hear from anyway. How's the cigarette situation out there now? I hope it's better than when I was there. I just bought myself a carton of Luckies here. I wish I could send some, but it's too conspicuous. Maybe I'll find a way to send Tony some in the future, okay? So-long for now and God bless you all.

Love To: Ma, Pa, Mary, Tony, Francie & Carlo
X X X X X X X X — Phil —

Tuesday November 14, 1944/Pratt, Kansas

Dear Mary,

Everything out here is all the same and I hope it's the same out there. . . . My days go by rather slowly, but without anything happening. It suits me that way and I hope everything can continue to be the same. Well, don't worry and so-long and God bless you all.

Love To: Ma, Pa, Mary, Tony, Francie & Carlo
X X X — Phil — X X X X

Wednesday November 15, 1944/Pratt, Kansas

Dear Mary,

. . . I was glad to hear that you received a letter from Frankie and that he sent you a ribbon with a battle star on it. Don't worry, he wasn't in the battle himself. Frankie told me all about his job. He has a lot to do about battles, but he doesn't go too close to them. He hasn't seen any actual battles and I doubt if he ever will, so don't worry about him. *[Frankie was in the Army Transportation Corps stationed in New Guinea. His job involved unloading supplies off ships, and then reloading them onto other ships headed into battle.]*

Well, so-long for now and God bless you all.

Love To: Ma, Pa, Mary, Tony, Francie & Carlo
X X X X X X X — Phil —

Thursday November 16, 1944/Pratt, Kansas

Dear Mary,

I received your letter in which you sent Frankie's picture and I'm sending it right back as you asked me. If you do get the negative to it, I'd like to have a picture for myself.

Well, everything out here seems okay. It's kind of cold out here, but I've got the top part of my gym sweat suit on underneath so I feel warm. I hope the weather out there is a little warm anyway and I hope you are all in the best of health.

So-long for now and God bless you all.

Love To: Ma, Pa, Mary, Tony, Francie & Carlo
X X X X X X X — Phil

Friday November 17, 1944/Pratt, Kansas

Dear Mary,

. . . Everything out here is going along pretty good so far, and I hope it continues to stay that way. And I hope the same is out there too. The weather is real cold out here but still it hasn't snowed yet.

I hate to talk about this watch I've got because whenever I say it's going good, something goes wrong with it. As yet it's running just as it did when I was there. When I was home I let my wife wear it, but, now I've got it with me.

Well, so-long and God bless you all.

Love To: Ma, Pa, Mary, Tony, Francie & Carlo
X X X X X X X X — Phil

Saturday November 18, 1944/Pratt, Kansas

Dear Mary,

Today I received a letter from you and a letter from Carlo. They were both swell letters. Tell Carlo I'll write to him when I find some time in the near future. You told me Shadow sent Tony a carton of cigarettes. That's swell. I just sent Tony a carton of Camels, too. Between Shadow and me, I think we can get Tony enough cigarettes to smoke. Here's what to tell Tony.

The cigarettes he gets from Shadow and the little bit I send him, he can keep some place and still try to buy them out there the same as usual. For instance, each time somebody goes to the store, try and get as much as you can. Shadow said he's trying to send Tony a carton each week. That'll be swell. You see, it's kind of tough out here for me to send cigarettes off the base. There's a shortage here, too, but the soldiers get 2 packs apiece whenever they want them. However, I can get them by the carton. My trouble is though to get them mailed. They keep eyeing the packages because they don't want soldiers sending cigarettes off the base. That's why I dumped a carton into another box.

If my wife was here in Pratt with me though like [Shadow's wife] June is in Memphis, I could easily take a carton off the base and let my wife mail it from town. But she's not here and that makes it tough.

Maybe for Xmas, I'll send Tony another carton of Camels, Luckies, or Chesterfield. Okay? I'll try my best.

I know Tony will want to pay me for the carton I sent, but tell him not to, because I'll get sore if he does and I'm not kidding. If he wants to dish out some dough, though, tell him to pay Ma for the cigarettes $1.33, including postage. Tell him to give Ma the money instead of sending it here because I'll phone up in the near future and I'll reverse the charges, okay?

So-long for now and God bless you all.

Love To: Ma, Pa, Mary, Tony, Francie & Carlo

X X X X X X X X — Phil

P.S. Peace with Germany by Christmas or New Year 1944 is my strong prediction.

Sunday November 19, 1944/Pratt, Kansas

Dear Mary,

Today is another Sunday and all is well out here. I got up at 11:30 a.m. so you see I rested kind of good. All day long I've been just resting and loafing around. The weather out here is pretty dismal. It's cloudy and cold, but it doesn't snow although it's cold enough. I'd say, with the exception of a few days, the winters in Buffalo are colder than out here.

I was glad to hear that the potatoes are still good. I should have bought a couple of more sacks for you.

If you get this letter Wednesday, tomorrow will be Thanksgiving. I hope you all eat well. We have a lot to be thankful for so don't feel too bad. No matter where all us guys are, you can picture us eating Turkey tomorrow. Yes, even Frankie will eat turkey. So-long for now and God bless you all.

Love To: Ma, Pa, Mary, Tony, Francie & Carlo

X X X X X — Phil — X X X

P.S. I hope by now Tony got the carton of Camels I sent. Tell him to keep them in reserve for himself.

Monday November 20, 1944/Pratt, Kansas

Dear Mary,

Not much to say for myself out here today. The weather isn't too bad and everything seems to be going along okay. I hope you can say the same thing out there. In one way, things are getting a little tougher, but that's to be expected and I'm prepared to meet and face anything that comes along for me.

Yesterday I told you I believed Germany would surrender before the year is over with. Yes, there's 5 big armies fighting Germany on one side,

2 more big armies fighting her on another, and also 8 more big Russian armies on another front, and they are all pushing forward. If Germany doesn't quit by New Year's, I'll quit making any more predictions. *[Phil had every reason to be optimistic. General Patton's forces had recently charged into the Saar Basin, Germany's second leading mining and manufacturing region. Germany clearly was on the retreat: in addition to the advancing American armies, the British had captured fields near Cologne; the French were at Strasbourg; and the Russians were about to break through German lines in Hungary.]* So-long for now and God bless you all.

Love To: Ma, Pa, Mary, Tony, Francie & Carlo
X X X X X X X X — Phil —

Tuesday November 21, 1944/Pratt, Kansas

Dear Mary,

Just another ordinary day going by out here. . . . The war is going along pretty good. I think my prediction about Germany still quitting for New Year's still goes. I've just got a feeling and if I'm wrong, I'll not make any more predictions.

The weather was very cold today. I stuck a thermometer outside and it read 28 degrees. I figure the thermometer is broke so it must've been about 20 degrees and that's pretty cold for November. Well, that's all for now so take it easy and God bless you all.

Love To: Ma, Pa, Mary, Tony, Francie & Carlo
X X X X X X X X — Phil —

Wednesday November 22, 1944/Pratt, Kansas

Dear Mary,

I received the swell letter you wrote last Sunday and thank you a great deal. I was glad to hear that you went over to see my wife. When she has somebody like you to talk to, it makes her feel better and less lonely.

You said you bought Shadow a wallet. That's swell. I've got 2 wallets here and I don't use them, because I don't like a bulge in my pocket. As for Ma sending Shadow some money, I'd say it's a good idea. It puzzles me how they get along with the little money they have. Why, the little time my wife was out here, it cost us about $400, so figure it out. Anytime Shadow gets into real financial trouble, I'll be ready to back him up myself.

Tomorrow is Thanksgiving, but we go to work as usual.

So-long for now and God bless you all.

Love To: Ma, Pa, Mary, Tony, Francie & Carlo
X X X X X X X X — Phil —

Thursday November 23, 1944/Pratt, Kansas

Dear Mary,

Today is Thanksgiving out here. The weather is beautiful. It's warm and the sun is shining. We had to work today, but they let us off from 11:00 a.m. to 2:00 p.m.

Boy what a meal I had. Heck, I couldn't get all the food on one tray so there was a lot I didn't take. All the soldiers who have wives here brought them along to eat and if my wife was here, I'd have brought her and she'd have enjoyed it. We had a band playing in the mess hall. As we went in they gave us each a pack of cigarettes. I had a big Turkey wing and a big chunk of turkey breast, mashed potatoes, salad, hot rolls, butter & coffee is all I took, but I could've taken some grape juice, pickles, dressing, cake, candy, cranberry, string beans & other things if I wanted to. Well that's my dinner. I hope you had a nice meal for yourselves out there. So-long and God bless you all.

Love To: Ma, Pa, Mary, Tony, Francie & Carlo
X X X X X X X X — Phil —

Friday November 24, 1944/Pratt, Kansas

Dear Mary,

Yesterday I received the letter you wrote last Monday. I also received the letter Tony wrote. I was glad to hear from you and him. You tell Tony, I think I ate more meat (Turkey) on Thanksgiving than he did.

You told me that Mrs. Mitri died. *[The Mitris were the Aquilas' neighbors and close friends of Phil's Aunt Josephine. One of the Mitris' sons had already been killed in action.]* I'm really sorry to hear that. I can't help but feel that this war ruined that whole family. I'll write [Aunt] Josephine a letter Sunday and pay my respects in that way.

I was glad to hear that Carmen may be home for December 2. You said he's bringing a French sailor with him. Well, I hope Carmen gets to stay home a few days this time. Well, I guess that's all for now. So-long and God bless you all.

Love To: Ma, Pa, Mary, Tony, Francie & Carlo
X X X X X X X X — Phil

Saturday November 25, 1944/Pratt, Kansas

Dear Mary,

. . . The weather here has been rainy and cold. Right now there's a 50 mile [an hour] gale blowing out side and according to some of these men who've been in Alaska, they say the weather reminds them of the Aleutian Islands near Alaska.

The war is still going pretty good and my prediction of peace with

Germany by Christmas or New Year's still goes. If Germany doesn't surrender, they ought to ruin her cities and kill off her population by the millions to make her suffer and pay. Same goes for Japan. Well that's all for today, but I'll be back again tomorrow. God bless you all.

> Love To: Ma, Pa, Mary, Tony, Francie & Carlo
> X X X X X — Phil — X X X

> Sunday November 26, 1944/Pratt, Kansas

Dear Mary,

Today I received the letter you wrote on Thanksgiving. Thanks a lot. You said you had roast chicken and potatoes and soup. That wasn't too bad. You tell Tony though that I was sorry he couldn't eat as much as I did. I was thinking of Tony a little as I was gobbling down the turkey. *[There was always a good-natured competition between Phil and his older brother Tony. But all of the talk about food also suggests that Phil, who came from a large and poor family that suffered greatly during the Depression, truly appreciated the quantity and quality of the food he received in the army.]*

Mary, I'm glad to hear you bought yourself a $200 fur coat. You really deserve it. I'm glad you visited my wife on Thanksgiving. You know you can deposit the money in the Main Street branch of the Liberty Bank instead of on William Street. I called them up when I was home and they said it was okay.

Well that's all for today. So-long and God bless you all.

> Love To: Ma, Pa, Mary, Tony, Francie & Carlo
> X X X X X — Phil — X X X

[This next letter was written on USO stationery.]

> Monday November 27, 1944/Pratt, Kansas

Dear Mary,

Tonight I'm at the U.S.O. in Pratt. I came here to call my wife on the phone. I'd have called you up, but I didn't want to reverse the charges on you so quickly. Maybe in 1½ weeks I'll call you up, okay, and I'll reverse the charges.

It sure was swell to hear my wife's voice after one month of being away. From now until the baby is born, I'll call her up every 2 weeks, so as to keep up her morale.

Well, everything out here is going along pretty good and I hope you can say the same for yourselves out there. . . . Well, that's all for now. So take it easy and God bless you all.

> Love To: Ma, Pa, Mary, Tony, Francie & Carlo
> X X X X X X X X — Phil

Tuesday November 28, 1944/Pratt, Kansas

Dear Mary,

This is just another of my very short letters. Everything here is okey dokey and I can't complain about anything, but I do have a little cold. It's the first one I've caught in about a year. It'll go away fast so don't worry. In fact don't even mention it because it'll be gone before I get your letter.

I hope everything there is okay with all of you. The weather here is pretty cold but it don't snow. Well so-long now and God bless you all.

Love To: Ma, Pa, Mary, Tony, Francie & Carlo

X X X X X X X X X — Phil —

Wednesday November 29, 1944/Pratt, Kansas

Dear Mary,

. . . Out here, everything is going along okay. My cold is getting better.

Yes, I know [Cousin] Johnny has been shipped. He also sent me a card telling me of his new address. I bet its kind of tough on Aunt Josephine and Uncle Pete [who already had one son killed in battle]. That was nice of you to have a high mass said for Cousin Joe. You said Frankie sent you a clearer picture of himself. I'd sure like to see it.

I'm glad you always ask my wife if she wants anything when you go uptown and thanks for depositing that $60 for me. Yes, it won't be long now I'll be a papa, but heck that don't make me an old man. I'm only 22, and that's the age every man young and old wants to be. Well so-long for now and God bless you all.

Love To: Ma, Pa, Mary, Tony, Francie & Carlo

X X X X X X X — Phil

P.S. I sent Tony the cigarettes 1½ weeks ago and you still didn't mention them. I hope they didn't get lost!

Thursday November 30, 1944/Pratt, Kansas

Dear Mary,

Well today is the last day in November. I got paid today. I get $42 each month after allotment, insurance, and bond is taken out. Well, that isn't too bad. . . . Pretty soon Christmas will be here: I'm not hinting, at nothing because there's nothing I want. But to make it simple for you out there, you can buy me a couple pair of army sox, and a couple of shorts. Leave the undershirt there because I don't use them. As for me buying gifts, I'm leaving it all up to my wife and I think she'll do a swell job of it. . . .

I received a letter from you today. You said Aunt Josephine sent a telegram to the President to keep [Cousin] Johnny here in the states. Of course the President hasn't got the time to read it. Who gives these people those brainstorms anyway? If a family has all the sons killed except one then people can write to the War Department about getting that son back.

Well, I guess I'll close for now so take it easy and God bless you all.

Love To: Ma, Pa, Mary, Tony, Francie & Carlo

X X X X X X X X — Phil

Friday December 1, 1944/Pratt, Kansas

Dear Mary,

Today is December 1st and it's the first day of the last month of this year. Whether we realize it or not, time is going by fast, even though the days seem to drag along. According to all the high officials in this war, the war with Germany will last until summer next year. I still go by my prediction, that Germany will quit by Christmas or New Year's of this year.

Well, things aren't going too bad out here at the moment. I just hope there won't be any changes made, but that's too much to hope for. I guess they'll still monkey around with me, until they actually get me into the heaviest fighting of this war. I hope not. I'd like to come back home after this is all over with, saying that I didn't have to kill nobody. *[Phil had every reason to be concerned. By 1944, the Army was transferring numerous soldiers from the Army Air Force into the infantry to keep up with the increasing demand for combat troops. Most American casualties occurred during the heavy fighting of the last fourteen months of the war.]*

The weather out here is pretty damn cold but no snow. The temperature is between 10 to 15 degrees above zero. Well that's all for now, so take it easy and God bless you all.

Love To: Ma, Pa, Mary, Tony, Francie & Carlo

X X X X X X X X — Phil —

Saturday December 2, 1944/Pratt, Kansas

Dear Mary,

. . . There's not much I can say right now because everything is going along okay. Naturally I get disgusted with the whole situation but I'll be okay in the end and that's what counts.

The weather here is pretty cold and it looks as if there'll be a blizzard at any moment. I don't care, I can sleep until 12:00 noon tomorrow. I'll go to work in the afternoon and quit at 4:00 in the afternoon. I'll do that because tomorrow is Sunday.

I was glad to hear that you are all feeling in good shape out there. As for my health, I couldn't be better. My cold is practically all gone. Well that's all for now so until tomorrow, so-long and God Bless you all.

Love To: Ma, Pa, Mary, Tony, Francie & Carlo
X X X X X X X X — Phil —

Sunday December 3, 1944/Pratt, Kansas

Dear Mary,

. . . Well, it won't be long now, Christmas will be around. I'm not buying any gifts from out here. I'm leaving it all to my wife out there. I've already sent Frankie a Christmas card to New Guinea, now I've got just 3 more cards to send. Yep, I'm getting off real easy this year. I guess when a guy has a wife, she usually takes charge of all that stuff, right?

You know, all week long I've been operating the gasoline station on this base. I'll probably work on it for just this next week and then I'll go back to my Chemical Warfare Supplies. It's rather an easy job. I've got a corporal and a private working with me. We give out about 1200 gals. of gasoline each day. Yep, when I was home, I paid $5.50 for 10 gallons of gas, and out here I let thousands of gallons run through my hands. I wish Tony had just the gasoline I see spilled on the ground. He wouldn't need any C card and he'd have to do more driving than he does now to use it up. [C Cards were used for gasoline rationing.]

In about one more month, our blessed event will take place, right? My wife can't wait, I can't wait, and I guess everybody else can't wait to see how things turn out.

Well so-long for now and God bless you all.

Love To: Ma, Pa, Mary, Tony, Francie & Carlo
X X X X X X X X — Phil

P.S. I told you once before that I had written a letter to a captain in [Cousin] Joe's outfit to see if I could find out how he got killed. Well I got the same letter back again and on it was stamped "Deceased" so that means this Captain was also killed. Probably Joe's outfit was all either killed or wounded, so information would be hard to get. So-long.

Monday December 4, 1944/Pratt, Kansas

Dear Mary,

Only 17 more shopping days left as I'm writing this letter. I know it's no use in my telling you this because no matter how much shopping you do right now, you'll still do a lot of last minute shopping. It never fails does it?

Well, today we have a thick blanket of heavy snow out here and all the roads are very slushy. It's a little cold too. I guess it could be worse. It's probably colder there in Buffalo right now.

Everything out here is sailing peacefully along and I haven't too many complaints to make. I hope you can say the same for yourselves out there. I was going to call you up this Thursday, but I won't because I want to call you up just before Christmas, okay? I'll let you know the exact date I'll call you up, alright? Well, I guess I'll close for now. So-long and God bless you all.

> Love To: Ma, Pa, Mary, Tony, Francie & Carlo
> X X X X X X X X X — Phil

P.S. I know I don't mention any body in particular in my letters, but just the same, tell Ma and Pa that I ask for them. When I write to you every day, I'm actually writing to Ma, so tell her that. So-long.

> Tuesday December 5, 1944/Pratt, Kansas

Dear Mary,

Today I received a letter from Carlo. It was swell to hear from him and tell him thanks for writing. . . .

December is well on its way now and in order for my prediction about the war to end to come true, something has to start popping mighty soon. As it is, though, the war is going at a pretty fast pace.

I tore out the editorial in the newspaper out here. This is sure a very radical newspaper. These editors out here really print about what they think. Show it to Tony and see what he thinks about it. I bet no Buffalo paper would carry an editorial like this about Canada. This is a pretty big newspaper too because it has about half the circulation the *Buffalo News* has. Anyway, it's a cinch they don't know Canada as we from Buffalo do or else they wouldn't talk that way about it. All I have to do is show this editorial to the *Buffalo News* and I bet I'd have an international fight on between all the newspapers in the country. Show it to Tony. . . . So-long and God Bless you all.

> Love To: Ma, Pa, Mary, Tony, Francie & Carlo
> X X X X X X X — Phil

P.S. Carlo said Nick Mitri was home. That's a swell break for him. I guess it sure is tough for him because he doesn't find his mother and father there *[The elder Mitris died recently. Phil included in this letter the following editorial from* The Wichita Beacon, *Tuesday, December 5, 1944, p. 16:*

Canada Betrays Her U.S. Neighbor

Canada, thru her prime minister, William Lyon Mackenzie King, compromising on the Canadian conscription issue, has betrayed most shamefully her loyal, patriotic, and close neighbor—the United States. The Canadian prime minister, who had said he favored conscrip-

tion in Canada to aid in supplying the manpower for the war, quickly changed his mind when the test of his conviction came. Public pressure was too much for him.

Reporting the quick change by Prime Minister Mackenzie King, Time Magazine says: "Reluctantly, Prime Minister King gave in. He told the House that 16,000 of the Dominion's 60,000 zombies, or home-defense draftees, would be compelled to go overseas in the next few months. But they would go only to Europe, not to the Pacific. And only to the extent necessary. They would not go at all should volunteers turn up. Great compromiser King had compromised again."

Thus, Canada's prime minister turns his back on the United States at the crucial moment of this nation's greatest emergency. It was the United States that said it would protect Canada when it appeared that Great Britain would be lost; that Britain would succumb to a German invasion; at the hour London was being blitzed by the Nazis; when the British were suffering appalling destruction at Dunkirk.

This is the neighbor Canada, forgetting America's pledge of protection when and if needed, that deprives this nation of Canadian support thru conscription at the time such aid is most imperative.

The United States should not let such action on the part of her Canadian neighbor go unnoticed. It should not be forgotten that Canada is running out on her best friend. We should not let Canada "sell us down the river." We should not permit betrayal by our closest neighboring country.

The United States has much in common with Canada. Trade relations are of the closest nature. In unity there is strength. Canada and the United States should be united in all ways for mutual benefit. Surely, there is something the United States could and should do about a betrayal of this nature. Canada, as an ally in the war, should measure up to her responsibilities—or else.]

Wednesday December 6, 1944/Pratt, Kansas

Dear Mary,

Today I received the letter you wrote last Sunday and I was happy to hear that you are all feeling fine out there. I was especially glad to hear that Carmen came home and it was too bad he had just a short time there. You said he may get shipped to the South Pacific. I hope not.

My watch is still running pretty good. You know those metal watch bands that stretch, like the one you sent Frankie. They cost about $12 I guess. Well, I bought one from some guy out here for $2. It's a pretty good bargain I think and it sure makes the watch look classy. Now, if the watch keeps on working, everything will be okay.

I was sorry to hear that Uncle Pete was sick in bed and I hope he gets well quickly, unless he's planning to get an emergency furlough for Johnny and I doubt it, because look at Nick Mitri, they wouldn't let him come home for anything. *[Pete's son, Joe, died shortly after D-Day, and the mother, Josephine, sent a telegram to the president trying to prevent her other son, Johnny, from being shipped overseas.]*

It's too bad about Pa's brother dying [back in Sicily]. As I told Ma when her mother died [in Sicily], there's no sense in causing a disturbance by wearing dark ties and etc. Feel sorry, sure, but there's nothing else that can be done about it. I know Pa, though.

Yep, that Nick Mitri certainly has been around Europe. He sure is lucky to get back the same way he left, a lot of guys don't. Well, so-long for now and God bless you all.

Love To: Ma, Pa, Mary, Tony, Francie & Carlo
X X X X X X X X — Phil

Thursday December 7, 1944/Pratt, Kansas

Dear Mary,

Today I received a letter from Carlo. It was swell to hear from him and tell him thanks for me. Right now, I'm about to call up my wife. Next time I call her up I'll call you up, okay? It'll be around the 21st or 22nd of December, I'll let you know for sure at an earlier date. I'd call you up now, but then I'd want to call you for Christmas and each time I call you I'd have to reverse the charges, because I haven't got that much change to pay for it out here. . . . So-long and God bless you all.

Love To: Ma, Pa, Mary, Tony, Francie & Carlo
X X X X X X X X — Phil —

Friday December 8, 1944/Pratt, Kansas

Dear Mary,

I got the letter you wrote last Tuesday and was glad to hear you are feeling the same as usual. I was glad to hear also that Tony received the cigarettes. You see, I sent them 3 weeks ago and you never told me he got them so I thought they got lost.

Out here today everything is going along pretty good and the weather has been real nice although there's still snow on the ground and everything is muddy. Well that's the dope for today, so until tomorrow, so-long and God bless you all.

Love To: Ma, Pa, Mary, Tony, Francie & Carlo
X X X X X X X X — Phil

Saturday December 9, 1944/Pratt, Kansas

Dear Mary,

Tonight I'm pretty mad. Mad because I'm restricted to the base for another week. I guess the major must've found something wrong with the way I made my bed for this Saturday's inspection. I also think the major's off his beam, because I've been making beds for a mighty long time and I took especially care this Saturday, because I wanted to go to town to buy my wife a gift. I'd also like to take a look at the major's bed. I bet he sleeps in a pig's pen compared to my neatness. Oh well, I'll take it on the chin.

The weather here is pretty cold. There was a little blizzard here today but everything is quiet now. Thanks to myself, I'm feeling fine. I say that because I feel the army hasn't done anything for me. I came in the army in good health and I'll stay that way because I live by my own ideas instead of the army's. Well, so-long for now and God bless you all.

Love To: Ma, Pa, Mary, Tony, Francie & Carlo

X X X X X X X X — Phil —

Sunday December 10, 1944/Pratt, Kansas

Dear Mary,

. . . I was glad to hear that you went with my wife to the doctor. Yep, it won't be long now. We can expect a new member any day after Christmas. Yep, he'll be a chip off the 'ole block', right?

As for Frankie, I haven't heard from him since he wrote me on October 11th. I haven't written him in about 2 1/2 weeks, but I'll write him this week some time. Well so-long for now and God bless you all.

Love To: Ma, Pa, Mary, Tony, Francie & Carlo

X X X X X X X — Phil

P.S. I'm enclosing the last letter I got from Frankie so you can keep it. So-long.

[The following is the letter that Phil received from his brother Frankie, stationed in New Guinea:]

Wed. Oct. 11, 1944

Hi Bub,

How are you feeling these days? As usual I'm fine and I hope you are the same.

Well, I know you haven't heard from me in quite awhile, but you know how it is. The Philippines have to be taken you know and we are just the babies who are going to do it. You know, even though I probably won't even leave New Guinea, I'll still have had as much to do with that campaign as if I'd been there doing the actual fighting. Don't you ever forget that. I'm one of the guys who sees that the boys up at the front get what they want, when they want it.

By the way, the Transportation Corps has a new shoulder patch. It's a gold shield with a ship steering wheel on it. Whenever you see a guy with one of them on his shoulder it would be a good idea for you to give him a salute because, hey, we really rate one. I don't know whether you realize it but the problem of supply lines down here is a pretty big job. In fact, it's practically a war on its own! Well, that's enough on that subject.

How are you getting along these days? I suppose you are probably worried about your wife. Well, there's nothing to worry about. People all over the world are having babies every day. While you are walking up and down in some hospital worrying, just think of me walking up and down in my foxhole doing the same thing! Maybe it will help you if you know that I'll also be worrying about your wife. (Purely brotherly love you know!)

Say, I guess that's about all for now. I have to go on duty now so I'll have to sign off. So-long and God bless you.

Love, Frankie

Monday December 11, 1944/Pratt, Kansas

Dear Mary,

Just another day going by out here and everything seems to be going along pretty good. I still didn't get anything done for Christmas, so it looks as if my wife will get her gift after Christmas passes, and also Tony will get his carton of cigarettes (Camels) after Christmas.

Well, I guess things don't work out as we want them at times. At times this army is stupid. It's dog-eat-dog in the army. It's funny how one man *[like the major who confined Phil to his barracks for not making his bed properly]* can keep another man from trying to make his wife happy for Christmas. Well, it was done to me, but I won't let it get me down. I can take anything this army has to offer me and still come up fighting.

Well, I hope you all feel in a better humor than I do, right now. So-long for now and God bless you all.

Love To: Ma, Pa, Mary, Tony, Francie & Carlo

X X X X X X X X — Phil

Tuesday December 12, 1944/Pratt, Kansas

Dear Mary,

. . . I read in today's paper that the East had a heavy snow storm so that probably included Buffalo. Out here we've been having mild weather, but the snow is still on the ground.

I wrote Frankie a letter and I'll mail it to him, as soon as I get an air mail stamp. I hardly hear from him any more, but just so he's feeling alright. As for Carmen, I hear from him at least once a week, but so far this week, I didn't hear from him. However, I hear from June and

Shadow twice a week. Well, I haven't much to say so I'll close for now. So-long and God bless you all.

Love To: Ma, Pa, Mary, Tony, Francie & Carlo
X X X X X X X X X — Phil

Wednesday December 13, 1944/Pratt, Kansas

Dear Mary,

This is just my daily little letter to you to let you know that everything out here is going along pretty good, and I hope you can say the same for yourselves out there.

I just wrote a letter to Frankie and I'm mailing it out with this. Today we had some pretty good weather out here. I know you got a lot of snow out there because I read about it in the paper. How's the car holding up in this cold weather? Does Tony take it to work every day?

Well, I'm going to shave, shower, and do some washing now, so I guess I'll close. So-long now and God bless you all.

Love To: Ma, Pa, Mary, Tony, Francie & Carlo
X X X X X X X X X — Phil

Thursday December 14, 1944/Pratt, Kansas

Dear Mary,

. . . I'm glad to hear that Tony is working as much as possible. You know, the Draft is getting stricter and I hope they leave Tony alone.

Incidently, I doubt if I can even call you up on Christmas Eve or Christmas, because the lines will be too busy, so I'm going to call you up on the night of December 22nd. At least that's what I'll do if nothing prevents me. You said you got 5 pairs of shorts and 3 pairs of stockings for me. Okay. I'll be waiting for them. I hope you didn't spend much though, because during these times there's no use of it.

Who said I don't like fried onions, with tomatoes and eggs? I like anything with eggs and in fact, the only way I like onions are when they are fried. Well, so-long for tonight, so until tomorrow, good night and God bless you all.

Love To: Ma, Pa, Mary, Tony, Francie & Carlo
X X X X X X X X — Phil

Friday December 15, 1944/Pratt, Kansas

Dear Mary,

. . . I just received a letter from Frankie. He wrote it December 5th and I got it today, December 15th, only 10 days since he wrote it. That's pretty fast mail, isn't it? He feels okay and in the best of moods. He asked me to send him the book entitled "Gone With the Wind." I don't know if he asked you to get him that book. If he did, don't get it no more, because I'll get it from here. At least, that is, I'll try to find one some place. I'll let you know how I make out. If I have any trouble sending it to him, I'll show them the letter from him requesting it. . . . So-long for now and God bless you all.

Love To: Ma, Pa, Mary, Tony, Francie & Carlo
X X X X X X X X X — Phil

Saturday December 16, 1944/Pratt, Kansas

Dear Mary,

Tonight I'm at the Pratt U.S.O. I came to town to do some shopping for a gift for my wife. This year I didn't have to worry about no gifts except hers. I didn't buy her anything special. I won't tell you right now what I bought her because I don't remember all the things, but I'll tell you in tomorrow's letter, okay, but you mustn't tell her. . . .

I was sorry to hear that little cousin Frankie was hit by an automobile. Yes, I guess our Aunt [Josephine] is running into a lot of heart breaking moments and I'm real sorry for her. Well, that's all for now, so take it easy and God bless you all.

Love To: Ma, Pa, Mary, Tony, Francie & Carlo
X X X X X X X — Phil —

Sunday December 17, 1944/Pratt, Kansas

Dear Mary,

Today I received the very swell Christmas package you all sent me. Thanks to you and tell Ma thanks also. It was swell and I appreciate it with all my heart. I received the soap, razors, razor holder, tooth powder, olives, cookies, cake, candy, gum, sausage, 5 pairs of shorts, and 6 pairs of stockings. It was one of the best packages I've ever received.

Yesterday I received a swell package from my wife also. Honest, those two packages were the same size and were both perfect. My wife sent me a pocket knife, a wallet, home made cookies, home made cake, shorts, stockings, tie clips, sausage, and salami. Yes, these two packages that you and my wife sent me made me very happy. Honest, if I was younger, I could sit down and cry because you both made me so happy.

Tell Francie thanks for sending me the razor holder. I wish I could buy each one in our family a gift. Someday, I will.

Today I packaged my wife's Christmas package. It sure took me a long time. I could've had everything packed by volunteer civilians at the Service Club, but I want to do things myself. I also packed a carton of cigarettes for Tony and one carton for my father-in-law. I wish I could send Joe a carton also, but as it is, I'm taking advantage of the Christmas rush to send these cigarettes through the mail undetected.

My wife's Christmas gift will get to her sort of late, but I couldn't help it. Last night was the first time I wasn't restricted in two weeks. . . . You know, the package I got from my wife I had to open with 10 hungry soldiers looking at me, so they finished up the food in a hurry. Today, however, I sneaked your package in and I've got all the food in my foot locker and I'll do the job to it each day. Out of $7 or $8 of food you and my wife sent me, I think I'm entitled to about $4 worth of it myself. Am I not right? Well, so-long and God bless you all.

Love To: Ma, Pa, Mary, Tony, Francie & Carlo

X X X X X X X X — Phil

P.S. Thanks again for the package!

Monday December 18, 1944/Pratt, Kansas

Dear Mary,

. . . I haven't much time right now to write many letters, so call up Aunt Josephine and tell her that I know [Cousin] Frankie was hit by a car and that I hope he gets well quickly.

Today I mailed my wife's gifts and Tony's cigarettes. I hope they get there before Christmas. I do hope Pa and Ma like what my wife bought them. It's not much and some day my wife and I hope to do better than that. So-long for now, and God bless you all.

Love To: Ma, Pa, Mary, Tony, Francie & Carlo

X X X X X, Love, Phil

[On December 18th, Phil Aquila signed and mailed two Christmas cards to his family: one was for his mother; the other was addressed to everyone else, that is, Pa, Mary, Tony, Francie & Carlo. The card to his mother read: "A Christmas Greeting for Mother: Here's a special greeting for Someone mighty dear/ It's brimming with good wishes, It's filled with joy and cheer/ It holds a Christmas message, And deep affection, too/ It's for the world's best Mother, That's why it's sent to YOU!" Phil signed the card: "Your Loving Son Always, — Phil — X X X"]

Tuesday December 19, 1944/Pratt, Kansas

Dear Mary,

I'm just relaxing after a day's work. I ate, read the paper, wrote my wife, and here I am writing you. Well, I guess it won't be long now for Christmas to be here. I said Germany would surrender by Christmas or New Year's. Well by the looks of things, Germany is still fighting back and it'll be a miracle if Germany does surrender, and I guess miracles don't happen so easily, but still you can't tell, you know. . . . *[Hitler surprised the Allies in mid-December by launching a fierce counterattack in the Ardennes.]*

Things are going along pretty good out here. I don't know how much longer all my good luck will hold out, but here's hoping. So-long for now and God bless you.

Love To: Ma, Pa, Mary, Tony, Francie & Carlo
X X X X X X X X X — Phil

P.S. On the Christmas cards I sent you yesterday, I forgot to add my wife's name, so write Mary's name in ink in front of mine, okay, don't forget. [Phil Aquila's sister did not write his wife's name on the cards. See previous entry.]

Wednesday December 20, 1944/Pratt, Kansas

Dear Mary,

Today I received two letters from you. One was an air mail letter which contained $5. Honest, Ma shouldn't have done it. She already sent me a large Christmas gift and that took care of everything. But, since she wanted to send it, tell her thanks an awful lot for me. You said, that it's costing you $150 to fix the windows in the back flat. That's a lot of money and I'm sorry you have to spend it. I told Ma once that this house is only her first one. The next house will be a very nice one in a good district.

You seem to expect me home pretty soon. I certainly hope I can come. A lot of times though a soldier won't be able to come home just because his baby is being born. [My wife] Mary is going to try to get me home though, and I hope they'll let me come. Well, so-long for now and God bless you all.

Love To: Ma, Pa, Mary, Tony, Francie & Carlo
X X X X X X X X X — Phil

P.S. The weather is fine and there's no snow on the ground no more!

Wednesday December 20, 1944/Pratt, Kansas

Dear Mary,

I'm on Charge of Quarters tonight and I have a little extra time, so I thought I'd write two letters for tonight. Yep, tonight I came to work prepared. I brought along a stick of sausage and the box of cookies which you sent me. With the pocket knife my wife sent me, I cut the sausage in little pieces and I already ate ½ stick with some of the cookies. These Salerno cookies are really the best I've tasted and they sure go good with hard sausage. I've got another ½ stick left and in about an hour I'll eat that up too. Yes, I wish Ma could see how I'm eating the food she sent me. She'd sure feel happy. I've also got a little can of ham which I'll open up about midnight and finish it off with the cookies. I've got a pocket full of nickels and a coca-cola machine here at my disposal, so you can picture me drinking cokes and eating sausage and ham with cookies.

Well that's all for this letter. I just wrote this because I wanted Ma to get a picture of me eating in this here office all alone. So-long and God bless you all.

Love To: Ma, Pa, Mary, Tony, Francie & Carlo

X X X X X X X — Phil

Thursday December 21, 1944/Pratt, Kansas

Dear Mary,

Everything is peaceful out here and going along pretty good so far. . . . I guess the weather there is just as cold as here, only here, when the sun comes out it warms up quicker than out there.

Well, the U.S. is taking one of the worst beatings of the war. Whether they'll trap the Germans and end the war or whether the Germans are really driving the Americans back remains to be seen. Anything can happen, though, so we'll just wait and see. Anyway a lot of guys are losing their lives and they are sure fighting like hell. *[Phil is referring to the German counterattack that began in Ardennes in mid-December. Initial victories by German armies created a bulge in the Allies' position. Eventually the fierce fighting became known as "the Battle of the Bulge."]*

Well, keep your chins up and God bless you all.

Love To: Ma, Pa, Mary, Tony, Francie & Carlo

X X X X X X — Phil

Friday December 22, 1944/Pratt, Kansas

Dear Mary,

I just got through calling you up. I talked to Ma, Tony, and Carlo. It sure was swell to hear them. I'm sorry I missed you, Francie, and Pa, though. I called you up tonight because it's probably the last time before Christmas I'm able to. Ma wanted me to call up again before Christmas. Honest, I wish I could, but that telephone bill will go up too high. I keep calling my wife up so often because I know that I'm paying for the calls. So tell Ma to understand, and tell her not to worry, because I will call up every little while.

Well, so-long for now and God bless you all.

Love To: Ma, Pa, Mary, Tony, Francie & Carlo

X X X X X X — Phil

P.S. I couldn't talk so loud over the phone because there were too many soldiers around listening, but I heard Ma and the rest real nice.

Saturday December 23, 1944/Pratt, Kansas

Dear Mary,

Just a few lines to let you know that everything out here is going along pretty good. I'm not working tomorrow or after tomorrow on account of the holidays. It's pretty good. Two solid days to rest. Out here, everybody is looking forward towards Christmas. A lot of soldiers can accept invitations to eat at people's homes if they want to. A lot of them go out and have a good time. And a lot of them, like me, will stay around the camp and take in a movie and write letters. It's just another day for me, but Christmas does make 9 months that I've been married. I'm getting to be an old married man.

Well, the weather out here is pretty cold and it looks as if there'll be snow at any time. So-long and God bless you all.

Love To: Ma, Pa, Mary, Tony, Francie & Carlo

X X X X X X X X X — Phil

Sunday December 24, 1944/Pratt, Kansas

Dear Mary,

T'is the night before Christmas and all through the barracks there's a lot of noise going on. I guess everybody is excited in his own way about the holidays. Last night I received the beautiful Christmas card from all of you there. It was swell.

You said a typewritten letter came from North Collins for my wife and me, and there wasn't any return address. Mary, when people don't put a return address on a letter they either don't know better or they're up to some trouble. Please, when you ever get anything like that, enclose it in an envelope and send it to me. Not that my wife can't take care of it, but I just don't want anything to upset her. So don't forget. You see, I know there's a lot of people who are jealous of Mary and me, and would do anything to hurt us. If I ever catch anybody though, I'm going to beat them up myself, because following the law doesn't help. As yet, I don't know what's in that letter. It may be a Christmas greeting or it may be some body trying to start trouble. If it is, my wife knows I'll fly into a rage and may not tell me, so you see, that's why I wanted you to send it to me right away.

I was glad to hear that June and Shadow sent each one of you a gift. That was swell of them. Someday though, I'll give Shadow plenty of competition in sending each one in our family a gift.

It was nice to hear that you bought a cocktail table and a dresser for your room. Yes, it's about time Tony had a dresser of his own to put all his stuff in. Ma can put his stockings, shirts, underclothes, and even handkerchiefs in his dresser and when he wants them all he's got to do is get them himself.

Well, so-long for today and God bless you all.

Love To: Ma, Pa, Mary, Tony, Francie & Carlo

X X X X X X X X — Phil

[Phil had ample reason to be suspicious about the typed letter with no return address. He vividly recalled the trauma surrounding the hate mail he had received following his marriage to Mary Cavarella in the spring of 1944. Now, just before Christmas 1944, this anonymous letter arrived. He feared that the police's intervention had not worked, so the hate mail was starting up again. That's why he says that if he finds out who sent the letter he'll beat them up himself, "because following the law doesn't help." Phil must have been relieved when he later learned that the anonymous letter was a false alarm. His comments to his sister on December 24th, however, demonstrate the frustrations and fears that plagued soldiers thousands of miles away from home. GIs not only had to deal with wartime issues involving life and death, but they had to worry about personal crises back home as well.]

Christmas Monday *** <u>DECEMBER 25, 1944</u> *** Pratt, Kansas
Dear Mary,

Today is Christmas out here and everything is going along pretty good. It sure was swell to hear all your voices real early this morning. I waited from 8:00 p.m. for that phone call and also for my wife's phone call. I really could actually see Ma with tears in her eyes as I was talking to her. You all seemed real close and I felt as if I was around the corner some place. I had to laugh though when Ma asked me where I was going after I hung up. I bet she thought I was all dressed up and out for a good time. No, it was Christmas Eve but I had on my overalls and I went right to bed. This morning I woke up at 8:30 and I went to the church. You know, I told you I wasn't going to call up because it would make the phone bill too big this month. But I thought Shadow and Carmen would call up and I didn't want to spoil Ma's complete evening by not calling up. It was also swell to say hello to Rae and Joe. I did talk to Carlo last Friday so it's okay that I missed him this morning. Some day I'll grab a nice sound proof telephone booth and I'll make Ma feel as if I'm on South Division. These booths here are just no good and every word I say is plainly heard by a dozen other guys.

Today I received the letter Francie wrote to me last Wednesday. She said this soldier friend of yours was back home. That's swell. Francie's letter was swell and tell her thanks for me. Well, so-long for now and God bless you all.

Love To: Ma, Pa, Mary, Tony, Francie & Carlo

X X X X X X X — Phil —

Tuesday December 26, 1944/Pratt, Kansas

Dear Mary,

This is the day after, and everything out here seems to be going alright and I hope it's the same out there. I won't expect much mail from you because I know that Sgt. friend of yours is out there. By the way, what's his full name? Maybe some day I'll run across him.

The weather here is cold and cloudy and it'll snow as usually is the case. I hope everyone out there had the best possible Christmas and here's wishing that the New Year will be a better one for all of us. So-long and God bless you all.

Love To: Ma, Pa, Mary, Tony, Francie & Carlo
X X X X X X X X — Phil

Wednesday December 27, 1944/Pratt, Kansas

Dear Mary,

Nothing to say today except I feel mad at everything in this world. It's one of those days when I feel I'm alone and nobody is on my side. I'm getting sick and tired of the war and life. I really have nothing to look forward to because my future is so darn dark. 1944 is practically gone. It's been a pretty miserable year, but next year will be worse. I'm through kidding myself and you that everything is going to be alright, because it isn't. We haven't even started to suffer yet and I'm talking about everybody in this country. I guess I feel bad because I'm discouraged in everything. So-long now and God bless you all.

Love To: Ma, Pa, Mary, Tony, Francie & Carlo
X X X X X X — Phil

[Perhaps Phil feels so depressed because he still has not learned that the anonymous letter referred to in the letter of December 24th was a false alarm. Or, it might be a post-Christmas letdown, or the fact that the United States isn't doing too well in the Battle of the Bulge that is raging in Europe. It could be a combination of the three. In any case, the tone of this letter certainly is more negative than anything he has written up to this point. The next two letters suggest that the source of his discouragement is probably the poor war effort. It appears that the United States will be fighting for a long time, or possibly might even lose the war.]

Thursday December 28, 1944/Pratt, Kansas

Dear Mary,

Right now I'm working, but I find I have a little time, so I thought I'd write you a little letter. Everything out here is going along as good as can be expected, and I hope to hear the same from all of you always. . . .

I guess once in a while I feel a little discouraged in my letters, like in yesterday's letter, but I guess it's the way I keep feeling from day to day.

Yesterday I got my good conduct medal. Two months ago I also received a medal for expert rifleman. All those are cheap and too common, so I'll not wear them, because too many soldiers have them. Well, that's all for now. Excuse the pencil, because I haven't any pen with me. So-long and God bless you all.

Love To: Ma, Pa, Mary, Tony, Francie & Carlo
X X X X X X X — Phil

Friday December 29, 1944/Pratt, Kansas

Dear Mary,

Today I received Tony's letter and it was good to hear from him. Yes, I received the $5 he sent me. He shouldn't have done it though, but tell him thanks a lot for it. . . .

Naturally I can't help worrying over the events taking place [at the Battle of the Bulge], but don't worry about me, because it won't affect me in any way, I mean the worrying, of course.

Right now, I'm waiting to call up my wife again. I'm trying to do everything possible to keep up her morale, especially at this time. Well, I hope you are all in the best of health. So-long and God bless you all.

Love To: Ma, Pa, Mary, Tony, Francie & Carlo
X X X X X X X — Phil

Saturday December 30, 1944/Pratt, Kansas

Dear Mary,

. . . I'm enclosing a letter I got from Frankie a few days ago. It was written Dec. 18th. If you look closely, you can see, Frankie is now a Corporal, so you better address him by that rank or else you'll offend him if you still call him a Private-First Class. A pretty smart guy that Frankie. If you notice, he doesn't mention it to me in his letter but he places "Corporal" on the envelope. I hope they keep promoting him. Promotions do make a soldier feel better especially overseas. . . . So-long and God bless you all.

Love To: Ma, Pa, Mary, Tony, Francie & Carlo
X X X X X — Phil

[Enclosed was the following letter that Frankie wrote to Phil from his post in New Guinea on December 18, 1944:]

Hello Bub,

How are you feeling these days? As usual I'm fine and I hope you are feeling the same.

Well, it's been quite awhile since I've heard from you so I decided to write and find out what's wrong. I hope everything is alright with you. I received a letter from home and I see where Carmen expects to be sent over here to the South Pacific. That's too bad, but I guess that's the way things go. Don't worry, though, from what I've seen, the Navy lead a better life overseas than the Army does back in the States.

Well, I hate to say this, but I guess I'll just have to say "I told you so!" There are only 13 more days left in 1944 and as far as I can see, there is no chance of Germany surrendering before the end of the year. Boy, that last prediction of your's really laid an egg! Oh well, don't let it get you down. You just keep guessing and sooner or later you're bound to guess the right date.

By the way, Phil, do you remember Joe Acanfora? He was out in North Collins with us a few years ago. You should remember him. Well anyway, I was down on the dock here and boy was I surprised to see him come walking up to me. His sister, Margaret, had written and told me that he was [also] in New Guinea, but I never expected to run into him. I was really tickled pink to see him. He's in the infantry so he'll be seeing plenty of action soon. He's not here, now. He was moved up and I guess you know where he's at. [Due to the censors, Frankie could not name troop locations.] *At least I managed to see him before he left. Well, I guess that's about all for now. So long and God bless you.*

Love, Frankie

[The next letter is addressed to Phil's older brother Tony, who had recently sent him five dollars to buy a few drinks that would help him forget his problems.]

Saturday December 30, 1944/Pratt, Kansas

Hello Tony,

I was glad to get your letter and I also received the $5 you sent me. Thanks a lot for you. You shouldn't have done it, though. I was also glad to hear that you had a lot to eat out there on Christmas day. Out here we had turkey and just about everything that goes into making a full course meal.

Don't worry about me getting old or having gray hair. No matter how much I worry about anything it won't affect my appearance. Whenever I shave real close, I'm almost ashamed of myself because I look about 18 or 19 years old.

As for buying a few drinks, well that won't ever happen, because I feel it won't help a bit in the long run. Well thanks again for your letter and $5. So-long and God bless you.

Love, Phil.

[On December 30, 1944, Phil sent a birthday card to his father, and signed it "Love, Son and Daughter, Mary and Phil." On the card was a postscript that read: "P.S. I meant to send this [card] last month but then I forgot until now. So tell Pa that!]

Sunday December 31, 1944/Pratt, Kansas

Dear Mary,

Today is Sunday, and it's the last day of 1944. Yep, the years slowly but surely go by. Every one thought Germany would quit in 1944 but they were all wrong, including myself. Let's hope that 1945 will be better and that there'll be less grief for everybody.

You asked me why I didn't say anything about you buying a dresser for your room, a cocktail table for the parlor, and switching your [old] dresser into Tony's room. Yes, I mentioned it all in a previous letter. Anyway, it's a good idea letting Tony have a dresser for himself and also, a new dresser in your room would look swell. I'll see them when I come home some day.

You said you had some pictures developed of Frankie. Well, as yet you didn't send me any, so I'll be waiting for one. Right now I'm calling up my wife again. My wife and I will have a real big telephone bill, but that's okay, I've got to keep up her morale at this time. Well, that's all for now, so until next year, that's tomorrow, I'll say so-long and God bless you all.

Love To: Ma, Pa, Mary, Tony, Francie & Carlo

X X X X X X — Phil — X X X

P.S. Yesterday I sent Francie and Pa a birthday card each. I knew Pa's birthday was December 11, but somehow after I remembered last month, the Christmas rush came on and I completely forgot about it until last night. So-long.

Monday January 1, 1945/Pratt, Kansas

Dear Mary,

Today is the first day of the new year. My prediction that the war would end by the last of the old year was wrong, so I'll quit making predictions from now on. When the war ends, it ends, but I won't try to predict it any more. *[As future letters will demonstrate, Phil did not stop making predictions. In fact, throughout the rest of his life he issued prediction after prediction about every imaginable political, social, and cultural event and issue.]*

Last night, I called up my wife again. By calling up every few days at times like these, we both feel better and worry less. I'll call her up some more yet and I don't care how much it'll cost, just so I get up to the minute news on how she is *[she's expecting the baby at any moment]*.

New Year's Eve and New Year's Day went by and I worked on both days. I had to work, because almost every army vehicle on the base depended on me for gasoline. Outside of that, everything out here is going along pretty good and I hope it's the same out there with all of you. . . . Well so-long for now and God bless you all.

Love To: Ma, Pa, Mary, Tony, Francie & Carlo

X X X X X X X X X X — Phil

P.S. Shadow said he'll get a leave in February. I was hoping he'd get one now so that in case I can come home I could see him. It's too bad, though. So-long.

Tuesday January 2, 1945/Pratt, Kansas

Dear Mary,

Just a few more lines I'm writing to you with hardly nothing at all to say, because as far as I can see everything seems to be going okay out here. Mind you now, I'm saying as far as I can see.

I hope you are all doing okay out there too. I know it's tough and lonely out there as it is out here, but heck, there's no sense in worrying about anything. You probably think I worry too much, but I don't. I just take everything on the chin day by day. . . .

I sure wish I'm able to come home soon [on an emergency furlough for the baby's birth]. Time will tell I guess, so we'll just have to wait. Tomorrow night I'll call up my wife again and see how things are.

Frankie asked me to get the book "Gone With the Wind." I couldn't find it around here, so I sent a money order to the book company in Chicago, and I hope I can get it so I can send it to him. That is all from this central part of the U.S. So-long and God bless you all.

Love To: Ma, Pa, Mary, Tony, Francie & Carlo

X X X X X X — Phil

Wednesday January 3, 1945/Pratt, Kansas

Dear Mary,

I'm taking time out from work to write to you today so pardon the pencil and government paper, because that's all there is around here. The weather is just cool but pretty darn windy today. I suppose out there it's cold and there's a lot of snow on the ground. Well, it won't be too long before March comes rolling by and spring will come again, and then Ma will be heading for the farm.

Tonight, I'll call up my wife again, to see how things are coming along out there. I wish her doctor is able to get me home [for the birth of the baby], although I know the army has to have a good reason before they give me an emergency furlough. But, it doesn't cost anything to try and keep wishing, so here's hoping that I'll be there soon.

Once in a while Carmen sends me a letter that's uncensored. The way it looks, he'll be heading out to sea to stay a while in the South Pacific. Let's be thankful that he's in the strongest navy in the world, so you can bet that nothing will happen to him. Yes, we've been very lucky so far and let's hope that it'll stay that way. Well that's all the good news for today, so until tomorrow, so-long and God bless you all.

Love To: Ma, Pa, Mary, Tony, Francie & Carlo

X X X X X X X X X — Phil

Thursday January 4, 1945/Pratt, Kansas

Dear Mary,

I received the letter you wrote last Sunday, or should I say last year? Yes, last year was a good year for my wife and me. We were married and we were able to be with each other for 4 months [in Pratt, Kansas]. Now, we are getting a baby. Well, I can't complain. I guess because I've had my share of happiness.

You said Tony may work at [the Bell Aircraft Plant at] Niagara Falls, because they are shutting down the Buffalo Bell plant. That plant is like the army. They always keep changing. Even when I was there [working at that Bell Plant just before the war], they'd be changing everything. Well, it won't be so bad if Tony had 6 riders as you say he has.

About this Sgt. Russell [that his sister is dating], well from what you say, he seems like a nice guy. You've got your own mind so, don't let nobody influence you in anything. You just go right ahead and do the things you think are right.

So-long for now and God bless you all.

Love To:

Ma, Pa, Mary, Tony, Francie & Carlo

X X X X X X X X X — Phil

Friday January 5, 1945/Pratt, Kansas

Dear Mary,

Not much today that I can say. The weather is really beautiful. It's cold at night and in the morning, but during the day-time, it's really like a day in autumn. I hope it stays that way. Today I received the book entitled "Gone With the Wind." I got it from Chicago for $1.49, and I'm going to ship it to Frankie, because he asked for it. It's a beautiful book and I'm sure he's going to like it. Well, everything out here is going along okay, and I hope it's the same out there. So-long and God bless you all.

Love To: Ma, Pa, Mary, Tony, Francie & Carlo
X X X X X X X X—Phil

[Stuck to this letter's envelope was a mailing sticker that apparently Phil had used to send a package to his mother one year before. The mailing sticker is from a store located in the Hotel Eccles building in Logan, Utah, called "The Jewel Box." The package is addressed, in Phil's handwriting, to his mother: Mrs. Calogera Aquila. On the back of the mailing sticker is a scrawled message that reads, "arrived here, tuesday, December 21, 1943. Cross for Ma." This probably means that Phil bought and mailed her a cross for Christmas 1943.]

Saturday January 6, 1945/Pratt, Kansas

Dear Mary,

. . . I was sorry to hear that there's so much snow out there, and I guess I'm really worried about my wife getting to the hospital [when the baby arrives]. I sure wish I could be there myself to make sure she can make it in time. I guess I'll have to just hope for the best to happen. . . . Everything out here is going along pretty good. I've got a lot of things to kick about if I wanted to, but no use doing that. Just so the big things go alright. Well, so long for today and God bless you all.

Love To: Ma, Pa, Mary, Tony, Francie & Carlo
X X X X X X X X — Phil

Sunday January 7, 1945/Pratt, Kansas

Dear Mary,

I just received the letter you wrote last Thursday. It's too bad there has to be so much snow out there at this time [when his wife is expecting]. I only hope everything turns out alright with my wife. I keep wondering if people can't get to work, how is she going to get to the hospital? I sure wish Buffalo and Pratt could trade weather for awhile. Today is the most beautiful day we've had since September. The sun is shining brightly and it's so warm that it makes me think it's June instead of January. California or Florida has nothing on Kansas today. I guess it's about 60 or 65 degrees outside today.

Well, I'll be waiting impatiently out here for all the news. Tonight I'm calling my wife up again to sort of see how everything is coming along. Well, I hope you are all feeling fine there. Out here I'm in the best of health. So-long and God bless you all.

Love To: Ma, Pa, Mary, Tony, Francie & Carlo
X X X X X X X X — Phil

Monday January 8, 1945/Pratt, Kansas

Dear Mary,

Just another day of patient waiting going by out here for me. Outside of all that, everything out here is going along pretty good and I hope to hear the same from you. . . .

I was glad to hear that Pa and Francie got the birthday cards I sent them. I'm glad I was able to put a smile on Pa's face. Next month, it's Frankie's birthday and he'll be 21 years old. He's getting up into the high brackets, too. I'll send him a card early so he'll get it in time. Well, so long for now, God bless you all and I hope everything turns out okay for us.

Love To: Ma, Pa, Mary, Tony, Francie & Carlo

X X X X X X X X — Phil

Tuesday January 9, 1945/Pratt, Kansas

Dear Mary,

I just received the letter you wrote last Saturday. That stationery you used, with your name and address, is sure pretty. You sent me Ralph Ferrara's address and I was glad to get it and I'll write him tonight. *[Ralph is a good friend of Phil's from his neighborhood.]* You said Frankie said that he asked everybody for a book each. He sure knows how to go about getting the things he wants. Well, I sent him the book he asked me to get, and I sure hope he likes it. How he can find the time to read all those books, though, is beyond me.

Yes, I'm sweating out all this suspense in waiting for the baby to be born, but, I guess nature takes its course, and I'll be patient. . . . So-long and God bless you all.

Love To: Ma, Pa, Mary, Tony, Francie & Carlo

X X X X X X X X X — Phil

Wednesday January 10, 1945/Pratt, Kansas

Dear Mary,

Tonight I'm at the U.S.O. I'm calling up my wife from here for a change, because I can talk more freely without so many guys to hear what I'm saying.

Yes, I'm sweating this baby out. When this baby grows up and he or she says not to rush him or her, because he or she wasn't born in a hurry, I'll say he or she is sure speaking the truth, because this baby sure is taking its precious time about being born.

Everything out here has been pretty good and I hope it continues to stay that way. The weather especially has been swell. It's more than 3 weeks now we've been having nice weather. . . . So-long and God bless you all.

Love To: Ma, Pa, Mary, Tony, Francie & Carlo

X X X X X X X X — Phil

Thursday January 11, 1945/Pratt, Kansas

Dear Mary,

I just received the letter you wrote last Sunday. Yes, I received Frankie's picture and I won't send it back because it's the only one like it you've sent me. It's a nice clear picture of him. He's still a skinny guy, by the looks of him.

So Tony is starting to learn his job and he's starting to get responsibilities. That's fine. Yes, I know they will draft a lot of 4–F's who are just monkeying around in civilian life. The papers said they'll draft 4–F's and place them in unattractive military jobs, meaning mainly as permanent K.P. workers. . . . So-long for now and God bless you all.

Love To: Ma, Pa, Mary, Tony, Francie & Carlo
X X X X X X X X — Phil

P.S. Mary, don't waste that good [stationery] paper with your name on by writing me. Why don't you use it especially to write your Sgt. friend!

Friday January 12, 1945/Pratt, Kansas

Dear Mary,

. . . I wrote Frankie a letter last night. I keep him always interested in some subject, and he keeps arguing and holding his own against me. *[He's trying to keep up his younger brother's morale by distracting him with debates about the war and politics. He's pleased that Frankie is able to hold his own.]*

I just got a letter from June and she said she'd be in Buffalo by today. I feel sorry for Shadow, because he's going to feel pretty lonely [when June leaves his base in Memphis], but he'll have to take it on the chin.

The weather has sure been swell out here. It's just like summer. According to the civilians here, February and March are the worst winter months. Well, I hope every one there is feeling fine so take it easy and God bless you all.

Love To: Ma, Pa, Mary, Tony, Francie & Carlo
X X X X X X X X — Phil

Saturday January 13, 1945/Pratt, Kansas

Dear Mary,

. . . It's Saturday night for everybody but me, because as usual I'm sitting down writing letters. . . . By now June is probably there. I bet [Shadow and June's baby] Ronnie sure grew up nice and big. According to June and Shadow he sure can talk pretty good.

Well, what does Ma think about Mary and me having a baby? I

know this is a fine time to ask Ma for an opinion. Well, we just want one. I won't follow in Shadow's footsteps, or Joe's footsteps, or Pa's footsteps. One is enough during war time, don't you think? After that Mary and I will go according to the money I'll be able to earn. Well that's all for now, so take it easy and God bless you all.

Love To: Ma, Pa, Mary, Tony, Francie & Carlo
X X X X X X X X X X — Phil

Sunday January 14, 1945/Pratt, Kansas

Dear Mary,

. . . I worked ½ day today because I wanted to. Tonight I'm going to call up my wife and see how everything is going along out there.

You know, I got to thinking about Frankie making corporal, and I bet he got his rating because they've already sent some body from his outfit back home. That's the way it works overseas. Of course I'm not sure so don't say nothing to Frankie. Sooner or later his turn will come up to come home.

Well so-long for today and God bless you all.

Love To: Ma, Pa, Mary, Tony, Francie & Carlo
X X X X X X X X X — Phil

Monday January 15, 1945/Pratt, Kansas

Dear Mary,

This is another uneventful day gone by. Last night I called up my wife and she said she was going to the hospital pretty soon. Maybe by the time you get this letter she is already there.

I bought 24 cigars and it cost me $1.68. It may be enough to give to the boys out here, don't you think? I've also got quite a few packs of cigarettes and if I can come home I'll bring a few extra packs along for Tony. I really am in suspense about the baby and I can't wait till it's all over with. . . . Well so-long for now and God bless you all.

Love To: Ma, Pa, Mary, Tony, Francie & Carlo
X X X X X X X X X X — Phil

[On January 15, 1945, Phil wrote the following poem, which he mailed to his wife back home. Not only do the rhyming couplets show how much he longed for his wife, but they describe what a typical day was like for him at Pratt Air Base:]

ODE TO ARMY LIFE

What did I do today
in this army far away?

While you at home are lonely,
loving and thinking of me only!
I awoke at seven this morn,
and saw the day being born.
In this land of few fences,
where the mighty West commences!
To the latrine with a rush,
I combed my hair, washed, and such,
and read a sign stating:
"Please flush, Pratt needs water greatly!"
Running to chow with a pain in my side,
I found scrambled eggs instead of fried.
But heartily my breakfast I ate,
hoping the best and trusting to fate!
To the barracks I dashed with a roar,
fixed my bunk and mopped the floor.
Lighted a cigarette and walked to work,
with a heavy heart and a smile of mirk!
I cleaned gas masks with disinfectant,
packed, for a depot, them I sent.
At noon, I waited in line to eat,
the meal was fair but not a treat!
After lunch, I went for mail,
As usual, me, you did not fail!
Back to work with a tired stride,
I missed the bus and could not ride.
Again I worked on masks till five,
and quit, feeling glad I was alive.
Straight to the mess hall I went,
which now was filled with cabbage scent.
But I ate so that I could survive
and some day see peace arrive!
I bought a paper and read on my bunk,
the war was slow and the news stunk.
Then I wrote your daily letter,
enabling our love to grow better.
When I finished, it was time for bed,
and I fell on it like a piece of lead.
And during all my prayers
I placed aside all my cares,
for I was thankful the day was through,
bringing me still closer to you!

Tuesday January 16, 1945/Pratt, Kansas

Dear Mary,

Another day is through out here and everything is going along pretty good. And I hope it's the same out there.

I found this [enclosed] picture of two Buffalo policemen in the Wichita, Kansas paper. Yes, it's very unusual when I read something about Buffalo in these Kansas papers. You sure had a lot of snow out there. Out here, the weather today has been cloudy and cool, but not so bad. *[The Wichita newspaper, the* Beacon, *January 16, ran a picture of two Buffalo policemen in a horse-drawn sleigh with lots of snow around. Phil read the Wichita newspaper every single day to keep up on the war, as well as other news.]*

I'm still sweating out the baby and tomorrow night if I don't hear any news from my wife, I'll call her up again. Well, so-long for now, and God bless you all.

Love To: Ma, Pa, Mary, Tony, Francie & Carlo

X X X X X X X X X X X X — Phil

January 17, 1945/Pratt, Kansas

Dear Mary,

Today it's dark, cloudy and rainy, and I feel as bad as the weather. Everything is going along alright though, and I hope to hear the same from you there.

I just got through calling up my wife again. And she's still home *[What he means is that she has not yet gone to the hospital. His wife, Mary, is living with her parents and younger brother in Buffalo]*. Well, I guess there's nothing to worry about, but why can't things happen to me on schedule? Nothing ever goes right with me I guess, and that's the way it'll always be. Just so she comes out of it okay. I guess everybody is in suspense by now. The baby will surely be born one of these days unless we didn't count the months right. Well, I'll be keeping my chin up. So-long for now and God bless you all.

Love To: Ma, Pa, Mary, Tony, Francie & Carlo

X X X X X X X — Phil

Thursday January 18, 1945/Pratt, Kansas

Dear Mary,

I received the letter you wrote last Sunday when [Joe's wife] Rae also wrote a paragraph in it. I had to laugh when she says she just got my Christmas gift and she's sending it. You know if she waits a little longer, she can kill 2 birds with one stone, by sending it to me for next Christmas. All kidding aside though, I don't expect anything from anybody, but I'll appreciate it anyway.

So [neighborhood friends] Joe Baldi and Angeline Christopher got another baby girl. It's okay and tell them hello for me, if you see them or write to them.

So Ma was sitting on the bench reading and looking at a book. Yes, I can picture her. I bet she's used that little bench more than anybody else in the family. As for reading, we should've taught her long ago. It's never too late to learn you know. *[Calogera did not know how to read English or even her native Italian. Apparently, she was sitting there just looking at the book's pictures.]*

Well, so-long for now and God bless you all.

Love To: Ma, Pa, Mary, Tony, Francie & Carlo

X X X X X X X X X X — Phil

Friday January 19, 1945/Pratt, Kansas

Dear Mary,

I got your letter which you wrote last Monday and I was glad to hear that you dropped in on my wife. She always likes to see someone from our family go up to see her. As for her coming down to our house, it will probably be a long time from now.

Yes, I know June's mother went down to Memphis to escort June home [from her visit with Shadow]. It's sure nice of her to go way down there to pick June up, otherwise June would've had a mighty tough time trying to come up to Buffalo alone *[She had her baby, Ronnie, with her, and may have been pregnant again]*.

I'm still waiting anxiously out here for the baby but I'm getting used to it now so I don't mind waiting. I feel like an experienced daddy. . . . So-long and God bless you all.

Love To: Ma, Pa, Mary, Tony, Francie, & Carlo

X X X X X X X X X — Phil

Saturday January 20, 1945/Pratt, Kansas

Dear Mary,

. . . Right now, I'm pretty excited about the Russians. They sure are doing a lot to end the war with Germany. I won't start predicting nothing, but as usual, I'll say, the war can end any day and any month or even any year. *[The Soviet army launched an offensive against the Germans on January 13. By the 19th, they had captured Warsaw, Lodz, Kracow, and Tarnow. As Phil writes this letter, the Russians are poised to invade Germany itself.]*

Still, the baby hasn't been born. Patience, is what we must have, I keep telling myself. One thing for sure, no matter how long that baby keeps us waiting, he'll have to come out. It's funny, how we can bring a poor innocent baby into this world that's cruel and rotten where a guy can't even live his own life. Let's hope that the next generation will get a better deal than this generation is getting.

Tomorrow is Sunday and I'll sleep until noon if I'm able to. Only, some of these guys are farmers, and get up at the crack of dawn, and start moving around or talking and it wakes me up.

It snowed today, and everything is white and the roads are slushy. It's not cold though.

I'll call my wife up tomorrow night again and see how she's doing. Well, I hope you are all well out there, so take it easy and God bless you all.

Love To: Ma, Pa, Mary, Tony, Francie & Carlo
X X X X X X X X X X X — Phil

Sunday January 21, 1945/Pratt, Kansas

Dear Mary,

Today is just another Sunday going by. All I'll do today is write letters, loaf around, call up my wife, and see a movie. I got up at 11:30 a.m. this morning and had a nice turkey dinner to eat. Incidently, I had a nice big drum stick. It wasn't too bad, and I can only think about Tony out there, eating a little meat once in a while, and I feel sorry for him. There's about 4 inches of snow outside but it's not cold at all. For my part, it can snow 10 more feet and it wouldn't make any difference to me.

Boy, those Russians are sure going to town lately. I know Tony must be following the war pretty closely. For my part, I'd say the war can end at any hour or at any year. *[The Soviet Army has invaded Germany and is pushing toward Berlin. German resistance is crumbling before the Russians' advance.]*

I haven't received any mail from Carmen in a long time, so I think the kid is probably headed for the South Pacific. But don't worry about him, because he's on a ship that won't sink as easy as regular ships do. Well, I'll close for now, but I'll be back again tomorrow. Until then, so-long and God bless you all.

Love To: Ma, Pa, Mary, Tony, Francie, & Carlo
X X X X X X X X X X X — Phil

Monday January 22, 1945/Pratt, Kansas

Dear Mary,

. . . I'm in the best of health and spirit, so I guess there's not much I can complain about. . . . I hope you are all feeling okay out there, but I know someone probably has a cold or a headache, because it's usual during this time of the year.

I called up my wife last night and still we are sweating out the baby. Just so everything is okay. So-long for now and God bless you all.

Love To: Ma, Pa, Mary, Tony, Francie & Carlo
X X X X X X X — Phil

Tuesday January 23, 1945/Pratt, Kansas

Dear Mary,

. . . I received this stationery from Rae and Joe today. It's really very nice stationery, in fact, it's some of the best I ever had. I'll write her and thank her for it either today or tomorrow. *[Phil is using stationery that says on the top "Philip Aquila ———— U.S. Army."]*

I'm sweating the baby out, but as I told you a few days ago, I kind of got used to it. I've been doing my own counting and I figure the baby to be born around February 5, 6, or 7th. That's my guess, because I think it's the latest date the baby can be exactly 9 months. . . .

According to the radio, the Russians are 138 miles away from Berlin. That's just a little more than it is from Buffalo to the border of Pennsylvania. Something has to happen. Either the Germans stop the Russians quick or the war with Germany will end. And then Japan, in my estimation, will quit very quickly when she sees herself fighting the whole armed world single handed. I'm not predicting now, I'm just thinking. That's pretty swell news isn't it? So-long for now and God bless you all.

Love To: Ma, Pa, Mary, Tony, Francie & Carlo
X X X X X X X X X — Phil

Wednesday January 24, 1945/Pratt, Kansas

Dear Mary,

Just another day gone by. Right now I'm waiting for a phone call to my wife. As usual, she'll be home. Yes, I guess we didn't figure it out right or something *[i.e., when the baby is due]*. Oh well, what's the difference just so everything turns out alright. You know, we may get twins. One never knows how such things turn out. Of course, if we get sextuplets, naturally I'll be made a Colonel or something and may even be discharged from the army. So, I hope it's 6 of them, and break all world's records.

I received a letter from you today. I've also received 3 air mail letters from Carmen yesterday and today. Yep, he sure has gone. He probably is in Hawaii for a while.

Well, so-long for today and God bless you all.

Love To: Ma, Pa, Mary, Tony, Francie & Carlo
X X X X X X X X X X X — Phil

P.S. Cousin Angelo said he saw my name in the paper for getting the good conduct medal. Yes, I got that ribbon a while back, but I don't wear it. I want the Congressional Medal of Honor or nothing.

Thursday January 25, 1945/Pratt, Kansas

Dear Mary,

I was just talking to you over the phone. You all sounded nice and plain. I'm real sorry about Ma. Honest, it came to me like a surprise and shock, but that's natural. I'd rather be told right away about such things. Everybody back home seems to think they save a guy a lot of worrying. It's not so. My wife told me last night to call you up. It was 10 p.m. out here and I had waited since 6 p.m. to talk to her, and when she told me to call you up, I thought nothing of it. I asked her if anything was wrong, but she wouldn't tell me, but she did tell me to call you tonight and I did.

If I'd have known Ma was in the hospital, I'd have waited until 2 a.m. to call up. Tonight, though, I called up my wife again, and she told me all about it, but I couldn't reach you. But, I finally did. If Ma is still in the hospital when you get this letter, tell her not to be afraid. I know she's never found herself all alone and she starts to think of Carlo and all of us. But tell her it's only for a little while and she'll be back home again. *[Carlo, the youngest child, is only ten years old.]*

I'll close now and I pray to God that everything will be alright. So-long and God bless you all always.

Love To: Ma, Pa, Mary, Tony, Francie & Carlo

X X X X X X X X X X — Phil

Friday January 26, 1945/Pratt, Kansas

Dear Mary,

I got your Air Mail letter today. Honest, I still can't believe Ma is in the hospital. Last night on the phone you said Ma would be operated on Saturday morning. I'll be thinking and praying that she'll be alright real soon. I know how Ma is, that she never complains of any ailment. It's always up to you at home to watch for things like that now, with both Ma and Pa. They are getting old right under our noses and we hardly realize it. We keep thinking always that Ma is made of iron and will stay that way, but we are wrong. It's up to us to force her in a chair and make her take life easy. *[Note: His mother is 56 years old; his father is 63.]*

One thing, you better get straightened out with Ma as soon as she's well again and that is to forget about going to work on a farm. When she goes to a farm from now on, it'll be just a pleasure trip and nothing else. She's been going to the farm for 16 years now, and that's too darn much. Why, an infantry soldier doesn't get as cold and wet and hot as

Ma used to get. So don't you forget, Mary, if Ma even mentions going to the farm again, you shut her up mighty quick. It's not worth it anymore. It's okay when a person is young.

Yes, I can't help worrying about Ma and my wife. Both things coming at the same time, too. When I heard Ma was in the hospital, it was just as much a shock as it would've been a month ago. Honest, I can't understand why you and my wife insist on keeping something like that away from me. It's okay to do it to Frankie or Carmen, but why me? Heck, here, I actually worry about how all of you take such things, and [then] you try it on me. I can take it, so don't ever keep anything from me again. I know both you and my wife meant good, but I'm no baby. Well, we'll let it go this time.

I'm sorry to hear about Tony, and that he might get drafted. Whatever he does, tell him to steer clear of the army and take the navy. It burns me up. We are four [brothers] in the service and still they want another. Some families live the life of Riley, while others have to do all the worrying and suffering.

I just read the part of your letter [again] where you said that you had to tell me about Ma because if I'd have come home and found out about it I'd feel bad. What if I'd have called up before I heard about it and didn't find Ma home? So, you should've told me long ago.

Yes, we miscounted the months for the baby to be born. I guess my wife and I are inexperienced at such things. Well, sooner or later the baby will be born.

Look, Mary, just one more thing. God forbid, but if Ma gets worse, I want to be near her, and don't worry about spoiling my chances to be with my wife when the baby is born. I think the baby will be born for sure in the next week and a half. But if Ma feels better then I'll wait for my wife to get me home. I'll close now, so God bless you all and I hope Ma feels much better.

Love To: Ma, Pa, Mary, Tony, Francie & Carlo
X X X X X X X X — Phil

Saturday January 27, 1945/Pratt, Kansas

Dear Mary,

I received the letter you wrote last Tuesday. I know you are the only one who does all the writing. Just do the best you can, although I'd like to know how Ma is each day. If some days you can't write, just phone up my wife and tell her how Ma is so she can tell me. And I want the truth.

I'm glad that you haven't told Ma that Tony might get drafted. Break the news to her easily. Tell her the war can't go on much longer. I know she says that she won't worry. She don't show it, but she keeps it all to herself. You've got to make her actually understand that nothing is going to happen to any of us. I know this war has been the main blame for Ma's sickness, so keep trying to pep her up. She needs confidence. *[Phil's mother was diagnosed as having a stomach disorder that later turned out to be cancer. Perhaps Phil was correct when he said that the stress of having four boys in the war had an impact on her health. It is also interesting to note that her health worsened as tension grew waiting for Phil's baby to be born. Exactly the same thing happens in the fall of 1946, when they were awaiting the birth of Phil's second child. Maybe all the stress was too much for her system?]*

Today is Saturday and according to you Ma was to have an operation. I do hope she went through it okay. I wish I could be there to help all I can. You are all worried because nothing like this has ever happened to us. Especially, tell Carlo to understand and not to be afraid. There isn't much I can do from out here except write letters to you each day. But tell Ma I'm always thinking about her, more than she thinks I do, and if I'm able to come home for the baby and my wife, I want her to cook a lot of spaghetti and a lot of meat balls. Especially I want a couple fried eggs each time I come home. You know, last time I ate most of the eggs at home so I thought I should go out and buy Ma a couple of dozen and I did. Heck, you tell Ma that just because I'm married makes no difference. I'm the same guy who's going to make her rich, and someday maybe I will. I'll close now, and keep Ma pepped up a lot. So-long for today and God bless you all always.

Love To: Ma, Pa, Mary, Tony, Francie & Carlo
X X X X X X X X X — Phil

Sunday January 28, 1945/Pratt, Kansas

Dear Mary,

I received the letter you wrote last Thursday. I'm glad you are keeping me informed about everything that goes on out there. You said Ma was on her feet for the first time in a week. That's swell. I hope she recovers quickly from the operation. I'll call you up tonight. I know our whole family must've been there last Saturday morning.

I wish I could be out there myself, but everything is complicated. However, if Ma's condition gets worse you can get me home, and don't worry about me coming home for my wife. You see, a lot of times a guy can't come home just because his wife has a baby. But if Ma is better, then forget my coming home. Well, I'll close now, hoping everything is going along better. So-long and God bless you all.

Love To: Ma, Pa, Mary, Tony, Francie & Carlo
X X X X X X X — Phil

Monday January 29, 1945/Pratt, Kansas

Dear Mary,

I hope Ma is feeling better today. Everything out here is going along the same as usual and I can't kick. I feel much better mentally, too, because I'm not nearly as worried as I have been for the past four days. I know my wife has a bad cold and I could hardly hear her voice on the phone last night. I sure hope she gets better.

That little baby must sure be a stubborn one. I hope he doesn't take after me, because we'll sure have a hell of a time with him. I'll put him in his place from the start, though. . . .

Well, so-long for now and God bless you all.

Love To: Ma, Pa, Mary, Tony, Francie & Carlo
X X X X X X X X X X X — Phil

Tuesday January 30, 1945/Pratt, Kansas

Dear Mary,

Today I received the letters you wrote last Friday and Saturday. You wrote one from the hospital and told me about Ma's operation. I sure was happy to know everything went okay with her. Now if she'd only recover and come home and my wife could have the baby and Tony gets that [draft] appeal okay, I'll be pretty happy.

Yes, my wife is lingering on, and I hope she can linger until Ma gets out of the hospital. It sure is tough on a guy to have his mother and wife in the hospital at the same time. If anybody is entitled to an emergency furlough I think I am in a case like that. But, if only everything would turn out okay, I don't care about a furlough. Well, let's hope for the best.

I still hope something comes up to defer Tony. Everybody else in the family I didn't mind too much to see leave, but Tony is the last guy home, and I should think they'd leave him home even to bolster up the morale of Carmen, Frankie, Shadow, and myself, because we'd sure feel a lot better knowing there was somebody home to take care of all the problems which might arise. Well, I'll close for now and let's hope always for the best. So-long and God bless you all.

Love To: Ma, Pa, Mary, Tony, Francie & Carlo
X X X X X X X — Phil

Wednesday January 31, 1945/Pratt, Kansas

Dear Mary,

Right now I'm waiting for the phone call to go through to you and one to my wife. There's a long delay tonight, but I'll wait. I hope you don't mind being awaken at such a late hour. . . . I do hope Ma is feeling better and I just can't wait for her to come home so that I can talk to her again.

My wife is still lingering on and I'll soon find out up to the minute news when I talk to her myself tonight. Well, anyway, each day that goes by brings us closer to the baby. It may be a boy, it may be a girl, and it may even be twins, nobody knows. Will I sure be surprised if it is twins. Somebody better catch me when I faint out here. Well, I'll close now and I'll keep waiting for the phone call to go through.

So-long and God bless you all.

Love To: Ma, Pa, Mary, Tony, Francie & Carlo
X X X X X X X — Phil

P.S. I just got the call through and I was glad to hear Ma is eating and feeling better!

Thursday February 1, 1945/Pratt, Kansas

Dear Mary,

No mail today from you, but that's okay, because I called up last night and know that Ma is feeling better. It was swell to hear you all last night and I'm sorry I couldn't talk to Tony. You see, I couldn't wait for him to get up because it would take too long and the operator would start to butt in to remind me to get off the phone.

You know, I got a letter from Ralph Ferrara [his neighborhood friend]. Poor guy was in Greenland for 19 months and he happened to come back and get stationed near Detroit. He only stays there a month, and they ship him to Utah. I guess now he wishes he was back in Greenland.

I hear from Carmen regularly and although he can't say where he's at, I can sure guess, and guess pretty accurately. He talks about getting a pass now and then and buying some souvenirs, so he must be in Hawaii, because he wouldn't be buying souvenirs in California or some other South Sea Island. So tell Ma not to worry about Carmen.

As for Frankie, I'm sending you the letter he wrote on January 14. He says he wishes he goes to the Philippines and I wish he does, because there's better living conditions there and the climate is much better, because New Guinea is near the equator and it's all jungles and heat, and I think the kid's spent enough time there. However, when Frankie gets there, he won't see no action. He'll be near a seaport that's already captured and there he'll work. You know, if it wasn't that I may get an emergency furlough, I think you'd see Frankie before you would me. Yes. I believe he'll get a furlough to Buffalo before I get my regular furlough.

Well, so-long for now, and I hope this letter finds Ma and all of you feeling well. God bless you all.

Love To: Ma, Pa, Mary, Tony, Francie & Carlo
X X X X X X X — Phil

[The following letter from brother Frankie was enclosed in Phil's letter home. The envelope to Frankie's letter is stamped "Passed By Army Examiner," meaning it was approved by a censor. None of Phil's letters have that stamp on the envelope. Letters from soldiers on the home front were not censored.]

Sunday January 14, 1945

Hello Phil,

How are you feeling these days? As usual I'm fine and I hope you are feeling the same. Well, by this time I'm pretty sure that your wife has had her baby. However, I'll wait until I get the news before sending you my congratulations. I received a letter from Mary which was dated December 30, and she told me that she expected the baby to be born within one week. I hope it's a girl!!!

Well, Bub, I think I told you this before, but I'm going to say it again. The New Year is 2 weeks old and as yet there is no sign of Germany collapsing. In fact, to me it looks like we've still got a tough fight on our hands in Europe. I'm going to change that prediction which I made. I don't think the war in Germany will end this Spring. I believe that it's going to last until sometime next fall. In fact, if they don't snap it up on the other side, we are liable to beat the Japs before the Germans are defeated!!!

I suppose you know how the war in the Philippines is coming along. By the time this letter reaches you, Manila should be in our hands. You know, I have very high hopes of going to the Philippines soon. I hope to heck it's real soon. I've had about all I can stand of New Guinea for one war!

By the way, Phil, you don't have to go to so much trouble for that "Gone With the Wind." When I asked for it, I thought you'd be able to get it without any trouble at all. I didn't think that you'd have to send directly to the publisher to get it. Well, Phil, I guess that's about all I have time for right now. I'll write again soon and I'll try to make my next letter a long interesting manuscript. So long and God bless you.

Love, Frankie

Friday February 2, 1945/Pratt, Kansas

Dear Mary,

No mail from you today, but I know you've got too much on your hands these days, so don't worry about writing too much to me. I hope Ma is feeling better today and I hope she comes home real soon.

I guess everybody is bawling you out for not telling us about Ma sooner, but don't worry about it. It's just the shock of learning that Ma is in the hospital, that's all. If I myself have hurt your feelings in any way, I'm sorry. You see, I even bawled out my wife for not telling me. I know you were trying your best not to worry any of us. So, if Shadow starts squawking about telling him late, just don't pay no attention to him. Yes, we are all thinking about Ma—Frankie in New Guinea, Carmen in the Pacific somewhere, Shadow and June in Tennessee, and myself in Kansas. We all hope that she'll be okay real soon. . . . I know you have a lot to worry about thinking about Ma, and keeping the house going. Just take it easy, that's all, because you, too, aren't made of steel. You can only worry and think so much and then you'll snap with a nervous breakdown and find yourself in a hospital too. So just take it easy.

Well, I guess my baby will have to show up pretty soon. It's inevitable. He can't stay in there always. So let's hope he's born real soon. So-long for now and God bless you all.

Love To: Ma, Pa, Mary, Tony, Francie & Carlo
X X X X X X X X — Phil

P.S. I'll let you know when I'll call up, okay? I'm calling up my wife Sunday and I'll tell her to tell you. So-long.

Saturday February 3, 1945/Pratt, Kansas
Dear Mary,

Today I received the letter you wrote last Wednesday. Yes, I know Ma must have suffered a great deal and I'm real sorry. I know if I was there to see her suffer like that I wouldn't have been able to bear it. Thank God that she is getting better.

Out here, the weather is pretty damp, cold, and foggy and I feel a little bad about it, because it gave me a cold, but I'll soon get rid of it so don't worry.

Yes, it'll sure be swell if I can see Shadow while I'm home and I know seeing both of us will be a much better medicine for Ma than anything the doctor can give her. Well here's hoping we both come home. So-long for now and God bless you all always.

Love To: Ma, Pa, Mary, Tony, Francie & Carlo
X X X X X X X X — Phil

Sunday February 4, 1945/Pratt, Kansas
Dear Mary,

I received a letter from you today and thanks for keeping me so well informed. I'm always glad to hear that Ma gets better and better everyday. . . .

I know there is a lot of snow out there and it makes traveling very hard, so I hope the car keeps running and that you can get enough gasoline for it.

Maybe by the time you get this letter the baby will be born. I sure hope so and I do wish I can get home for my wife, Ma, and the baby. Yes, I've got three persons to look forward to mainly see now.

The war is going on pretty good and the Russians are 25 to 40 miles of Berlin. So-long for now and God bless you all.

Love To: Ma, Pa, Mary, Tony, Francie & Carlo

X X X X X X X X X X — Phil

Monday February 5, 1945/Pratt, Kansas

Dear Mary,

Today I received the letter you wrote last Friday. As I said before don't let anybody bawling you out [for not telling them about Ma sooner] worry you. Heck, you are completely right in keeping that news from us from your point of view.

I'm calling you up tonight, so I'll not finish this letter until I hear you talking on the phone. I know Ma must be worrying about the cost of her hospital expense, but talk to her and tell her not to worry about that. You only live once, while on the other hand money is always made.

You aren't kidding when you said that we do a lot of things to upset Ma, and when she's sick we sure do realize it. I've been a pretty bad boy when I was small, but when I'd see Ma work so hard on the farm, I changed. She never knew it, but I used to watch her quite a bit.

I guess, as I grew older, I became a bad boy with Pa [because he always argued with Ma]. I didn't mean to be but I just couldn't stand it to see Ma suffer and hit herself, and Pa insulting her like he did. I just couldn't stay as calm as Tony always is, because I knew a lady has to break down under the hard blows she'd give to herself. I love Pa, but I love Ma still more, and there just wasn't any choice for me. Anytime I acted rough with Pa, it wasn't because of something between him and me, no, it was because of him and Ma. I tried to talk to both of them, but it would never help. A lot of times I wonder out here if they still fight. Anyway, when I did get rough with Pa, that would take his mind off Ma and he'd talk about me. I don't care what Pa ever told people about me, but one thing he can never say and that was I struck him or threw him out of the house. I could've if I wanted to, but I'd carry him to the door and just let it go at that. So I hope he doesn't carry any hate in his heart for me, because I do like him and I'll always help him whenever I can. . . . *[There is a break in this letter, because Phil went to place a long-distance phone call.]*

* * * *

Well I just called you up and my wife's mother up. It's a boy and I'm so happy that my wife is alright. Wow, 8 or 9 lbs. I never thought it would be that much. I sure feel proud. And I'm glad Ma and all of you feel happy, too. I'm telling Frankie right now, so he'll know far before you tell him. I'll close now because I'm going to see about a telegram. I sure wish I can get to come home. Here's hoping. So-long and God bless you all.

Love To: Ma, Pa, Mary, Tony, Francie & Carlo

X X X X X X X —P hil

[There is a gap of three weeks before the next letter, so apparently Phil received his furlough and left immediately for Buffalo to be with his wife, baby, and mother.]

Monday February 26, 1945/Pratt, Kansas

Dear Mary,

I arrived [back] here tonight. Yes, I feel pretty bad, but that's to be expected and can't be helped. I still feel a little dizzy from the long train ride, but I'll soon get over that. You know as soon as I got out of N.Y. state, I didn't see any snow until I passed Chicago. Out here there's about 2 inches of fresh snow and the temperature is about the same as Buffalo.

Ma was nice and brave about my leaving. I'm glad she came out of the hospital and I hope that as each day goes by she becomes stronger and stronger. Everytime you write, let me know how she feels. I'm sorry that Ma couldn't see the baby while I was there. I hope she likes him when she sees him.

Right now I'm going to take a bath, because I need one. I'm all situated again and I hope I can stay that way for a while at least. That's all for today and I hope everybody there is feeling fine as usual. So-long and God bless you all.

Love To: Ma, Pa, Mary, Tony, Francie & Carlo

X X X X X X X X X X X — Phil

Tuesday February 27, 1945/Pratt, Kansas

Dear Mary,

Just another day out here. I've nothing to look forward to anymore. Most of my worries are gone. My wife and baby are getting along swell. Just Ma is left now and I hope that she gets stronger as each day goes by.

You know, when I was there, I tried to come down to the house as much as possible and I hope I was able to make every one happy. . . .

I received 3 letters from Carmen today. He told me about passing through the Panama Canal. He's somewhere in the Pacific by this time. Well, that's all for today. Everything here is going along pretty good so tell Ma not to worry.

So-long and God bless you all.

Love To: Ma, Pa, Mary, Tony, Francie & Carlo

X X X X X X X X X — Phil

[Phil received the following two letters from his brother Frankie, who was still in New Guinea in late February:]

Tuesday, January 23, 1945

Hi Bub,

How are you feeling these days? As usual I'm fine and I hope you are feeling the same. You know it's been quite awhile since I've received a letter from you. Don't worry, though, I understand. You're probably worried about *[your wife]* Mary, so you don't have to feel bad about not writing. I had a letter from your wife dated December 30, and she told me that she expected her baby within a week. By this time I suppose she has already had it, so your worries are over. I'll be waiting to hear the news, so let me know as soon as possible.

Well, I suppose you've been hearing about that snowstorm that Buffalo had a couple weeks ago. All the letters coming in have been filled with news about it. Boy, I'll bet it must be lulu. I only wish to heck that I were somewhere where I'd be able to get caught in a blizzard. Anyplace at all would do, just so long as there would be a little snow. It certainly will be nice to throw snowballs at a guy instead of those coconuts that we have been using!!!

Well, I suppose you know about how the war is going these days. As usual the Russians are tearing hell out of Germany, while England and the U.S. are still managing to gain their one mile a day. The Battle of Luzon is also going along pretty good, as you know. Boy, all I can say is that my outfit handled an awful lot of that ammunition that is being used there.

You know, I have very strong hopes of going up to the Philippines soon. All I can say is that the sooner the better. I've been in New Guinea for 19 months now and it's about time I had a little change of scenery. Well, I guess that's about all for now. So long and God bless you.

Love, Frankie

[The following is the other letter that Phil received from his brother Frankie in late February.]

Sunday, January 28, 1945

Hi Bub,

How are you feeling these days? As usual I'm fine and I hope you are feeling the same. I received your letter of January 11th and I was awfully glad to hear from you again. By the way, I'm going to ignore that reference of your's about how I got promoted!

I was awfully glad to hear that you have mailed me that book which I asked for. Don't try and kid me because I know you did go to some *trouble to get it. Whether you like it or not I'm still going to thank you. No kidding, I really appreciate it.*

Well, now I'm going to tell you something and I hope it doesn't make you sore. I thought I had told you this, but I guess I didn't. When I told you that I asked everybody back home for a book, I really meant "everybody." That also included your wife, Mary, too. Don't get the wrong idea on that. I'm not sponging from you two only. I'm getting books from Shadow and June, I already got one from Francie, Mary is sending me one and Joe and Rae are sending me one, also. I plan on asking Joe and Rae for another one as soon as I come across the name of a good book. I'm also going to ask Tony for a book. For some reason or other I decided not to ask Carmen for a book. The reason I'm telling you this is that I don't want you to get sore because I asked both you and Mary for books. I hope you follow my line of thinking. I'm just trying to sponge a little from everybody without any one person shouldering too much of the burden.

By the way, I've decided to stop ribbing you about your predictions. You probably thought just what a hundred million other people were thinking. As far as I'm concerned it was just wishful thinking [that the war would end by the end of 1944].

I don't think you'll have to worry about Germany getting what she deserves. By the looks of things the only way that we will beat Germany is by doing just what you said. That is by practically destroying every village and city. If I'm not mistaken, there isn't too much in Germany [left] to be destroyed. As for us using "Mustard Gas," all I can say [in reply] is that I hope to God nobody uses it. You see I've had a little experience with that stuff. My outfit has handled that stuff as part of our job in getting these ships unloaded [here in New Guinea]. Let me tell you that it's powerful. You don't have the least idea of what it can do if it ever gets unloaded on some crowded ship. War is war, but using gas is altogether different. I only hope that nobody uses it. [Phil, who works in chemical warfare, apparently had written to Frankie suggesting that mustard gas should be used to bring about a quicker end to the war. Obviously, Frankie disagrees. Their debate anticipated the later controversy over the atomic bomb. Some took Phil's position that any weapon that can end the war more quickly should be used; their opponents basically argued similar to Frankie, that morality places limits even on weapons of destruction.]

Well, I see that you have the idea that I'm not sun-tanned. Well, you're wrong because I'm burnt almost to a crisp. I guess the photos just don't show it. I also see that you think I'm a little on the skinny side. When I left Camp Stoneman I was up to about 163 pounds. Then I got to New Guinea, and I lost a little of that weight. Did you ever try to live on dehydrated and canned food? Well, let me tell you that it's not a very nourishing diet. We don't get much fresh fruits, vegetables, and milk. We also get very little fresh meat or eggs. Don't get me wrong, I know darn well that I'm better off than a lot of the troops that are overseas. At least we don't have to live in fox-holes and eat just plain C rations, or K rations. The food I'm getting may not be the best in the world, but it's a long way from being the worst. It's just that it's not the type of food that puts weight on a guy.

Well, I guess that's about all for now. Don't forget to let me know what [your wife] Mary has. I hope it's a boy, because you do. So long and God bless you.

Love, Frankie

Thursday March 1, 1945/Pratt, Kansas

Dear Mary,

Everything out here is going along pretty well. I hope Ma is getting stronger each day and that all of you are feeling well.

Let me know how Tony is coming along with the draft. I hope his plant is able to defer him again. If he can only get another deferment, I think he'll be all set as far as the war is concerned because by the time his next deferment is up I believe most of the war will be over with.

The weather here today was nice and warm like a spring day. Yesterday it was snowing and cold and today it's warm and sun shiny. That's Kansas for you.

I bet my son must sure be getting nice. Go see him once in a while and let him get to recognize all of you.

Well so-long for now and God bless you all.

Love To: Ma, Pa, Mary, Tony, Francie & Carlo
X X X X X X X X — Phil

Friday March 2, 1945/Pratt, Kansas

Dear Mary,

Everything is going along okay . . . and I hope that you can say the same for [yourselves] out there, and also I hope Ma feels better. I received a letter from Shadow today. He feels pretty lonely, but he's getting used to it. I just wrote a letter to Carmen and Frankie and I'm enclosing a little picture of Shadow and myself together that we took at Sattler's [department store].

I receive a letter from my wife everyday and I'm happy that she and the baby are getting along fine. . . . Well so-long for now and God bless you all.

Love To: Ma, Pa, Mary, Tony, Francie & Carlo
X X X X X X X X — Phil

Saturday March 3, 1945/Pratt, Kansas

Dear Mary,

Tonight I'm on Charge of Quarters out here. It's not so bad. I've got a nice radio to listen to. I bought a can of ham for 16 cents and 2 red points [used for meat rationing] and a box of crackers and I'm having some nice snacks and to top it off, I've got a pocket full of nickels and there's a coca cola machine full of coca cola. Well, I'll have a little feast by myself out here.

As yet I [haven't] received any mail from you, but that's okay, just so everything out there is going along pretty good.

I just sent my wife a first wedding anniversary gift. I won't say what it is until maybe a couple days from now. . . . Well so-long for now and God bless you all.

Love To: Ma, Pa, Mary, Tony, Francie & Carlo
X X X X X X X X X — Phil

Sunday March 4, 1945/Pratt, Kansas

Dear Mary,

I still didn't hear from you yet. Today is one week since I've been away from home. It's kind of lonely and time is going slow, but there's no way out of it. Today also makes one month that the baby was born. It won't be long and he'll be a big boy.

The weather here has been pretty good and everything is going along okay too. I hope Ma is almost normal again.

Well, so-long for now and God bless you all.

Love To: Ma, Pa, Mary, Tony, Francie & Carlo
X X X X X X X — Phil

Monday March 5, 1945/Pratt, Kansas

Dear Mary,

I received the first letter from you since I've come back, and it was swell to hear from you again. Also, I'm happy to hear that Ma is feeling more normal as each day goes on. Just let her always take it easy, and let's hope that she'll always be alright. I received the clipping you sent me from the *[Buffalo] Evening News* about my baby being born. Thanks a lot for it.

You know, I've been at this camp exactly one year now. Well, I'm shipping out tomorrow, March 6, so by the time you get this letter I'll have arrived at my other camp. It's at Wendover Field, Utah. I guess I can't get away from that Utah. Now don't be alarmed, it's not overseas. I'll have exactly the same job I've got now. My address will be: 216th Base Unit, Wendover Field, Utah, but don't write there until I tell you.

Meantime write me here at Pratt. So-long, don't worry, and God bless you all.

Love To: Ma, Pa, Mary, Tony, Francie & Carlo

X X X X X X X X — Phil

[The reason why Phil says he can't seem to get away from Utah is because he was stationed there back in 1943, when he attended the Air Cadets Training Program at Utah State Agricultural College. Though he isn't exactly thrilled at the thought of returning to Utah, he knows it is far better than any overseas alternative. Just a few weeks earlier, Phil had applied to Officer Candidate School, because he was almost certain that he was going to be sent into combat. He knew that OCS would delay his being shipped out for a while. And, if he did have to go into combat, he preferred going in as a lieutenant than a sergeant. As soon as he learned that his new assignment would be in Utah instead of overseas, he immediately withdrew his application to OCS.]

Tuesday March 6, 1945/Pratt, Kansas

Dear Mary,

Just a few lines just before I leave this base. In a few hours I'll be on a train going back into the West. The more I hate Utah, the more they send me there. This is the third time I've been stationed there. Incidently Ralph Ferrara *[Phil's close friend from the old neighborhood]* is stationed there at Wendover, Utah, so no doubt I'll see him. He'll be the first guy from home that I know at a camp since I was inducted.

This will be the last letter you'll get from me from Kansas. The next one will be from Utah. Tell Ma not to worry, because everything will be alright. So-long till the next time I write and God bless you all.

Love To: Ma, Pa, Mary, Tony, Francie & Carlo

X X X X X X X X X — Phil

P.S. Tell June I received her copy of the overseas *Buffalo News* and that I said thanks.

Wednesday March 7, 1945/Dalhart, Texas

Dear Mary,

Here I am in Texas for a few hours. My trains are a little off schedule so I have a little time. This isn't much of a town to look at. It's pretty small and is about the size of Gowanda, New York. *[Gowanda, near North Collins, had a few thousand people.]*

Everything is going along okay. Last night I pulled in here. It was 3:00 a.m. so I slept on a bench in the station till 8:30 this morning. My train pulls out from here about 1:00 p.m. this afternoon. I should be in

Fig. 2.2. Trains such as this one allowed Phil Aquila and other soldiers to come home on furloughs during the war. (Ball State University Photo Services)

Wendover, Utah, by midnight tomorrow (Thursday). Well that's about all for now. So-long, don't worry, and God bless you all.

Love To: Ma, Pa, Mary, Tony, Francie & Carlo
X X X X X X X X — Phil

Thursday March 8, 1945/Denver, Colorado

Dear Mary,

I'm in Denver, Colorado, today. Connections are very poor so I had a layover of 14 hours. Everything is going along pretty good, though, and I think I should be at my next camp by Friday afternoon. The weather isn't too bad out here. I told you about this city once before 1½ years ago when I was here. It's a large city almost like Buffalo only it's practically surrounded by mountains.

I hope Ma is feeling fine. Tell her not to worry about anything. So-long for now and God bless you all.

Love To: Ma, Pa, Mary, Tony, Francie, & Carlo
X X X X X X X — Phil

Friday March 9, 1945/Wendover, Utah

Dear Mary,

I just arrived here at Wendover Field. I may as well be overseas as far as civilization goes. It's way out on the Utah-Nevada border where there's actually nothing for hundreds of miles around except desert and mountains. As yet I'm not used to it here and my first impressions make me feel pretty bad. But I guess I'll have to take it on the chin and get used to it.

You know, Ralph Ferrara is here. I knew he was here and you should see how surprised he was to see me. I've had few friends in my life, but this Ralph is one of them.

Well, everything is going along okay, so tell Ma not to worry about me anyway. Tonight for a change I'll have a bed to sleep in. I've spent 2 nights on station benches and one night on a rocky train that made me so sick, I thought I'd die. So it'll be sweet to sleep in a nice warm bed again. As for food, I've been eating pretty good on my trip, and now here I'm eating regularly again. We can't kick you know. At least I can talk, but some guys on the battle fronts can't do that no more.

This camp handles mighty secret work, so I can't tell you too much about it. I'll still have my old job. [*Wendover Field was the training site for the crew of the* Enola Gay. *No wonder the camp was in the middle of nowhere. Phil was the NCO in charge of chemical supplies and the training of personnel in chemical warfare.*]

The weather here is summer time in the afternoons and winter at nights.

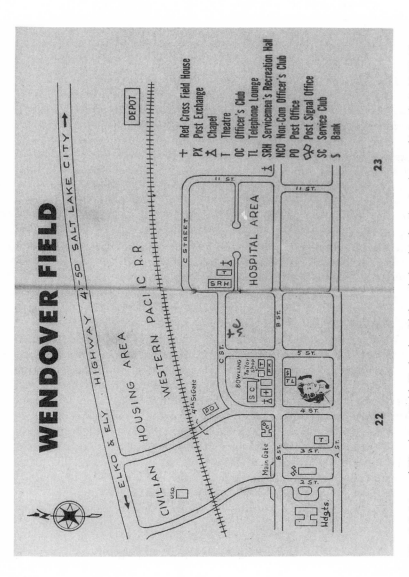

Fig. 2.3. Map of Wendover Field, Utah, that Phil mailed to his family. See letter of March 9, 1945. Note how he indicated the location of his barracks on the map. (Philip L. Aquila Collection)

I bought my wife a nice birthday gift in Denver. Ask her to let you see her birthday gift and also her anniversary gift. Well, I close for today but I'll be back again tomorrow.

So-long and God bless you all.

Love To: Ma, Pa, Mary, Tony, Francie & Carlo

X X X X X X X X X X — Phil

[Phil enclosed in this letter a small pamphlet that described his new base. It was called "Wendover Field Army Airbase, Information Handbook." The booklet contains several brief chapters, including: history of Wendover, information about nearby cities, how to place long-distance calls, rates for three-minute calls, and general information about the Red Cross, the base chapel, the base hospital, the enlisted men's service club, post theaters, post office, post cafeteria, post exchange, transportation, and housing. It also contains a map of Wendover Field that shows where everything is. Phil placed an "X" on the map designating where his barracks was. He wrote "Me" next to the "x." There were four movie theaters on the base. The handbook explains: "New films are shown frequently, with only the best in movie entertainment offered. Admission is 15 cents but theater books may be purchased at 20 per cent discount. Weekly USO Camp Shows are also featured at one or more theaters."]

Saturday March 10, 1945/Wendover, Utah

Dear Mary,

Another day is going by in which I'm trying to settle down and get used to this place. The weather is very sunny. It hardly rains or snows out here. There's nothing growing, not even weeds, so I guess I'll miss out on spring for this year. Oh well, that's war for you. It makes everybody miss out on a lot of things. The food out here isn't too bad. It's typical army food. Incidently, I just found out that Nevada is only about 1 mile away and I can easily see it, so that places me practically on the Nevada-Utah border or in other words in the middle of nowhere. If Frankie thinks he's far from lights and civilization and women [in New Guinea], he should see this place. There aren't even any WACs out here. I rather like it this way, though.

Well, for now, so-long, don't worry and God bless you all.

Love To: Ma, Pa, Mary, Tony, Francie & Carlo

— Phil

Sunday March 11, 1945/Wendover, Utah

Dear Mary,

Just another Sunday as far as I'm concerned. The weather here has been swell. It's very sunny and warm outside. I hope you can say the same for out there.

I'm situated pretty good out here and tomorrow I'll be reporting for work the same as usual. I don't know how long I'll be here. I may be here a few months, or even for the duration of the war. It's not such a hot camp, but I'll get used to it. I just hope I won't get moved because I sure hate all the fuss that goes with moving from one place to another.

I sure hope Ma is feeling fine these days and I hope she continues to feel that way. Just tell her not to worry about any of us boys, because we are perfectly capable of taking care of ourselves. I also hope everyone else is feeling okay.

So-long for now and God bless you all.

Love To: Ma, Pa, Mary, Tony, Francie & Carlo
X X X X X X X X X — Phil

P.S. I have only received one letter from you since I left home.

Monday March 13, 1945

[Actually it is March 12th. He usually doesn't err on these things. It's probably all the travel and trying to get into the flow of the new environment.]

Wendover, Utah

Dear Mary,

I haven't received no mail for a long time, so I hardly know how everyone is feeling out there.

Today I started to work. It's as if someone threw a jig-saw puzzle at me and told me to put it together. Whoever had my job before I came here sure left it in a mess. But as usual, I'll try my best at things. *[As the NCO in charge of Wendover's chemical warfare supplies, Phil is responsible for keeping the supplies in order and inventoried.]*

The weather here is perfect and I can't kick about that. I'm eating and sleeping okay too. All in all everything is going along as best as could be expected. I hope everyone there is feeling as well as could be. So-long for now and God bless you all.

Love To: Ma, Pa, Mary, Tony, Francie & Carlo
X X X X X X X X — Phil

Tuesday March 13, 1945/Wendover, Utah

Dear Mary,

Today I received 11 letters *[Apparently the mail just caught up to him at his new base]*. It was swell to hear from all of you. I wish I could have been there when the baby was baptized, but that's alright, it wasn't too important anyway. *[Obviously, Phil was not a dedicated Catholic. But that doesn't mean he wasn't religious. His letters all indicate that*

Phil prayed quite a bit and trusted in God to help him and his family through the hard times and problems.]

Thanks for everything you've done for the baby, even though nobody appreciates it except me. Well, that's life. You know I went to confession the other day and then to church. But that won't help me any. It's getting so that I'm getting mighty disgusted with life as a whole and don't be surprised if I join some fighting outfit pretty soon. Tell Ma never to worry about me. I make my own decisions. Until my next letter, so-long and God bless you all always and don't worry.

Love Always To: Ma, Pa, Mary, Tony, Francie & Carlo
X X X X X X X X X — Phil

[This letter suggests that Phil is getting annoyed by what appears to be the beginning of in-law problems. His sister Mary apparently has suggested that the Cavarella family, perhaps even Phil's wife, does not appreciate all she is doing for the baby. She even seems to be suggesting that Phil's loyalties are with his wife rather than his parents and siblings. Obviously, Phil's wife, who was also a strong-willed person, had her own ideas about how to raise the child. This contest for control of a newborn child and the divided loyalty of the man between his "old" and "new" families was probably being played out in millions of other families on the home front. The birth of a baby frequently changed the dynamic of in-law relationships. Exacerbating the problem was the fact that soldiers like Phil were hundreds or thousands of miles from home and had no easy way of mediating the differences between their new wives and old families. Of course, Phil's agitation could be traced to other causes. Perhaps he was having problems adjusting to the new base in Utah, which he apparently hated. Making matters worse, he was having a difficult time organizing the chemical supplies, which apparently had been left uncataloged and disorganized by his predecessor. Also, the tensions that resulted from being so far from home when his mother was ill, his new wife had just had a baby, and family squabbles were occurring were probably taking their toll on his morale.]

Wednesday March 14, 1945/Wendover, Utah

Dear Mary,

. . . My job is pretty complicated, but that's the way I found it and I can't make it any worse than it is, but as always I'll try my best even if I do have a more complicated job than the President has. . . .

I get disgusted and lonely at times, but I can't help it. I guess I'm plain sick and tired of wasting time. The war seems as if it won't end, but I hope it does although I think of it less and less. *[This sense of wasting time must have been especially bad for men stationed on the home front, who didn't feel like they were really in the war.]*

I hope Ma is feeling fine and getting stronger. You just make her understand that hard work isn't good for her in the long run. I hope Pa's back is better by now and that all of you are feeling as best as possible. So-long for now and God bless you all.

Love To: Ma, Pa, Mary, Tony, Francie & Carlo

X X X X X X X X X—Phil

[A birthday card was sent to his mother on March 15th. It read: "Thoughts of You on your Birthday" [and he wrote in by hand, "Mother!"] On the inside, he wrote "Ma" and then the verse read: "There's Just this pleasant little way/ To Wish you luck and greet you now/ But may it gladden your Birthday/ And bring you joy, someway, somehow." He signed the card: "With All Our Love! Your Loving Daughter & Son—Mary & Phil —"]

Thursday March 15, 1945/Wendover, Utah

Dear Mary,

Today is just another day out here on the Utah-Nevada border line. Just get a U.S. map and draw a line straight from Salt Lake City and when you get to the border of Nevada, that's where I'm at. . . .

Incidently today my wife is 20 years old. She's still a young, tender, chick. I bought her a picture to hang on the wall. It's really not a picture. It's a desert, hand-made[,] set in a case. It's really beautiful, so tell her to show it to you.

For her anniversary [coming up on March 25th] I bought her 8 sheets and 2 pillow cases. It cost about 13 dollars. I didn't know what to get her for her cotton anniversary so after a lot of red tape I finally was able to buy the sheets.

Well, I hope Ma is feeling fine today. You are probably working by now, if so tell Ma to take it easy. And how is Tony making out at Linde Air Corp? And what about his draft board? *[Phil's sister Mary went back to her job making boxes at a box company. Tony quit his job at Bell Aircraft, because they had transferred him to their Niagara Falls plant, which was too far from his home. His new job is at Linde Air Corporation in Buffalo.]* So-long for now and God bless you all.

Love To: Ma, Pa, Mary, Tony, Francie & Carlo

X X X X X X X X X X X X — Phil —

Friday March 16, 1945/Wendover, Utah

Dear Mary,

I received the letter you wrote last Tuesday and it came to me direct from Buffalo.

The weather out here today was pretty nice and warm. You know, there's no more need for you to tell me how the weather is out there. Ralph [Ferrara] works for the weather department here and he knows how the weather is in Buffalo before you even know it. In fact he can forecast Buffalo weather thru his work. I guess we'll be together for some time yet.

I was glad to hear that Ma is getting back to normal again. Just tell her not to do any heavy work or worry too much about anything. I am very sorry to hear that Tony is about to leave. I hate to see him go. It's alright for myself and our other brothers to be here, but I hate to see Tony join us. Sometimes they treat everybody like babies. It's all a big joke. I've been disgusted with the army and the war for a long time now. I sure hope they give him a 30 day extension like you said they might. And tell Ma not to worry.

This war is bound to be in its last stages. If it keeps going, 80,000,000 Germans are bound to all get killed. They are sure blasting heck out of it. The longer they keep fighting the worse they are suffering. If Tony must go though, I hope he gets into a good branch of the service. Let me know how he makes out, right away.

Well, out here, I'm up to my neck in work. I'm sure feeling like a jig-saw puzzle *[Phil still feels like he's trying to put together a puzzle because the previous person in charge of chemical warfare supplies had made such a mess.]* I'll try my best and if they don't like it, they can fire me and that will be okay with me. Mind you, I'm doing the work of a couple guys. I have to run my own desk in the office and I have to handle about 4 small warehouses, plus two areas where all my supplies are at. I'm what you'd call a Chemical Supply Man as rugged as they make them. But I'll try my best.

So-long for now and God bless you all and don't worry because a lot of things can happen for the best in no time.

Love To: Ma, Pa, Mary, Tony, Francie & Carlo

X X X X X X X X X — Phil

Saturday March 17, 1945/Wendover, Utah

Dear Mary,

Today I received two letters from you which you wrote Friday and last Monday. I'm glad you like the baby. Yep, he sure is growing bigger everyday. My wife told me that she was coming down there last week. Tell Ma not to be afraid to hold him all she wants. I know with Joe's baby and Shadow's baby Ma would think both Rae and June would watch her. But honest, with my baby I want Ma to feel just as if it was her own. As far as I'm concerned, I really would like Ma to be near him as much as Alice [his mother-in-law] is. I want the baby to grow up and really know everyone in our family real well. I would hate to come home and find that my baby was practically a stranger to you all.

Yep, I guess he won't know me when I come back, but that's to be expected. In time, everything will be worked out, I'm sure.

Yes, I know poor Shadow must be feeling mighty lonely, but it can't be helped. We can't say he did wrong by getting another baby, more power to him, but if he didn't he still could've had June and Ronny with him. As for me, it was understood from the beginning that Mary would come home as soon as she was pregnant. As for letting Mary come out here, it just can't be. There's no towns or villages around and besides it's just too far and there's too many train connections to make. Do you realize that from Kansas to here, I had to sleep two nights on benches in railroad stations, and one night I slept on a dirty, old-rickety train, and each time I think of it I get sick all over again. No, I would never let my wife come all this way and then back again all alone.

I know how Ma feels herself get better and worse according to the weather. In time, her pain will fade away and without her knowing it. I sure wish she's not suffering too much, though.

You told me about Pa's income tax. I'm glad he doesn't have to pay anything. It sure is tough to see Tony inducted, but it's tougher on a mother to know five of her sons are in the services. At least we know there aren't any 4–F's or even limited service men in the army from our family. Some of those people in Buffalo should be ashamed of themselves compared to the sacrifice Ma has made. Don't worry, though, God is on our side. The war has gone on for almost 4 years now. We've been lucky and God must be on our side because none of us are hurt and I'm sure none of us will get hurt. So tell Ma to be thankful of that fact.

So-long for now and God bless you all and don't worry.

Love To: Ma, Pa, Mary, Tony, Francie & Carlo
X X X X X X X X X X X — Phil

Sunday March 18, 1945/Wendover, Utah

Dear Mary,

It's Sunday once more and I got up late. Tonight I'll go to church with Ralph. I like it that way. Instead of getting up early in the morning to go to church, they hold a mass at 5:30 in the evening, so now I'm able to go. For Easter I'll go to communion.

I just got letters from Shadow and Carmen. Carmen sent his letter air mail and the stamp is still good, so I'll just stick it on an envelope and use it to write him a letter. . . .

I sure hope Tony doesn't have to leave this week [for the induction center]. I don't know why they take so many out of one family while other families are barely touched. We'll just keep hoping for the best though.

I hope Ma is getting better as each day goes by. No doubt she feels the pain each day, because she's always thinking about it. Well that's all for today, so-long, God bless you all and don't worry.

                    Love To: Ma, Pa, Mary, Tony, Francie & Carlo
                    X X X X X X X X X — Phil

                    Monday March 19, 1945/Wendover, Utah
Dear Mary,

I just received the letter you wrote last Friday and I was happy to hear that you were all feeling fine, and I hope you all stay that way. I'm glad Ma really likes my son, and I wish I could have seen how cute he was when my wife brought him over to the house.

It was nice of Frankie to give you 5 dollars to buy a gift for the baby. Yes, the scale is a mighty nice gift. The baby has a lot of clothes so I'm glad you didn't get him anymore. I'll write Frankie and thank him for the gift. Thanks to you also, for going through everything to buy it.

I received a letter from Carmen yesterday and one today. He hasn't much to say. He knows I got a baby boy and he's happy about it.

You said Tony may leave on the 20th of March. I sure hope he got that extension. I'm going to send some cigarettes in the letter. I'll try to get 10 in or maybe less. Let me know if they get there okay. If they do, I can send some every day, that is if Tony is still there. So let me know if these are alright.

Well, everything out here is going slow as usual, but then it could be worse. So-long for now and God bless you all.

                    Love To: Ma, Pa, Mary, Tony, Francie & Carlo
                    X X X X X X X X — Phil

P.S. If the 14 cigarettes I'm sending are a little flat, it's because I flattened them out so it wouldn't look too fat. [But, they are actually] fresh cigarettes out of a new pack.

                    Tuesday March 20, 1945/Wendover, Utah
Dear Mary,

Today, I received two pictures of the baby which my wife sent me. You were in one picture and I think they came out pretty good. The baby looks real nice. Maybe someday, I'll be able to see him again. . . .

I'm enclosing two sticks of gum. This P.X. [post exchange] hardly has any gum, but once in awhile they get some in. I hardly chew gum so it don't bother me any.

Today Tony was supposed to leave, but I hope he got an extension. I hope Ma is feeling as fine as possible and that she isn't worrying too much. So-long for now and God bless you all.

                    Love To: Ma, Pa, Mary, Tony, Francie & Carlo
                    X X X X X X X X X — Phil —

Fig. 2.4. Photograph taken at the baptism of Phil's baby in March 1945. *Left to right:* Jimmie Cavarella (Phil's brother-in-law was the baby's godfather); Philip L. Aquila Jr.; Mary Aquila (Phil's sister was the baby's godmother). (Philip L. Aquila Collection)

Wednesday March 21, 1945/Wendover, Utah

Dear Mary,

I just received the letter you wrote last Sunday. Yes, I get all your mail regularly now. Everything out here is going along alright and I can't kick. Yes, they've got places for wives out here. But the only way anyone can get a home is if the wife works on the base. You should see the outskirts of this camp. There's government homes and a lot of trailers, so if Mary, my wife, came out here for a few weeks, I wouldn't know where she could stay. She'd sure have to go through a lot of suffering on these trains and the round trip ticket would run up to a good $100. All in all, we'd get set back a good $200 if she came here. I can't think of anything I'd like better than to see her but it just can't be.

I sure hope Tony got his extension, if not, he's gone by now and I'm sorry. Here's hoping though.

I'm glad Ma bought my wife a couple pairs of stockings, she knows Ma didn't forget [her birthday] anyway. Even if Ma did, it's nothing because we are so many [children and in-laws], and there's too many birthdays. So-long for now and God bless you all.

Love To: Ma, Pa, Mary, Tony, Francie & Carlo

X X X X X X X X — Phil

Thursday March 22, 1945/Wendover, Utah

Dear Mary,

. . . If I sound disgusted once in a while, I just can't help it. Things just won't go right. Of course I'm speaking about my work. I can't ever complain about my wife and baby, because they are doing swell. You know, you shouldn't have gone through all that bother about the baby. I mean, putting initials on his ring and so forth. But, if you wanted to do it, it's okay and I appreciate it.

I still don't know if Tony left or not. I sure hope they gave him an extension.

You said I received some religious papers and scapulas from Santa Ana, California. You see while I was down [there], I somehow joined a Catholic Knights of the Sky club, because I was going to fly. But, all I did was just join.

I hope Ma is feeling alright today. The war looks dark for Germany and here's hoping that she can't last much longer.

So-long for now and God bless you all.

Love To: Ma, Pa, Mary, Tony, Francie & Carlo

X X X X X X X X — Phil —

Friday March 23, 1945/Wendover, Utah

Dear Mary,

I was waiting for a letter from you telling me if Tony had left [for the army] or not, but I didn't receive any, so that means I'll have to wait until tomorrow. You know, I bet I'm sweating this out more than he is. I wish so much that he doesn't have to go. It burns me up, because they don't do anything fair. There's a lot of guys they can take from that neighborhood. If you think some of those guys are 4–F's, you should see the guys out here in uniform. Why one guy was almost as old looking as Pa with white hair. A good friend of mine at Pratt, and my wife knows him, has a glass eye. Another guy is a cripple as a result of an auto accident and still he can't get a discharge. When I see these guys here and think of all the 4–F's who can do things any normal man can do, it burns me up, and yet they've got to clean out a family like us. Well, at least there's no 4–F's in our family. I just hope it doesn't affect Ma too much. You tell her that this war is in its last stages. Everything from now on is going to happen fast and expectedly, so tell Ma to feel a little cheerful, because when all of us come back we want to find her well. So-long and God bless you all.

Love To: Ma, Pa, Mary, Tony, Francie & Carlo

X X X X X — Phil — X X X X

Saturday March 24, 1945/Wendover, Utah

Dear Mary,

. . . I was very glad to hear that Tony has a 30 day extension. Yes, it's better than nothing at all. A lot can happen in the next month. Germany looks as beaten as she ever will be and I personally don't see why she doesn't surrender at any hour now.

I'm sorry to hear that Ma has a cold. I hope she takes good care of it, so it'll go away. I never forget anybody's birthday in our family. They come almost every month so all I have to do is think of whose birthday it is each month. I'm glad Ma got her birthday card alright and I hope the table-cloth my wife got for her is okay. It's not much, but it'll have to do until peace comes when we can go about getting gifts in a big way.

So-long for now and God bless you all and don't worry.

Love To: Ma, Pa, Mary, Tony, Francie & Carlo

X X X X X X X — Phil —

Sunday March 25, 1945/Wendover, Utah

Dear Mary,

Sunday again out here, only today it's my wedding anniversary. Time sure goes by whether we think so or not.

My wife told me she was down there for Ma's birthday and she said she enjoyed it. I hope you all liked the pie she made. It was nice for you and Josephine Mitri [a neighbor] to go get her and bring her home.

Now that Tony got his extension, I would like to send him some cigarettes, but honest, I just can't. I think they open up every package that leaves the camp. There's a cigarette shortage out here and I think they wouldn't allow cigarettes to be sent. Well, once Tony gets in the army, he won't have any cigarette problem. . . . So-long for today and God bless you all.

Love To: Ma, Pa, Mary, Tony, Francie & Carlo

X X X X X X X X X — Phil —

[The next entry is a postcard that pictures the telephone lounge at Wen-dover Field, where soldiers are making calls. Phil wrote the following message on the card:]

Dear Mary, I'm putting in a call to you tonight, and I hope I find most of you home. This card is a picture of the place here. *[It's March 25. He's calling his wife because it's their anniversary, so he figures he might as well call his parents also.]* Love, Phil

[The next entry is an Easter card. The front of it says "Happy Easter Mother" and he wrote in by hand "& Dad". Inside the card, the verse reads: "Happy Easter, Mother/ Just These words to say/ Wishes over-flowing/ From my heart today/ Wishes warm and tender/ Hopes that have to do/ With a love that always/ reaches out to you!" He signed it, "Your loving daughter and son, Mary and Phil."]

Monday March 26, 1945/Wendover, Utah

Dear Mary,

Last night I called you up. It was good to hear all your voices again. I'm sorry I didn't catch you, Tony, and Francie there. I'd have talked a little longer, but, it runs up to $10 in no time at all from out here. It was sure swell to hear Ma's voice again and convince myself that she's alright. Yes, I know my baby is sure growing big and cute. I guess all Aquilas have fine children. It runs in the family, don't you think? . . . Ma told me that you sent me a package. You really shouldn't have done it, but I guess it's alright. I told Ma that the war wasn't going to last much longer. The way it looks, the news since is making every body happy. So keep tuned to your radio, and any time it ends, they'll inter-rupt any program to tell everybody.

Well, so-long for today and God bless you all.

Love To: Ma, Pa, Mary, Tony, Francie & Carlo

X X X X X X X X X — Phil —

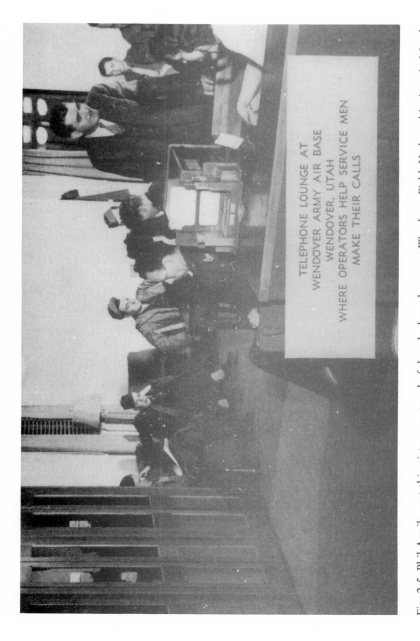

TELEPHONE LOUNGE AT
WENDOVER ARMY AIR BASE
WENDOVER, UTAH
WHERE OPERATORS HELP SERVICE MEN
MAKE THEIR CALLS

Fig. 2.5. Phil Aquila sent this picture postcard of the telephone lounge at Wendover Field, Utah, to his sister in March 1945. He placed his long-distance calls from this lounge. (Philip L. Aquila Collection)

Tuesday March 27, 1945/Wendover, Utah

Dear Mary,

Today I received the letter you wrote last Friday and the letter you wrote last Saturday. It was swell to hear from you, as always. I feel always happy to know that Ma is feeling as well as possible.

I'm glad you received the 14 cigarettes I sent you for Tony. I wish I could send him some, but there's too much of a check on them. Even if I enclose cigarettes in a letter, they may return the letter to me, so you see what I'm up against. I'm glad he still has a few packs left. Tell him to smoke those cigarettes, only if he can't get any no place.

I couldn't help but laugh my head off when you told me that you sent $100 to Frankie and that he bought ½ of a horse with it. Buying a horse is a joke itself, but buying a horse in New Guinea is double a joke, but to top it off, you said he bought ½ horse, either he buys the other half at the end or sells his half. No doubt he's probably got the wrong end of the horse. That really tops anything Shadow ever did, and I've got to laugh everytime I think of it.

You said Tony's going to jack the car up and remove the tires and battery. Just so he keeps the nuts and bolts all in one place, and before he jacks it up he should give it a good grease and oil job, then when he or any of us come home on furlough we can change the oil and give it another grease job. Of course one other thing, he could've taught you to drive and you could get your license. Well, I'm sorry, it's got to be parked but that's the best way I guess. Every once in a while some one of us will be home and we'll run it so don't worry.

The war still looks swell and it may be a few days and may be a few more weeks longer, but not much more. So-long for now, Happy Easter as much as possible to all of you, and God bless you all.

Love To: Ma, Pa, Mary, Tony, Francie & Carlo

X X X X X X X — Phil —

[Phil and his family seem extremely upbeat, because it appears the war will soon be over. Over the past few weeks, the Allies have fire-bombed Dresden, crossed the Rhine, taken control of the Balkans, captured Cologne, defeated the Germans in the Saar Basin, and invaded Austria. In addition, in February and early March, thirteen additional nations, including Turkey, Egypt, and several Latin American countries, have declared war on Germany. Germany is not only in retreat, but on the brink of collapse.]

Wednesday March 28, 1945/Wendover, Utah

Dear Mary,

I received the package you sent me today. Everything was in it exactly as you put them. The two sticks of sausage, the cakes, cookies, and the loose candy and the box of candy chocolates. It is a swell package and thank you all very much for it. I guess no matter how much I tell you not to send me packages, you'll keep on anyway. Honest, I know it costs you money, time, and energy to make up a package and then you have to bring it to the post office to mail it. I appreciate it, but I don't want all that trouble over me. Well, at least I've got Ralph [Ferrara] to help me with the sausage at this camp and I'd rather give some to him than anybody else.

Well, everything out here is going along pretty good and I can't kick. Slowly but surely I'm getting used to this place and I'm catching on to the ropes. I hope Ma is feeling nice today and tell her I enjoyed the package very much and I really did, and of course Ralph said thanks a lot for the food too. Why don't you call up his house and tell his mother. I see the guy everyday. He only lives a few barracks down from me. We go to church and shows together. We don't work together, though, because I'm in a different line of work.

You know I still can't get over the 1/2 horse Frankie owns. Worse comes to worst, he's got some horsemeat to eat anyway.

Well, that's all for tonight. The war is still going great and here's hoping for the best. So-long and God bless you all.

Love To: Ma, Pa, Mary, Tony, Francie & Carlo
X X X X X X X X X X X — Phil —

[The following letter is written on stationery that has four photographs in the left-hand column: the Mormon Temple; the Great White Throne; Bryce Canyon; and Rotary Headquarters Hotel Utah.]

Thursday March 29, 1945/Wendover, Utah

Dear Mary,

Today, I received the letter you wrote last Sunday. I'm always glad to hear that you are all feeling alright, and especially that Ma is getting along as best as possible. Yes, the war certainly looks swell. Maybe by the time you get this letter, a lot will have happened in this war. Here's hoping anyway. If I had my way about it, I wish it would end by Easter Sunday *[that's in three days]*.

Yes, I went to church on Palm Sunday and I got a little palm. There's a half of what I got enclosed in this letter. For Easter, I'll go to communion. I'm so glad that Ma holds the baby for a long while. I'd give anything to see Ma hold my baby, and hear her talk to him. And any one of you there can hold him all you want to. Don't ever be afraid of my wife. She wants you all to hold him. He sure is a nice quiet baby, and it takes a lot for him to cry. I'm glad you see him as much as possible.

I got a letter from Frankie today dated March 16th. He told me he bought ½ horse. You know, I got to thinking, he won't lose the money. He'll have a lot of fun and yet when he ships out, he'll be able to sell his share easily to somebody else. You see those bases like the one he's at will be permanent American bases. Well, so-long for now and God bless you all.   ⁄

Love To: Ma, Pa, Mary, Tony, Francie & Carlo
X X X X X X X X X — Phil

Friday March 30, 1945/Wendover, Utah

Dear Mary,
. . . I didn't eat no meat today. I'm fasting for the first time in maybe twelve years. Yep, I'm going to do my Easter Duty this year.

You said Tony cleaned the car and that it looks good. Well, no doubt it still looks good, but, it's nothing to worry about too much. When he parks it in the yard with the tires off, tell him to take out most of the tools, so they won't be lost. And if he has to really leave this month tell Ma not to worry. All this is all temporary and someday we'll all be back again.

Well, I hope Ma and all of you are feeling in the best of health. So-long for now and God bless you all.

Love To: Ma, Pa, Mary, Tony, Francie & Carlo
X X X X X X X X X — Phil —

Friday March 30, 1945/Wendover, Utah

Dear Mary,
I've got a little extra time, so I thought I'd write you two letters for tonight instead of just one. I just ran out of ink so I'm using pencil. It's 9:30 p.m. out here right now, so it's 12:30 early in the morning out there. You see, this western part of Utah just falls in the Pacific Coast Time Zone and it really makes me feel as if I'm in California or Washington again. I like this weather up here. It's a little cold, but it's not the kind of cold that's in Kansas where it rips through the clothes. The weather here is nice and dry and hardly no body has a cold. From where I am, I can see the Great Salt Flats that lead to Salt Lake. Actually I'm only a five minute walk from the state of Nevada because it's about ¼ of a mile away, so everyday I see both Utah and Nevada. The scenery here is actually really pretty. High mountains all on one side and the Salt Flats on the other. Yep, you'd never be able to imagine how big this country is until you've travelled around it like I have. But, no matter what I see or no matter into what kind of climate I land into, still there's no place like Western New York.

The food out here isn't so bad. It just burns me up when people squawk about the army food. Like Aunt Josephine's son Johnny telling her he traded a few things for an egg. When I tell Uncle Pete it's not that way, he says I talk like that because I'm not in no place like the Philippines. You never heard Frankie squawk about the food and he's been in New Guinea for 19 months and it's twice as hot there as it is up in the Philippines. I've been in the states, okay, but I know more about fighting and army life than ¾ of the guys across [the ocean]. If and when I go across I know just what to expect. I'm practically one of the few guys here who hasn't been overseas. The rest of the guys are like Ralph Ferrara, who've been all over, from South America, Africa, Italy, France, New Guinea, Saipan, Greenland, and all over. So when I say something, about overseas and how they treat them, I know what I'm talking about, so you just tell Aunt Josephine, that if Johnny does get hurt, he'll be alright.

Well, the war looks pretty good as usual. All the armies are driving across Germany and as far as I'm concerned, the war there has ended. From now on it'll be just a mop up operation in Germany. As for Japan, they're blasting the hell out of her. So as I said in the first letter, all this army stuff is just temporary, because some day the war will be over with, so tell Ma not to do too much worrying about us guys.

Well, it's past 10:00 p.m., so I guess I'll take in some sleep. Until tomorrow though, so-long and God bless you all and don't worry.

Love To: Ma, Pa, Mary, Tony, Francie & Carlo
X X X X X X X X X X — Phil —

P.S. I got an Easter card from School #6 [*that's the elementary school he attended*].

Saturday March 31, 1945/Wendover, Utah

Dear Mary,

Just a Saturday night out here. I may take in a show later on in the evening and maybe not. . . . Tomorrow is Easter. Last year [my wife] Mary was with me on Easter, in Kansas. Well, it'll just be another day out here and I know it'll be the same out there.

I'm glad to hear that Ma feels strong enough to go to the Novena [*a special Catholic Easter service*]. I hope she continues to be that well. As for Pa, I'm glad he comes home early. He has no reason to stay out late anyway.

You said you received a roll of cards from Carmen from Hawaii. By now, he's probably taking part in all those big naval battles and bombardments against the Japanese Islands. But tell Ma not to worry about him, he'll be alright. That Carmen is young [*Carmen is twenty*]. Yes, he's the youngest grown man in the family, but he can take care of himself very well. I wish I could be facing the things Frankie and Carmen are facing instead of them, but they have to do their own jobs I guess. So-long for now and God bless you all.

Love To: Ma, Pa, Mary, Tony, Francie & Carlo
X X X X X X X X X X X — Phil

Sunday April 1, 1945/Wendover, Utah

Dear Mary,

Today is Easter Sunday, but nothing special. I got up early this morning because there was too much noise going on in the barracks. This afternoon though I slept for a couple of hours. It's pretty chilly and cloudy here today, but it's alright. Later on this evening I'm going to church and communion.

I feel pretty lazy today and don't feel like doing nothing at all. I know you all didn't have such a happy Easter there, but maybe next year it'll be better for all of us. I hope you are all feeling in the best of health out there. I can't kick about my self out here.

The war still looks good. The Americans landed on a pretty big island 325 miles south of Japan itself. Here's hoping for the best. Well, so-long for now and God bless you all and don't worry.

Love To: Ma, Pa, Mary, Tony, Francie & Carlo
X X X X X X X X X X — Phil —

Monday April 2, 1945/Wendover, Utah

Dear Mary,

Just the day after Easter and everything is going along pretty good out here. You know, last night I heard a commentator on the radio who said Germany would quit this month, and Japan would quit this year. He's just a commentator but still we can never tell. You probably know that the Americans and Russians are less than 200 miles from meeting in Germany. And you know that the Americans landed on a large island only 325 miles from Japan. Yep, things are being done in a big way and we can never tell.

I hope you all are feeling as well as possible. Tell Ma not to worry about taking pills. Why even some of these soldiers take pills everyday. As for Carmen, don't worry about him, he's probably on the sea somewhere and it takes a long time to get a letter mailed and it takes a long time to get it to the U.S.

Well, so-long for now and God bless you all.

Love To: Ma, Pa, Mary, Tony, Francie & Carlo
X X X X X X X X X X — Phil —

Tuesday April 3, 1945/Wendover, Utah

Dear Mary,

. . . I didn't receive any mail from Buffalo today except a copy of the *[BUFFALO EVENING] NEWS* that June sent me.

The war is going on the same as usual. There's a lot of peace rumors, but that's about all. One thing though, Germany has to quit mighty soon because everyday they're taking a terrible beating from the air and on the land. So we can expect anything at any time. Just stay tuned to the radio and they'll let you know mighty quick when it ends.

The weather out here has been pretty chilly, but it's not too bad. I figure, I'm from Buffalo, and according to a lot of magazines and newspapers all over the country, Buffalo is the Snow Queen of the U.S.A., so cold weather doesn't bother me.

Well, so-long for today and tell Ma not to worry. God bless you all.
Love To: Ma, Pa, Mary, Tony, Francie & Carlo
X X X X X X X X X — Phil —

Wednesday April 4, 1945/Wendover, Utah

Dear Mary,

I received the letter you wrote last Saturday. I also received the swell birthday card with the $2 enclosed. Honest, you shouldn't have sent the $2. Thanks a lot for it though, and thanks for the card because it was very pretty. I'm glad Ma liked the plant my wife and I bought for her. It wasn't much. Two women I'll always love are Ma and my wife, so tell that to Ma. I think of her, and when holidays come around I think even more.

You said my wife seems different lately in that she talks and laughs more when she's there. Yes, I know it. Don't worry, I won't tell her about it. You see, I quit trying to force her to like anybody. It's up to her. You know when this war ends, I'll have my own home and I promise you that she'll see our family exactly as much as she'll see hers.

I'm enclosing a letter from Carmen. You said you didn't get any for quite a while. He wrote this on March 6th and he must've been past Hawaii, because he talked about it. You know, you can't expect a letter from Carmen as you do from Frankie. Carmen sails around and sometimes letters don't get off the ship for a few weeks and then until a couple more to get to Buffalo. You figure it out. So-long and God bless you all.

Love To: Ma, Pa, Mary, Tony, Francie & Carlo
X X X X X X X X X — Phil

Thursday April 5, 1945/Wendover, Utah

Dear Mary,

Just another day out here, even if it is my birthday. Yep, 23 years old, and I feel as if I'm still about 16 years old. I guess I've still got a long ways to go though. Today I got a birthday card from my wife, one from my son, and one from my mother-in-law and father-in-law. Yep, my wife got a birthday card for my son, but of course she wrote my name on it, even though my son could've done it. *[His son is two months old!]* It really makes me happy to know that both you and my wife and her family remember me on my birthday. If no body else remembers, it makes no difference to me.

Everything out here is going along pretty good. The weather is fine and warm and I'm struggling along alright in my job. I hope Ma is feeling fine out there today and also the rest [of you]. So-long for today and God bless you all and don't worry.

Love To: Ma, Pa, Mary, Tony, Francie & Carlo
X X X X X X X X — Phil —

Friday April 6, 1945/Wendover, Utah

Dear Mary,

Not much to say for my self today. I feel a little tired, but not because I worked hard. It's just that it gets so monotonous out here. Everything is going along alright though, so I really can't kick. The weather has been swell, too. I hope everybody there is feeling alright too.

When is Tony supposed to leave? According to the radio, if Germany quits they are going to draft only 18 year olds. But you can't go by the radio. They keep saying too many wrong things. I sure hope Tony has this last bit of luck to stay out just a little while longer. Well, that's all for now so till tomorrow, so-long and God bless you all.

Love To: Ma, Pa, Mary, Tony, Francie & Carlo
X X X X X X X X X — Phil —

Saturday April 7, 1945/Wendover, Utah

Dear Mary,

Everything is going along pretty good out here and I can't kick. The weather has been rather warm. I guess it'll be warm from now on. I hate to think of the heat out here when summer time comes along.

The war seems like it'll never end even though it's going fast, but one look at the map and you can see that Germany is pretty small and can't hold out much longer. Each letter I write to you I keep wondering that maybe part of this war will have ended by the time you get it in Buffalo.

Today I got my cigarette ration card. Yep, they started to ration cigarettes on this base. They're giving us 12 packs a week. That's really too much for me, but I'll get them and save them up.

I hope Ma and all of you are feeling fine today and stay that way. So-long and God bless you all and don't worry.

Love To: Ma, Pa, Mary, Tony, Francie & Carlo
X X X X X X X X X — Phil —

Sunday April 8, 1945/Wendover, Utah

Dear Mary,

. . . I'm glad to hear that you started to work again [at F. N. Burt's box factory], and I hope you get used to it quickly. Did they give you the same job back again? Out here I'm doing my job as well as I can. Yes, it's getting a lot easier and maybe someday I may even learn to like it a little. I never quit any job though just because I don't like it.

Yep, my son is growing and growing. I know he didn't lose his hair like June, Rae, and Shadow said he would. When I came home, he won't recognize me, and I won't recognize him. That's the way it goes.

Well, I hope Ma and all of you are feeling well and fine. Out here I am feeling fine. My wife bought me a real good wallet and sent me a package with candy, salami, cookies, cake, olives, peaches, pretzels, and bread. I'll be eating for the next week now. So-long and God bless you all.

Love To: Ma, Pa, Mary, Tony, Francie & Carlo
X X X X X X X X X X — Phil —

Monday April 9, 1945/Wendover, Utah

Dear Mary,

. . . I hope Ma is feeling very well. Has she talked about the farm yet? If she has, you shut her up mighty quickly. Let her rest from now on.

By the way, I talked it over with my wife and I want her to pay you for the phone call I made last month and also any other phone calls I make. It's only fair. We pay for them at her house so we want to pay for them there also. So I want you to accept the money when she gives it to you, or else I'll send it from here. I know Ma hasn't got much money, so by paying for my phone calls, I feel as if I'm helping out.

I wrote to Frankie and Carmen yesterday and I sent Carmen a picture of my son and he's supposed to send it to Frankie and Frankie will send it to me back again. I just want them to see the baby before my wife sends them a picture they can keep.

Well so-long for now and God bless you all.

Love To: Ma, Pa, Mary, Tony, Francie & Carlo
X X X X X X X X X — Phil

Tuesday April 10, 1945/Wendover, Utah

Dear Mary,

. . . I received mail only from my wife today. She bought a nice new coat. I've been telling her to buy one for a long time. She hasn't any spring-summer coat at all. The only thing she had was that old [three-year-old] coat from her suit, which her mother bought her for Easter when she was 17 years old. I bet she sure looks pretty sharp with her new coat.

I hope you are all feeling fine, especially Ma. Out here, I'm in the best of health. One thing I can say, I never have become really sick. I've never been on sick call or anything. Well, that's all for tonight. Until tomorrow, so-long and God bless you all.

Love To: Ma, Pa, Mary, Tony, Francie & Carlo
X X X X X X X X X — Phil —

Wednesday April 11, 1945/Wendover, Utah

Dear Mary,

I received the letter you wrote last Saturday. I also found the clippings you had in it about Mike Ferrara's case. It's very interesting. You said Pa lost 4 days work because he's a witness. I guess nothing can be done about that. You just put Pa straight that all he's supposed to tell is what he actually saw. Whatever happened in the past is none of his concern.

I'm glad to hear that Ma is getting along pretty good. I know it's tough on you to work and then write letters. Well, you don't have to write me too much. Just about once a week is alright. Of course, though, some body should write to Carmen and Frankie a few times a week. . . . Well, I'll close for tonight. So until tomorrow, so-long and God bless you all.

Love To: Ma, Pa, Mary, Tony, Francie & Carlo
X X X X X X X X X — Phil —

Friday April 13, 1945/Wendover, Utah

Dear Mary,

Today is Friday the 13th and if a person is superstitious, it'll sure worry him or her. Well, to me, it's just another day.

Well, everybody is mourning for the President. You can't find any orchestras on the radio, and you don't hear nobody crack jokes or laugh on the radio either. Roosevelt was a great man and I think he deserves every bit of respect that he's getting. His death isn't affecting the war none, so don't worry. Germany is being cut to bits and as far as I'm concerned the war in Europe has ended. Japan is the one that's left, and I don't think this country feels like playing around any too long. The death of Roosevelt makes it worse for Japan, because the soldiers will feel more hatred towards them than before. Well, let's keep hoping for the best. So-long for now and I hope Ma is feeling well and so are the rest of you. God bless you all.

Love To: Ma, Pa, Mary, Tony, Francie & Carlo
X X X X X X X X X X X — Phil

Saturday April 14, 1945/Wendover, Utah

Dear Mary,

. . . I'm glad [to hear] my letters come in regularly. I try my best to write everyday and I see no reason why every serviceman shouldn't write everyday. But, because I write everyday, my letters are pretty short because I've hardly got much to say or tell you. Whereby, if I wrote just once a week my letters would be much longer. We'll let it go at once a day though, because I know you all want to hear how I'm doing everyday. I bet Ma is so much in the habit of hearing from me every day that if two or three days go by that no letter from me comes she'll start to worry. But, you tell her not to, because maybe some days I'll work too hard and I'll not feel like writing, but I doubt it, so don't worry about it. Then again, I may get in an argument with my wife and I won't write no letters to any body for a week or two. But that has seldom happened, I'm just referring to it in case it does so you don't worry.

Well, they're still mourning over President Roosevelt. All the radio has is news about the funeral and etc. concerning the president. They even closed down the [movie] shows on the camp so now nobody has no place to go. Oh well, a man as great as Roosevelt deserves the respect. He really was like a father to this country, and in my opinion he'll go down as a greater man than Washington or Lincoln.

I'm glad to hear that Ma gained two pounds. When people pass 50, they lose weight normally and here Ma has been sick and she gained two pounds. I sure hope she continues to be well. She's got the happiest days of her life to live yet. One of the reasons why people feel so sorry to know that Roosevelt died was because the guy poured his heart to first putting the country on its feet [in the Depression] and then winning the war and here he couldn't live to see Victory. The same with Ma, she's been battling all her life to get us all on our own feet and now when the war is over, she can really relax and be happy. So I sure hope that she'll always be alright.

You said Carmen was in the Battle of Iwo Jima. I bet he's in the Battle of Okinawa, too. I'm sure happy that guy is in the navy, because he'll be alright. The odds of him getting hurt as compared to a land soldier are very small, so tell Ma not to worry too much about him.

I'm glad you can start seeing the Aquila features in my son. Yep, he sure is growing up into a nice boy.

Well, so-long for now, and God bless you all.

Love To: Ma, Pa, Mary, Tony, Francie & Carlo
X X X X X X X X X X — Phil —

Sunday April 15, 1945/Wendover, Utah

Dear Mary,

Not much to say for today. It's just a Sunday and I've been loafing around doing nothing at all. Right now I'm going to shave and shower and then go and eat a baloney sandwich and drink a cup of coffee. That's the way it is, sometimes you get a nice meal and at times you don't, so we'll have to take the good with the bad.

I received a letter from Carmen today which he wrote on March 25th. He didn't say too much and he's feeling alright, so don't worry about him. I just wrote to him and Frankie.

Everything out here is going along alright and the weather is okay too. I hope Ma and all of you are feeling okay too.

So-long for now and God bless you all.

Love To: Ma, Pa, Mary, Tony, Francie & Carlo
X X X X X X X X X X — Phil —

Monday April 16, 1945/Wendover, Utah

Dear Mary,

. . . It was swell of Ma to go over to see my wife and baby. It's alright, just so Ma is feeling well, but if some times she wants to see the baby and doesn't feel well enough to go over, all she has to do is ask my wife and I'm sure she'll come over. You said you haven't missed a week to see my son. I'm glad. I want him to see all of you often so that he'll know you all just as good as he'll know my wife's family. I don't want him to look up to my wife's family more than our family, so just keep winning your way into his heart.

I received a swell letter from Carmen today. He said he fought in the Battle of Iwo Jima and that he saw the marines put up the flag on that island.

Well, so-long for now and God bless you all.

Love To: Ma, Pa, Mary, Tony, Francie & Carlo
X X X X X X X X X — Phil —

Tuesday April 17, 1945/Wendover, Utah

Dear Mary,

. . . I hope Ma and Pa and all of you are feeling fine out there. I'm glad Tony hasn't heard from his draft board yet and I hope they hold it off a little longer.

The war is slowing up some, but I think it's the last pause before they finish it. At least with Germany. It's funny how Germany keeps fighting. It has nothing to gain and a lot of men are getting killed for nothing. It just burns me up, but the heck with them. If the German soldiers haven't got sense to quit, they deserve to stop a bullet.

Well, that's all I can say for tonight. Tell Ma not to worry. So-long and God bless you all.

Love To: Ma, Pa, Mary, Tony, Francie & Carlo

X X X X X X X X X — Phil —

Wednesday April 18, 1945/Wendover, Utah

Dear Mary,

Today has been a swell day out here. The sun was shining and it was real warm. I bet, if I'm out here this summer, I'll be sending you the temperature readings and I'll bet it'll reach 115 degrees easy. You see, this land out here is a desert, so you can imagine how hot it must get. Anyway we'll soon find out, provided I stay out here. My job hasn't been so bad and who knows, I may even learn how to do it yet. All kidding aside, I try my best. If Generals aren't perfect, how can I, just a sergeant be perfect? I'm feeling pretty good and I can't kick about anything, but then, I always take good and bad on the chin. In fact, I consider myself to be lucky I'm alive everyday the dawn appears. I could've been fighting a long time ago, if God wanted.

I hope Ma is feeling fine today. Maybe, she can get rid of those pains she gets once in a while, some day. Does Pa get some yet? I hope not. I hope all of you are feeling well. Make Carlo go to school everyday. I sure pity my son, having a father like me. I've always tried to boss Frankie, Carmen, Francie & Carlo. I used to be rough with them, but I tried to tell them right from wrong. I'd take an interest in everything they'd do, and in the future whenever I can help any one of our family I'll gladly do so. So-long for now and God bless you all and don't worry.

Love To: Ma, Pa, Mary, Tony, Francie & Carlo

X X X X X X X X X X X X — Phil —

P.S. Only a stick of gum for Ma <u>today</u>!

Thursday April 19, 1945/Wendover, Utah

Dear Mary,

. . . You said you haven't heard from Frankie in over 3 weeks. Well, I hope he's on his way home. You said he's been over there [in New Guinea] 21 months now. They usually keep them overseas 2 or 2½ years, but then again you can't tell when they let guys come back.

You said Aunt Josephine bought another house next door to hers. That's fine. As for Ma buying another house, I don't see why not. I only wished we'd have bought a new house someplace nice. I can't help but feel that I'm the fault for Ma buying the house you now have. The only thing I have against it is the neighborhood. The house itself and the yard are really nice and you can't ever lose on it. *[Phil wanted his mother to have her own house. So, when a house next door to the one they rented went up for sale, he convinced her to buy it. He also gave her his savings so she could buy the house.]*

Well, I'll close for now. So-long and God bless you all.

Love To: Ma, Pa, Mary, Tony, Francie & Carlo
X X X X X X X X X X — Phil —

P.S. I was surprised to get a letter from Tony today and I'll write him as soon as I can.

Friday April 20, 1945/Wendover, Utah

Dear Mary,

. . . I'm glad to hear that Ma is feeling alright and that the specialist found her in good shape. I hope when she gets X-rayed that she's as well as ever.

You told me that [Joe's wife] Rae hasn't received an answer to the letter she wrote me. I couldn't help but smile a little. How could I answer her letter when I didn't receive any? If she wrote, she must've made a mistake in my address, because ever since I've been in the army, I've received every single letter my wife writes me and she writes everyday without missing. So you tell Rae, she must've made a mistake, but I'll write to her anyway as soon as I can. . . . So-long for now and God bless you all.

Love To: Ma, Pa, Mary, Tony, Francie & Carlo
X X X X X X X — Phil —

[This next letter is addressed to Phil's brother, Tony.]

Friday April 20, 1945/Wendover, Utah

Hello Tony,

I received the letter you wrote, and after I decoded it, it didn't sound so bad. I was really glad to hear from you. Yes, it's too bad Roosevelt had to die. I don't know about this Truman fellow. He may turn out to be alright. They can always impeach him if he isn't. Then again a president can only be as strong as the 100,000,000 people of this country. Of course in my figures I'm excluding the bums of Michigan Avenue and etc. all over the country.

Yes, Carmen has seen some action. No doubt he's got a better chance of getting through everything by being in the navy. But I still worry about him. According to figures on the Battle of Okinawa more than 50% of all the American casualties so far have been Navy personnel, and no doubt Carmen has been in that action too. He'll be alright, I guess. *[Phil is never this worried or pessimistic when writing to his sister.]*

I suppose, me being with the longest military service in our family, I should tell you what to expect when you are drafted, but I won't, because there's nothing to it. You won't have to worry about what clothes to wear, what or where you'll eat, or where you'll go every day. It will be all taken care of for you. It's alright to be polite in the army, but it's mainly "Hooray for me and the hell with the other guy!" Maybe you may get a chance to go to Officer Candidate School. I just had an application in, but when I got shipped to Utah, I withdrew it right away, so I didn't tell nobody anything about it.

Well, I'll close for now, and I hope the [draft] board forgets your name a little longer. So-long till the next time.

Your brother and Pal, Phil

P.S. Yep, my kid is sure coming along okay. No matter what happens to me, there'll always be a Phil Aquila—personal strategy! *[The baby is named Philip L. Aquila Jr.]*

Saturday April 21, 1945/Wendover, Utah

Dear Mary,

Another week has gone by and everything seems to be going along alright out here and I hope it's the same out there. Time sure goes by pretty fast, no matter how slow we think it goes by. It really is going by too fast for me. When we come right to the point, all this war business is just a waste of time. As if the human life wasn't short as it is, but science has to make it shorter by war. Oh well, we can just take it on the chin and have patience.

I received a letter from cousin Johnny and I think he's seen some action, too. I hope he doesn't get hurt.

I hope Ma is getting along pretty good and the same goes for the rest of you. I wrote Tony a short letter yesterday. I'll write him more often I guess. If he gets into the service, he'll be another guy on my regular list of letter writing. I don't mind it though.

The weather here today has been cloudy but warm and now it's raining with thunder, and rain is very unusual for out here. I probably won't see rain again for 6 months.

So-long for now and God bless you all.

Love To: Ma, Pa, Mary, Tony, Francie & Carlo
X X X X X X X X — Phil —

Sunday April 22, 1945/Wendover, Utah

Dear Mary,

Today is Sunday and everything is going well. The sun is shining brightly and it's nice and warm. I sure wish I could be where I could see Spring come. Out here there aren't any flowers or trees or grass. Just snow capped mountains on one side, dry rocky mountains on the other, and a big desert on another side. No trees whatsoever, except maybe a couple off the base. If Pa was out here, he'd feel lost because there's not even dandelions. *[Many Italian immigrants loved to pick dandelion greens early in the spring to eat in their salads.]*

I had a picture taken in front of Ralph's barracks on Easter morning and I just got it back. I sent one to my wife and one to you. It didn't come out so very good, but I'm sending it any way so that you can slap it in the album.

I hope Ma is feeling alright today. Each day I can't help wondering how she actually feels. I can only hope for the best though.

The Russians have entered Berlin and probably have made a connection with the Americans, so actually as far as real war goes, it really is finished in Europe. Germany hasn't got an organized army with all the modern equipment to fight a real war any longer. Here's hoping for a fast finish. Well so-long for now and tell Ma not to worry because everything will turn out for the best. God bless you all.

Love To: Ma, Pa, Mary, Tony, Francie & Carlo
X X X X X X X X X X — Phil —

[The next letter is addressed to brother Tony.]

Sunday April 22, 1945/Wendover, Utah

Dear Tony,

I just thought I'd write you another letter to boost your morale a little. If you are going to be drafted, I may as well get used to dropping you a line once in a while. *[Phil writes regularly to his brothers in the service to boost their morale, as he says, and probably to keep the family going too. He writes less frequently to cousins and friends in the service.]* Incidently, it's a good idea if you glanced over some algebra because they'll give you a test right away and how you make out on the test depends a lot as to what branch you'll actually get into. That's the way they worked it before, anyway. *[Phil's excellent performance on his induction exams got him admitted into the Army Air Force. However, in late 1943, the military did away with its skimming policy that allowed the Army Air Force to select the best inductees. It's interesting that he's advising his older brother to study algebra. That seems to have been the main reason for writing this let-*

ter. He apparently thought about the algebra suggestion after he had mailed the previous letter, and he thought it important enough to send another letter.]

The Russians have just about taken all of Berlin, and as far as the German war goes, it's mainly mopping up operations now. Next is Japan and we seem to be doing things in a mighty big way in the Pacific. Well, I hope you are getting along pretty good out there. So-long for now.

Your brother and Pal, — Phil —

Monday April 23, 1945/Wendover, Utah

Dear Mary,

. . . It was nice of Carmen and Frankie to send Ma all those nice presents. I know if only this war would end and we can all come home again, we will make Ma very happy.

You said you got a letter from Frankie. I also got one today. I'll say he's busy with his horse. He said a lot of other guys have also bought horses now. I bet his camp must be like a race track. Well, just so he has his fun. According to him, he's learning how to ride the hard way, if you get what I mean, but I'm sure he'll make a good cowboy.

I'm enclosing a picture I took on Easter Sunday with Ralph. The shadow hit part of my face and gave me an English profile, but it didn't come out too bad. Stick it in the scrap book.

So-long for now and God bless you all.

Love To: Ma, Pa, Mary, Tony, Francie & Carlo
X X X X X X X X X X — Phil —

Tuesday April 24, 1945/Wendover, Utah

Dear Mary,

Just another day going by out here. Same old stuff day in and day out, but I can take it like the rest. . . .

I'm sending you a picture that I took on Monday April 2nd. You can paste it in the scrap book. I sure look pretty rugged in this picture, and in my opinion I really am. Yep, this picture shows "the fighting sarge himself" at the Battle of Wendover, Utah. If you notice, the slope of a mountain [is] in the background. I'm standing in front of Ralph's barracks. My barracks is down the line. It's the last one way in the end. It's the fifth one counting the barracks I'm standing in front of. If you see anything growing such as grass or flowers, tell me right away so that I, too, can look at them. Of course, that trash can belongs to Ralph's barracks. Also, these barracks are more like barns, but they're alright. While you are at it, you may as well see my army shoes. My working clothes are a little too big, but that isn't unusual. I never get anything

Fig. 2.6. Phil Aquila (*left*) with his friend from the old neighborhood, Ralph Ferrara. The picture is taken at Wendover Field, Utah, on Easter Sunday, 1945. He mentions it in his letter of April 23, 1945. (Philip L. Aquila Collection)

Fig. 2.7. Picture of Phil Aquila, "the fightin' sarge," taken at Wendover Field, Utah, on April 2, 1945. He describes the photo in his letter of April 24, 1945. (Philip L. Aquila Collection)

just right in the army anyway. As I said, go ahead and paste it in the scrap book. I've sent my wife these pictures also, so she's got some exactly like these.

Well, I hope you are all feeling fine, especially Ma. And I hope the draft board forgets Tony for a while longer, anyway. I didn't receive any mail from anyone today, and that's unusual, so tomorrow I should get a lot. So-long for now and God bless you all.

Love To: Ma, Pa, Mary, Tony, Francie & Carlo
X X X X X X X X X — Phil —

Wednesday April 25, 1945/Wendover, Utah

Dear Mary,

Don't expect no picture in this letter, because I only had 3 and I sent them all to you in the last 3 days. Today I received two nice pictures of my son from my wife. He sure looks real nice and chubby. I bet he's real tough. I'm feeling alright out here today. The weather has been chilly and cloudy. I hope Ma is feeling in good health and in good spirits. And I hope the rest of you feel okay too. Well, so-long for now and tell Ma not to worry about anything. God bless you all.

Love To: Ma, Pa, Mary, Tony, Francie & Carlo
X X X X X X X X — Phil —

Thursday April 26, 1945/Wendover, Utah

Dear Mary,

. . . My wife told me that you and Francie were down to see her and that you brought my son a nice little suit. Thanks a lot for it and it was nice of you to go down. You don't have to buy some thing everytime you go down there though.

I hope Ma is getting along alright. Maybe with summer she'll feel real nice.

Two weeks ago the radio was filled with news about Roosevelt's death. Now it's filled with news about the San Francisco Conference which is being held to form a permanent peace. It's the same old story every time a bunch of old men get together. They forget the young man who is laying 6 feet under. Well, I hope there will be peace after this war, a little longer than after the other. *[Apparently Phil is skeptical about the conference that opened in San Francisco on April 25 to discuss the creation of an international organization, the United Nations.]* Well, so-long for now and tell Ma not to worry. God bless you all.

Love To: Ma, Pa, Mary, Tony, Francie & Carlo
X X X X X X X X X X X — Phil —

Friday April 27, 1945/Wendover, Utah

Dear Mary,

. . . I think I'll call you up tonight if everything goes along alright. One thing though, I wish you'd accept the money [from me] when I reverse the charges. . . .

Yes, my son is sure a lively baby, and he's beginning to understand. I know he won't recognize me when I see him again but that's to be expected. But in time everything will be alright and we'll get together okay. Well, I have no more to say for today so take it easy, don't worry and God bless you all.

Love To: Ma, Pa, Mary, Tony, Francie, & Carlo
X X X X X X X X X — Phil

P.S. I just called you up and it was swell to hear all your voices with the exception of Francie and Tony. But that's okay. Honest, I could hear Ma as if I was a few blocks away instead of three days traveling away. Ma told me you got two [of the pictures] so far, and I'm glad you liked them. Well, so-long again and God bless you all.

Saturday April 28, 1945/Wendover, Utah

Dear Mary,

As I write this letter, the radio is filled with news about Germany's surrender, but as yet it's not official, and everybody is waiting for the official announcement by President Truman. Everybody feels happy about it, and I can't blame them. I know Ma must feel happy, too. Yep, [sometimes] it seems as if war is endless, but the day always comes when it ends, and that goes for Japan, too.

Last night I called my wife up and I just caught her as she came in, so I couldn't talk to her too long. So tonight I called her up again. It sure was swell to hear her voice. I wish I could stay on the phone longer when I talk to you or to my wife, but it costs too much.

Everything out here is going along pretty good and I'm feeling fine. I hope Ma is in the best of health and so are all the rest [of you]. God bless you all.

Love To: Ma, Pa, Mary, Tony, Francie, & Carlo
X X X X X X X X X — Phil

P.S. Thanks a lot for buying the high chair for my son. My wife and I really appreciate it.

Sunday April 29, 1945/Wendover, Utah

Dear Mary,

. . . I do hope Ma is feeling better than she did when you wrote that letter [last Wednesday]. Out here, I'm feeling fine.

That rumor about Germany surrendering was false, unless we'll hear more about it pretty soon. Well, anyway, if Germany quits or not, she'll be completely over-run in a matter of weeks so it'll be the same thing.

Today is a swell day out here. It's not so warm but it's just nice. I'm laying on a blanket outside my barracks in my gym trunks and I hope I can get a little sun tan. Well, so-long for today and God bless you all.

Love To: Ma, Pa, Mary, Tony, Francie & Carlo
X X X X X X X X X X X X — Phil —

Monday April 30, 1945/Wendover, Utah

Dear Mary

. . . The weather out here has been really swell. My back and legs are nice and red by the sun burn I got, but it don't hurt. Sun burn never did hurt me like it did other persons.

I hope Ma is feeling fine today and that her pains are fading away and I hope the rest of you are also feeling alright.

I'm glad that there hasn't been any notice for Tony to report to his draft board, and I hope it continues to be that way. I'll write Frankie and Carmen tonight and I'll also try to write [Cousin] Johnny a V-Mail letter too.

I guess that peace rumor [about Germany] Saturday was really a rumor, but we can expect something big to happen at any time, so tell Ma when she hears a lot of bells and whistles like New Year's Eve, it means that half the war is over with. Well, so-long for now and tell Ma not to worry. God bless you all.

Love To: Ma, Pa, Mary, Tony, Francie & Carlo
X X X X X X X X — Phil —

Tuesday May 1, 1945/Wendover, Utah

Dear Mary,

. . . The weather here is swell and I'm getting a nice tan. After work, I lay in the sun and try to get as much as possible. Why don't you buy Ma a nice bathing suit and let her get some sun tan around her body this summer? Go ahead and laugh at me, but I think it sure will help her to get her strength back.

The war with Germany is finished as far as a lot of people are concerned. At this peace conference [in San Francisco] though, these politicians aren't doing so hot. Maybe they ought to carry a rifle and do some fighting instead of trying to build a world peace right now. Well so-long for now and God bless you all.

Love To:
Ma, Pa, Mary, Tony, Francie & Carlo
X X X X X X X — Phil

Wednesday May 2, 1945/Wendover, Utah

Dear Mary,

I received the letter you wrote last Saturday and I was glad to hear that you are all feeling fine. Yes, I'd like to see Frankie's picture on a horse with his head shaved. I bet he looks comical. . . . You said a guy named Frank C. moved in the rear [flat]. Yes, I know him quite well. I guess he's okay, but he's the sly type of guy and pretty reckless, so just kind of keep an eye on him. He used to do acrobatics on the stage with me about 16 years ago. *[When Phil was a youngster, he participated in an acrobatics club sponsored by a local charity group.]*

Today I sent Tony 12 packs of cigarettes. They are rationed out here but I get more than I can smoke. I sure hope he has time to smoke them before he gets drafted. Let me know if he gets them alright. I sent them in Ma's name so as to throw off suspicion. Well I guess I'll close for now so till tomorrow, so-long and God bless you all and tell Ma not to worry.

Love To: Ma, Pa, Mary, Tony, Francie & Carlo

X X X X X — Phil — X X X X

Thursday May 3, 1945/Wendover, Utah

Dear Mary,

. . . Well, the war in Europe is going along swell. The Germans are surrendering all over and I'll bet by the time you get this letter every inch of Germany will be in Allied hands. Well, Japan is the only thing that's keeping us from coming home.

Don't forget to let me know if Tony got the 12 packs of cigarettes, okay? I sure hope that they let him stay a while longer now that Germany is beaten. I hope Ma is feeling fine today. Let me know how her X-rays came out, because I'm waiting to hear that she's as well as always. So-long for now and God bless you all and don't worry.

Love To: Ma, Pa, Mary, Tony, Francie & Carlo

X X X X X X X X X X — Phil —

Friday May 4, 1945/Wendover, Utah

Dear Mary,

. . . Out here, I'm feeling as well as ever and my work and the weather are alright too. I know, it's pretty chilly out there, according to Ralph who is in the weather service. Well, soon it'll warm up out there.

You said that now that summer is coming Ma feels pretty bad about not being able to go out to the farm. You just tell Ma that I said to get that farm idea out of her head once and for all. God only knows how scared she had everyone of us and now she wants to go to the farm and really worry us all. Nope, it can't be done. It'll be a good idea though, if Tony is still there to take Ma for a nice drive on Sundays to the farm and get some nice fresh air. Well, that's all for now so take it easy and don't worry.

Love To: Ma, Pa, Mary, Tony, Francie & Carlo
X X X X X X X X X X — Phil —

Saturday May 5, 1945/Wendover, Utah

Dear Mary,

. . . It rained quite a bit today and I was surprised. It sure cooled everything off real nice, and if there were only trees and flowers around the air would sure smell sweet.

I received a nice letter from Carmen today. He said that after they got through with the Battle of Iwo Jima, they stopped at an island called Alihti where he got off for a few hours of recreation. The kid sure is seeing a lot of the world.

Well, that's all for now, so till tomorrow, so-long, God bless you all and don't worry.

Love To: Ma, Pa, Mary, Tony, Francie & Carlo
X X X X X X X X X — Phil —

Sunday May 6, 1945/Wendover, Utah

Dear Mary,

. . . I was going to church this morning but here's what happened. I got up at 6:45 a.m., I ate breakfast, I went back to bed at 8, I woke at 11:00 a.m. So I missed Mass.

Everything out here seems to be going along pretty good. The weather is very nice and cool, provided one doesn't move around too much to work up a sweat. I had a nice piece of steak to eat this afternoon. All in all, I'm eating pretty good and I hope you all are too. I hope by now Tony got his cigarettes. With those 12 packs plus what he can buy, I figure he should be set for at least 2½ weeks without worrying about cigarettes.

Well, I hope Ma and all of you are getting along alright and in good health. So-long and God bless you all.

Love To: Ma, Pa, Mary, Tony, Francie & Carlo
X X X X X X X X — Phil

Monday May 7, 1945/Wendover, Utah

Dear Mary,

Well, today Eisenhower declared the war with Germany has officially ended. Gen. Eisenhower's word is good enough for me, although the President hasn't said anything yet. Well, it's really one down and one to go. Whether the Japs turn yellow and quit or keep fighting remains to be seen. . . .

I hope Ma and all of you are getting along fine. I'm enclosing a stick of gum for Ma and one for anybody else there who wants it. I get it whenever I find some. I personally don't care for gum. Well, so-long for now and God bless you all.

Love To: Ma, Pa, Mary, Tony, Francie & Carlo
X X X X X X X X X — Phil —

P.S. I'm about to write a letter to Carmen and Frankie also tonight. So-long.

Tuesday May 8, 1945/Wendover, Utah

Dear Mary,

Today the war with Germany has ended forever officially. It's the second time in 30 years that Germany has had to be defeated. I guess everybody all over the world celebrated, but not here at Wendover. Work went on as usual. I did drink a coca cola though. When Japan ends, it's a different story, but I won't drink anyway.

I received the long letter you wrote last Saturday and it was swell. I'm really sorry to hear that Ma still feels those pains. You said that the doctor found Ma's condition spreading. What's spreading? You just tell Ma to keep eating and getting a lot of rest and fresh air. Sometimes these doctors don't know what they're talking about. Soon summer will be here and I know Ma will feel fine with all that good weather.

Yep, I know my son is really growing. Yes, my wife tells me all about him, but still I like to hear you tell me about him. For some reason, that baby is the least of my worries. He's a real champion and I'm about the proudest father there is. I would be so happy to see him and Ma and my wife but that can't be for a long time. I know I can't get a furlough before October. My emergency furlough doesn't count, but the one I had last October does, so I'm stuck till next October. Well, a lot can happen to change the rules, so don't worry. You see, I get 15 days a year and the year ends July 1st, and I already got my 15 days for this year when I took it last October.

I sure hope the German War's end has a good effect on Tony not being drafted. I'd be really happy if this war just passed him by. There isn't a thing he can gain in the army. Here's hoping. So-long for now and God bless you all.

Love To: Ma, Pa, Mary, Tony, Francie & Carlo
X X X X X X X X X — Phil

P.S. 5 sticks of gum enclosed. I found some Beech Nut and my wife doesn't like it. I can only get 1 pack a day when they do have it. And I split it up between you, my wife and myself.

Wednesday May 9, 1945/Wendover, Utah

Dear Mary,

. . . The weather is fine out here and I hope it's nice there too, for Ma's sake. I got a letter from Carmen yesterday and he said he is now a petty officer 3rd class, just like Shadow. Shadow said he's trying some tests to make another rating. Yep, they may as well get ratings whenever they can.

Yes, I know [Shadow's wife] June must be having a hard time of it. I sure wish I could help Shadow out financially, but I've got to set myself up first. Yes, my wife is planning on buying a bedroom suite. It'll save us from getting it later on. I don't know what's on Joe's and Shadow's minds, but I want to buy my own home as soon as possible. I never did like the idea of paying rent every month and still not owning anything. Right now I can't save much. I've been coming home on furlough quite a bit. Each time I came home, after I got married, it cost me over $100. But, I can't help it. If I'd get another furlough, I'd willingly spend another $100.

You said Pa picked a bag of dandelions and gardoons. Well, I don't like dandelions, but I do like gardoons fixed in a pie. I sure used to eat a lot of them, if Ma remembers. *[Gardoons are the stems of a burdock-like plant that many Sicilians enjoy in the spring.]* Yesterday I enclosed 5 sticks of gum. Tonight I've got 4, because I'm chewing one myself.

Well, now when we talk about the war, we mean Japan only. The war with Japan will only last as long as it takes the U.S. to transport the military equipment and men there. No one knows, Japan may give up any day now. It depends on them. They're fighting a useless war because they lost it from the start. So keep your chins up and tell Ma not to worry. So-long and God bless you all always.

Love To: Ma, Pa, Mary, Tony, Francie & Carlo

X X X X X X X X X — Phil —

P.S. My champion son is sure coming along okay. He sure is the best baby I ever heard about. I guess that's because he's my son.

[The next entry is a Mother's Day card, with the envelope postmarked May 9. On the front of the card, it reads: "Mother's Day Greetings to Mother and Father." Inside the verse says, "May this dearest of days/ In the whole happy year/ Bring both Mother and Dad/ All the finest good cheer!" He signs it, "Your Loving Son, Phil." It is interesting that some Mother's Day cards in the 1940s apparently also honored the father.]

Thursday May 10, 1945/Wendover, Utah

Dear Mary,

. . . I sure hope the weather out there is getting better. I know it's been pretty chilly. I hope Ma is feeling better than usual today. Last week everyone out here was squawking about their impatience about Germany still fighting. Now that Germany has surrendered, they are all excited about discharges. Well, very few will be discharged from the Air Corp[s] until after Japan quits. You see, discharges are going to be worked on the basis of points. These points will be gotten from 4 items. They are: Total Length of Service, Total Length of Service Overseas, Total Amount of decorations and medals, including ribbons and etc., and then the last is dependents, but wives don't count. Frankie has a fine chance of getting out, except for one thing, and that is he's in the service forces and provides equipment to troops and he may be essential. One thing, though, now with Germany's surrender they will try to send replacements to the Pacific and Frankie may come back as soon as that happens. As for the Navy, that's just like the Air Corp and will be fighting till the last shot is fired. I've only got length of service and the baby as a dependent. If I'd have put about 1½ years across someplace, I'd have a pretty good chance in the future. Oh well, I've got to get out sometime, I'll always be grateful to God that I'm still in good shape. Here I am, as tough as any marine or infantry man, and I'm still taking it easy, so when I come home doesn't bother me, it's the way I'll be when I do come [that matters].

No kidding, though, if Japan doesn't quit within the next couple months, she's going to be really destroyed. They ruined the German cities so they won't be able to build them on the same spot for the next 20 years, but Japan is going to get plastered worse than that. The airplane is going to do it with fire bombs. Incidently, the bombs they use over Japan are Chemical Warfare bombs, and that's right in my line of work. I say I don't do much for this war, because I really can't measure what I do in blood, except in sweat.

Well, I'll close for now and let's hope for better days. Tell Ma not to worry. Germany was the toughest to whip. So-long for now and God bless you all.

Love To: Ma, Pa, Mary, Tony, Francie & Carlo
X X X X X X X X X — Phil —

Friday May 11, 1945/Wendover, Utah

Dear Mary,

Enclosed is 4 sticks of gum and $2 (Brand new $2). I hope you get them all alright. I received the letter you wrote last Monday. I'm glad you all were so happy over Germany's defeat. We certainly have been real lucky with the German War. None of our family was involved and it was a shame that Cousin Joe had to be killed to make those Germans quit. What did the Germans gain by fighting the last 2 years? They lost and we won, but that was to be expected. Now that Germany's beaten they should keep her beaten for all time. Just so we don't have to fight

Germany no more, I'd gladly let my son go across for 1 year to still keep Germany down in 20 years from now.

You asked me what idea I had on how long Japan would last. Well, I don't even think Japan will be fighting by Christmas. Japan is going to be ganged up on in several months and they'll plaster her with everything, from dynamite, rockets to fire bombs. The super fortress bomber especially will be used by the thousands. Japan is going to get it more than Germany got in all the 6 years they've been fighting. So let's see if we'll have a real peaceful Christmas this year. Yep, Japan is prepared to lose 10,000,000 men in this war and I think they will. It's really going to be a one-sided massacre.

I was glad to hear that you received 2 letters from every one of us guys last Monday. That was really a coincident and I bet Ma was real happy. You are wondering why I sent you the $2. Well first of all, I was glad to hear Tony received the cigarettes I sent. He sent me the $2 and I didn't ask [to be paid] for them, so I'm taking them anyway and I'm giving them to Ma to pay part of the phone bill. Honest, I wish I could help you out as much as I could. If I had a lot of money, I'd buy myself the best house in the best part of Buffalo and right next door I'd buy one for Ma. Maybe some day that might happen.

Yes, my wife got $140. They hadn't paid the baby's allotment for 3 months and now they paid all at once. That was pretty good. Yep, most of it went in the bank. I'd like to see my bank account go up, but first I want my wife and son to get everything they need. I want her to be dressed as well as any girl, and I want my son to be fed and clothed as well as any other baby, too. I hope Ma is feeling good today. Tell her not to worry. So-long and God bless you all always!

Love To: Ma, Pa, Mary, Tony, Francie & Carlo
X X X X X X X X X — Phil —

Saturday May 12, 1945/Wendover, Utah

Dear Mary,

Just another day going by out here and everything is going along pretty good. I hope Ma and all of you are getting along fine. The weather out here is pretty hot. The thing is though everything turns to salt. I sweat and after my clothes dry it takes on that salt appearance. The salt comes right out of the ground and when one looks out on the desert it looks as if there's all snow around. It's really nice healthy weather out here because it's real dry. I haven't had a headache or any kind of cold since I got here. Well that's all for today. So till tomorrow so-long and God bless you all.

Love To: Ma, Pa, Mary, Tony, Francie & Carlo
X X X X X X X X X — Phil —

Sunday May 13, 1945/Wendover, Utah

Dear Mary,

Today is Mother's Day. I hope Ma liked whatever my wife got her for mother's day. I got up at 10:45 this morning and now I feel pretty lazy. Too much sleep I guess.

It rained last night out here. I can notice some weeds on the mountain sides that turned green during the last few days. It's nice and warm out here though.

Also today V-E day is supposed to be remembered. It's not even a week that Germany quit and yet it seems like a long time ago. Well, as Germany quit, someday Japan also must quit.

Well, right now I'm going to shave and take a nice hot shower to regain my pep back. So-long for now and God bless you all and don't worry.

Love To: Ma, Pa, Mary, Tony, Francie & Carlo

X X X X X X X X X — Phil —

Monday May 14, 1945/Wendover, Utah

Dear Mary,

. . . It rained pretty hard out here today. Everyone sure is surprised. Some of the guys who've been here since last year said it's more rain than they ever saw for out here. So, I just can't figure out why nothing wants to grow out here. Today this base switched from Pacific Coast time to Mountain War Time. Now I'm only two hours behind Buffalo time.

Yesterday, 500 B-29's bombed Japan. They dropped 7½ million pounds of incendiary bombs and blasted heck out of a city 3 times as big as Buffalo. That war with Japan is sure going to be a fast one from now on. I personally expect the Americans to make a landing on China or Japan any day now.

I just got a letter from Carmen dated May 2nd, twelve days ago, not bad eh? He's alright. You know a couple weeks ago I told him that I thought he should be in the Battle of Okinawa by now and although he didn't mention Okinawa, he said my guess was right, if I remembered what I had guessed at. I sure try to get to know where they [Carmen and Frankie] are at and the kids catch on. But tell Ma not to worry about Carmen, because when he wrote this letter May 2nd, the naval battle of Okinawa was almost over with. Don't mention anything of what I said to Carmen, because a censor may just happen to read your letter. Wait till he tells you himself. I hope Ma and the rest of you are feeling in tiptop shape. So-long for now and God bless you all.

Love To: Ma, Pa, Mary, Tony, Francie & Carlo

X X X X X X X X X X X — Phil

[The following letter is addressed to Phil's brother Tony.]

Monday May 14, 1945/Wendover, Utah

Hello Tony,

Just figured I'd drop you a few more lines. I wrote to almost everybody so, I didn't want to exclude you. Well the mighty German Wehrmacht (Army) has been defeated. Germany is just a mess of ruins right now and I doubt if they can build her up in the same spot for a long time. Japan is next and I think when the U.S. gangs up on her, she's going to crack. If they don't, millions of Jap civilians are going to get killed when the combined super forts, aircraft carrier planes, and former European airplanes attack her by the thousands. It's going to be a slaughter house, but they are asking for it, because they haven't got the sense to quit.

By the way, once in a while kind of let Ma know how the war is going on. You know when I used to work your shift, Ma and I would be all alone in the early hours of morning because she'd want to cook for me. I'd eat and talk with her at the same time. You'd be surprised how interested Ma is in geography, history, and world events. *[Phil was extremely close to his mother, and is trying to get his older brother to discuss events with her. He is telling his brother not to be fooled by his mother's appearance. Sure, she is an Italian immigrant who can't read or write, or speak English. But still she is intelligent and interested in world events when someone actually explains them to her.]*

I just heard a rumor that they won't draft anyone over 32 years of age. I sure hope they lower it a little more, so you won't get into this war. *[Tony is twenty-nine.]*

Well Tony, so-long for now and God bless you. Love, Phil

P.S. Take it easy going to work. I'm a brave soldier but you scared hell out of me on Delaware Avenue going to work. I don't know how you manage to pass so many cars but you do. If I tell Carmen, he'll worry about you too.

[The next letter is one of the few sent directly to Phil's parents. Since neither could read or write English, his letters were always addressed to his sister, Mary.]

Monday May 14, 1945/Wendover, Utah

Dear Ma and Pa,

I wrote to everyone [today] and I thought you two would feel hurt if I didn't write to you. I hope some one would translate this to you. Ma,

I know, you still have a lot of pains, but you just rest a lot and go out for a walk and get a lot of fresh air. Watch what you eat. What I mean is don't mix up your food so that it'll get sour in your stomach. I know too that you keep worrying about Frankie, Carmen, Shadow, Tony, and me. Well there's no sense in worrying. Nothing is going to happen, and if it had to happen, all your worrying couldn't stop it. It's up to God. Pretty soon Frankie should be coming home. He's been there [in New Guinea] a long time and I think they'll send him home in a few months, so don't worry.

As for Pa, I can only tell him to watch himself when he walks across the streets. When I was home, he looked pretty old and he needed good glasses. I hope he's got a new pair by now. I sure wish I could eat a pie of the gardoons he picks. Well, when I come home again, I may taste them. Well, so-long for now, don't fight, and God bless you both always.

Your Loving Son, Phil

[Usually Phil's letters are handwritten, but the next two are typed. There aren't too many typos either, which indicates that he learned to type very well in school.]

Tuesday May 15, 1945/Wendover Field, Utah

Dear Mary,

. . . Last night I wrote off quite a few letters. I'd write to one person and I'd figure the other would also like to hear from me so I kind of kept that up for a while until it got too late and I couldn't write anymore. Really though I had just got through fixing my pen and I was sort of trying it out.

Right now I'm on my lunch hour and I thought I'd write now instead of tonight. *[He usually writes his letters at night after dinner when he is resting on his bunk.]* A few days ago you said that Rae told you she had written to me. Well, I still haven't received it and I doubt if I'll ever get it, but I wrote her a letter a few days ago and I also sent Joe a Birthday card, because his birthday comes along a day different than Tony's. I think Tony's birthday comes before Joe's but I'm not too sure about it.

Everything seems to be going along pretty slow out here. Same old thing day in and day out. But I hope I can stay here for the duration even if [Wendover Field] is one of the loneliest camps in the country. Well, I hope Ma is feeling fine today and I hope she stays that way. So-long for now and God Bless you all.

Love To: Ma, Pa, Mary, Tony, Francie & Carlo
X X X X X X X X X X — Phil —

Wednesday May 16, 1945/Wendover, Utah

Dear Mary,

. . . I received a letter from Frankie today, which he wrote on May 8th, only 10 days ago. That's pretty fast mail, I think. Sometimes a letter from Buffalo takes 5 or 6 days to get to Wendover and here it only takes 10 to get from New Guinea. He feels pretty good and is a little mad because he thinks the soldiers here in the states are getting all the credit for winning the war. Of course I won't tell him, but the government did leave the best soldiers here in the states to protect the U.S. itself. *[Phil was joking, of course, but very likely he did tell the same joke to Frankie, which is why Frankie was mad. Ironically, there was some truth to Phil's claim. The Air Corps did skim off many of the best recruits and some of them were stationed at this top secret base in the United States.]*

I hope Ma and all of you are feeling in tip-top shape today. So-long and God bless you all.

Love To: Ma, Pa, Mary, Tony, Francie & Carlo
X X X X X X X X X — Phil.

Thursday May 17, 1945/Wendover, Utah

Dear Mary,

. . . A little more rain has fallen and the weather is cloudy and cool. It never gets damp out here, though. It don't rain for more than a few minutes at one time. There's nothing new that I can tell you about because everything's the same for me out here. I hope Ma is feeling as well as possible and I hope she hasn't as many pains as she used to. I hope the rest of you are also getting along good in your work and feeling in the best of spirits. So-long for now and God bless you all.

Love To: Ma, Pa, Mary, Tony, Francie & Carlo
X X X X X X X X X X — Phil —

Friday May 18, 1945/Wendover, Utah

Dear Mary,

Yesterday I received the letter you wrote while you were at work. It sure was a big sheet of paper, but I enjoyed reading it anyway. I believe Ralph is going to be transferred. You see he was in Greenland for a long time and he requested a transfer closer to home, and finally they gave it to him. He'll go to Rome, New York. That sure is pretty close to Buffalo. I think if he gets a chance he'll drop by the house. . . .

I was glad to hear that Ma has a nice appetite and I think just so she eats good she'll be alright. . . . Well so-long for now and God bless you all.

Love To: Ma, Pa, Mary, Tony, Francie & Carlo
X X X X X X X X — Phil —

P.S. Today I received the letter you wrote last Monday. I'm glad Ma received the card I sent her and I'm glad she liked what my wife bought for her on Mother's Day. Incidently don't tell anybody that Ralph may come to New York, because he wants to surprise his folks. So-long.

Saturday May 19, 1945/Wendover, Utah

Dear Mary,

Just another Saturday out here and everything is going along pretty good. . . . When I haven't even received the slightest cold or headache since I got here in early March, there sure must be something to this [desert] weather, don't you think?

Yep, Ralph is going to Rome, New York, and I think he'll drop by the house to see you when he stops in Buffalo. I hope you didn't tell his family anything, because he wants to surprise them. I hope Ma and all of you are feeling alright today. I'm in tip-top shape out here. Well, so-long for now and God bless you all.

Love To: Ma, Pa, Mary, Tony, Francie & Carlo

X X X X X X X X X — Phil —

Sunday May 20, 1945/Wendover, Utah

Dear Mary,

. . . I was glad to hear from you and know that Ma is feeling alright. I hope she continues to feel that way. I'm sorry Frankie says that he doesn't receive any mail. Who does he get mail from, except from you and me? I know you write him as often as possible, and I write him almost every week. June writes him and also my wife. So why don't you remind June, my wife, and Rae, and Shadow to write to him more often?

I sure hope Tony continues to stay there. I should think they'd have enough men now by just drafting the 18 year olds. So let's hope for the best. . . . So-long for now and God bless you all.

Love To: Ma, Pa, Mary, Tony, Francie & Carlo

X X X X X X X X X X — Phil

P.S. I just finished writing letters to Frankie and Carmen.

Monday May 21, 1945/Wendover, Utah

Dear Mary,

Everything out here is going along pretty good and I can't kick. I hope you all are feeling fine out there and I hope Ma is also well. I'm enclosing 2 sticks of gum. One for Ma and one for any body else who wants it. . . .

Well they lowered the discharge age to 40 years of age. That don't help any, but it's a step closer anyway. So-long for now and don't worry. God bless you all.

Love To: Ma, Pa, Mary, Tony, Francie & Carlo
X X X X X X X X X — Phil —

Tuesday May 22, 1945/Wendover, Utah

Dear Mary,

Not much to say for today. Everything is going along bearable, but I feel a little disgusted with my military affairs. I'm really getting sick of this war. I guess it'll end as soon as some of these big companies and munitions manufacturers make enough money for themselves. Japan must be beaten and beaten for good, though, no matter who's making the money.

I'm enclosing a stick of gum for Ma and one for anybody else if you don't want it. I hope Ma and the rest of you are feeling in the best of health and spirits. I'm in good health out here, so I'm the least of any worries.

Well so-long for today and God bless you all always.

Love To: Ma, Pa, Mary, Tony, Francie & Carlo
X X X X X X X X X — Phil —

[Phil wrote the following poem to his baby, which he mailed to his wife on May 22, 1945. The advice he gives the baby reveals his pride in the little boy, as well as the values he cherished. He encourages "Little Phil" to always do the right thing, to thwart evil, and to be strong and noble. And he promises to be there for whatever help the boy needs.]

MY LITTLE SON

Little son so small and sweet,
    Kicking with uplifted feet.
Making noises with your throat,
    Sweetly like a musical note!
Oh baby of my dream,
    Drink all your milk and cream.
Be contented, as the day is long,
    Soon, you'll be big and strong!
Ever since your day of birth,
    You've been champion on this Earth.
You won't fail me in my plan,
    Of growing up to be a man!
You will be right, not wrong,
    You'll not be weak, but strong.

Keep your thoughts in the sky,
    Never live the life of a lie!
Crush crime at every turn,
    Make all evil bleed and burn.
Destroy the hopes of evil seeds,
    Live your life by noble deeds!
You understand, as if you knew,
    What the future holds for you.
Your eyes shine in a different way,
    Your smile is like a sunny day!
Little Phil, I'm proud of you!
    Sons like you are rare and few.
I'll try to be the finest dad,
    a little son has ever had!
As the years come and go,
    Through sunshine, rain, and snow,
My thoughts will always include you,
    My Little Son, so brave and true!

                    Wednesday May 23, 1945/Wendover, Utah
Dear Mary,
    . . . I put in a pretty hard day of physical work today and I'm a little tired, but then nothing can defeat me, so I'm really in good shape.
    I hope Ma is feeling fine and I hope the weather there is nice so that she will feel good. I can't tell what kind of weather Buffalo has anymore until I hear it from my wife's or your letters, because Ralph left here early Monday morning. That Ralph sure got himself a good break by going to Rome, New York, which is only about 4½ hours from Buffalo by train. Things like that can only happen to me in a dream. *[Yesterday Phil was rather depressed; probably Ralph's leaving the morning before had a lot to do with that. Ralph was an old friend from the neighborhood and Phil used to like to hang out with him. Phil also enjoyed knowing what the weather was like in Buffalo. Now he can no longer find out. Plus, Ralph was one of the few friends he could go to movies with and talk to about Buffalo.]* Well so-long for today but I'll be back again tomorrow. God bless you all.
            Love To: Ma, Pa, Mary, Tony, Francie & Carlo
               X X X X X X X X X X X — Phil —

                  Thursday May 24, 1945/Wendover Field, Utah
Dear Mary,
    Yesterday I felt a little tired, but today I don't feel too bad. Everything out here is going along pretty good and there isn't a thing I can complain about except being away from home.

Tomorrow night I'm going to call up my wife and I'll also call up there. Only it will be a little of a surprise, because I've got it all arranged with Shadow so that both he and I will call up tomorrow night. I wrote him and I told him that it would be a good idea to have Ma hear both of us in the same night, and it would make Ma feel a little more happier, don't you think?

Well, the war with Japan is going along pretty good. They are bombing Japan with these big B29's and they sure are causing a lot of damage. Of course big things can't be expected as yet because it takes a long time to transport men and equipment to the Pacific to do the job. But, after we are all ready, then it's only a matter of time until Japan does quit like Germany did. . . . Well, I guess that's all for today so till tomorrow, so-long and God bless you all.

Love To: Ma, Pa, Mary, Tony, Francie & Carlo
X X X X X X X X X X X X — Phil

Friday May 25, 1945/Wendover, Utah

Dear Mary,

. . . I was glad to hear that Ma is taking some nice rides. It'll help her physically and mentally. *[He had suggested they take her for rides out to the farm, so she could visit friends and breathe fresh air.]* I also was glad to hear that Pa has a pair of new glasses and I hope he can see well now.

Tonight Shadow and I will call up home. . . . [W]e both should get through to Buffalo at about the same time. Yes, June will have her new baby in a few weeks. The doctor told her it would be a boy, but no one can tell yet. Yep, my son can sure giggle now. I sure hope I could see him grow, but that's not possible, so I'll not even think about it. . . .

[There's a pause in the letter at this point, while Phil went off to make his long-distance calls.]

Well, I just got through talking to you, Ma, and Carlo, and it was swell. I guess I got my call in before Shadow. I was glad to catch you because you were over [the neighbor] Mitri's house. Well, so-long for now and God bless you all.

Love To: Ma, Pa, Mary, Tony, Francie & Carlo
X X X X X X X X — Phil

Saturday May 26, 1945/Wendover, Utah

Dear Mary,

. . . Yesterday, I called you up. I placed a call in at the same time to you and my wife. Your call came through in 10 minutes after I placed it, but my wife's call, well that didn't come through at all. I waited all night till midnight and then I even got up at a quarter after 5 this morning, and called as early as I could so that she wouldn't worry. *[A soldier had to place a long-distance call with the operator and then wait in a lounge until the call went through. It could take a few minutes, hours, or apparently, it might never go through.]*

I was glad to hear that Ralph Ferrara came down to the house to see you all. He said he'd drop by if he had time. . . . Well, I'll close for today, but I'll be back again tomorrow, so till then, so-long and God bless you all.

Love To: Ma, Pa, Mary, Tony, Francie & Carlo

X X X X X X X X X — Phil —

Sunday May 27, 1945/Wendover, Utah

Dear Mary,

Today I received the letter you wrote last Wednesday and the letter Francie wrote last Tuesday. I was glad to hear from both of you. I hope Ma and the rest [of you] are feeling okay. Out here, everything is the same and I can't kick. I'm just taking it as easy as I can. It sure is swell that they are letting Tony stay a little longer and I sure hope he continues to stay. The war looks alright and Japan is taking a beating from fire bombs.

I just got a letter from Carmen dated May 5th and he's feeling in good shape. I'll write Frankie and Carmen again tomorrow. Well, so-long for now. I'll shave and shower and take in a show for tonight. So-long and God bless you all.

Love To: Ma, Pa, Mary, Tony, Francie & Carlo

X X X X X X X X — Phil —

[The following letter was addressed to "The Mr. Anthony J. Aquila." Tony apparently had written Phil a letter bragging about various things. This is Phil's humorous reply:]

Monday May 28, 1945/Wendover, Utah

Dear Big Brother Tony,

I received your very modest letter of May 21st, and I was glad to hear from you. Yes, speaking for myself, Shadow, Frankie, and Carmen, we are fortunate to have an older brother such as you. Gee, you are 29 years old. You don't look it. You look about 23 years old, or as young as I do. Of course you've got the edge on weight by 48 pounds, but then you haven't got your weight proportioned around the way I have. For example, there's a slight difference in the width of our shoulders. I don't know if my shoulders are wider than yours naturally, or because I've worked harder in my life.

I'm glad that the draft board is leaving you home for a while longer.

Really, the fighting man of this war is between 23–25 at the age where they have no fear.

Well Anthony, I was surprised to learn that you've been promoted to Victory Garden supervisor of the Aquila Estate, although I did know you were president of the Parlor Loafer's Union. So long for now and I'll write you another picturesque letter as soon as I find time.

Your Younger Brother, Philip L. Aquila I

Monday May 28, 1945/Wendover, Utah

Dear Mary,

Today I received a letter from Carmen which he wrote on May 17th. He's getting along alright, so tell Ma not to worry about him. I just wrote the Supervisor of the Parlor Chairs (Tony) a letter to bolster up his morale a little. What's Ma feeding that guy to get him up to 208 pounds? Well, a lot of sleeping and eating does put on weight.

Well, I'm doing a little resting up myself out here and I can't kick. The weather isn't too warm or too cold. All in all everything is going along pretty good out here. I hope it's the same for Ma and everyone there. I hope Shadow called up alright on the 25th of May, and I hope we made Ma happier than usual. Well that's all for today, so till tomorrow, so-long and God bless you all.

Love To: Ma, Pa, Mary, Tony, Francie & Carlo
X X X X X X X X X — Phil —

P.S. So Tony is only 29 years old. I thought he'd be 32 years old this year. I'm only kidding. Tony does look younger than he is. He'll pass easily for 28½ years old.

Tuesday May 29, 1945/Wendover, Utah

Dear Mary,

. . . The weather is fine out here and I managed to get a little more sun tan. All in all, I'm nice and tan. I hope by now Buffalo is having good weather. How's Ma feeling today? Gee, I hope her pains would go away. I guess in time they will. I'm glad Ma doesn't mention the farm any more. Heck, she can't spend all her life out there. There had to be a stop to it and this year is as good as any year.

Maybe Shadow can come home [from Memphis on furlough] for when his next baby is born. I sure hope so. As for me, in time I'll be home again. It's a matter of months again.

Well so-long for today and tell Ma not to worry about anything. God bless you all.

Love To: Ma, Pa, Mary, Tony, Francie & Carlo
X X X X X X X — Phil —

Wednesday May 30, 1945/Wendover, Utah

Dear Mary,

Today I received the letter you wrote last Sunday and I'm glad to hear that you are all feeling fine. I'm glad Ma looks forward to the rides on Sundays and I hope she continues to have them. I was sorry to hear that Shadow wasn't able to call you up on the same night I did. I probably spoiled your whole evening when I told you he would call. I just got a letter from him and he said he couldn't get through to Buffalo that night. I also got another letter from Carmen which he wrote on May 11th. The kid sure writes a lot of letters.

Yep, my kid is sure getting up in the world. No use in even wishing I could see him. Maybe someday though.

. . . I took a 3 day pass last Sunday and I loafed all the time till today. Not bad eh! I didn't go no place, though, just stood on the base and loafed around. Well so-long for now and God bless you all.

Love To: Ma, Pa, Mary, Tony, Francie & Carlo
X X X X X X X X X X X — Phil —

Thursday May 31, 1945/Wendover, Utah

Dear Mary,

Tomorrow will be June again. Time sure goes by. It seems as if only yesterday that Christmas was here and already ½ year has gone by. Today I got paid again. It wasn't much, but, after all deductions I got $40.50.

I'm enclosing a couple sticks of gum for Ma and 1 for anybody else.

Well, from all reports, I hear my 17 pound, 4 month old son is doing alright for himself. He eats pretty good. He's a chip off the old block I guess.

. . . How's the Plymouth running in this nice weather? It sure held up pretty good during all those winter months. Well I'll be closing for now so take it easy and God bless you all.

Love To: Ma, Pa, Mary, Tony, Francie & Carlo
X X X X X X X X X X — Phil —

Friday June 1, 1945/Wendover, Utah

Dear Mary,

Things are going along pretty good out here and I hope they continue that way. But, I guess I can take anything that comes along. *[This last sentence can be explained by the fact that he is worried he might be shipped overseas. See below, second to the last paragraph.]* I hope Ma and the rest of you are feeling alright.

I just saw a picture with a whole lot of laughs in it entitled "Murder He Says" with Fred MacMurray. If you want to laugh a lot, just go see that picture. It's funnier than a Bob Hope picture. *[Since Phil always goes to the movies but has never before mentioned any particular one by title, this film must have really impressed him.]* Enclosed are 2 sticks of gum. One for Ma and 1 for any one else there. . . .

Well, I guess that's all for now. There's not too much news lately, and besides, you have the radio and can listen to it there. All men below 30 will be drafted and all men physically fit who haven't been across will be sent [overseas] soon, and I guess I'm no exception.

So-long for now and God bless you all and don't worry.

Love To: Ma, Pa, Mary, Tony, Francie & Carlo
X X X X X X X X X — Phil —

Saturday June 2, 1945/Wendover, Utah

Dear Mary,

Today I received a letter from Carmen which he wrote on May 22. It took just 11 days to get here and that's pretty good. He sure writes me a lot of letters. I can only write him once a week and I sure wish I had more time, but I haven't. That goes for Frankie, too. Carmen says he feels pretty good and is getting along pretty well, so tell Ma not to worry about him.

Well, everything out here seems to be running smoothly. It gets a little tough at times, but that's to be expected. There's a lot of talk about furloughs again. I know just about where I stand and when I'll get mine if I'm still here, but I won't say nothing because everything is very uncertain. But I think I'll spend part of the summer in Buffalo this year. I hope that little hint helps you a little. Well, I hope everything out there is going along nicely and I hope Ma and the rest of you are all feeling fine. So-long for now and God bless you all.

Love To: Ma, Pa, Mary, Tony, Francie & Carlo
X X X X X X X X X — Phil —

Sunday June 3, 1945/Wendover, Utah

Dear Mary,

I received the letter you wrote on Memorial Day and I was glad to learn that everything is going along okay out there. It's too bad you weren't home when Shadow called up, but that's okay. I was glad to hear that you and Ma went over to see my son. Yep, he sure does change quickly. I was surprised to hear that Joe [finally] went down to see him with Rae. I thought if he didn't see my son [pretty soon], they wouldn't recognize each other on the street in later years, so I'm glad he went down.

. . . I got up at 11:30 this morning so I slept for almost 12 hours. Right now, I'll write to June, Shadow, Frankie, and Carmen and then I'll take in a movie. So-long for now and don't worry. God bless you all.

Love To: Ma, Pa, Mary, Tony, Francie & Carlo
X X X X X X X X X — Phil

Monday June 4, 1945/Wendover, Utah

Dear Mary,

Everything out here is going along nicely. The weather wasn't so good though because it rained harder than I ever saw it rain out here. I believe if this soil didn't have so much salt, this land would be pretty fertile. I'm telling you, you can see the salt stretch out like a blanket of white snow, real flat, as far as the eye can see. I guess I can see clear across the flats to the mountains on the other side which are about 100 miles away. It's like looking from Buffalo clear to Pennsylvania. If there are any questions you have or any of the kids [i.e., Francie and Carlo] have about this land, just let me know.

I hope Ma and the rest of you are all feeling fine. So-long for today, but I'll be back again tomorrow. Till then, God bless you all and don't worry.

Love To: Ma, Pa, Mary, Tony, Francie & Carlo
X X X X X X X X X X — Phil

Tuesday June 5, 1945/Wendover, Utah

Dear Mary,

Just another little letter for today. . . . It rained almost all day long and everything is quite damp and muddy. I hope the weather out there is fine so that Ma will feel better.

Well, the war against Japan is going on full fury with the B-29's blasting heck out of the Jap cities. *[Notice Phil uses the word "heck" in his letter to his sister, while his letter to his brother, Tony, used "hell" as an adjective. This demonstrates accepted behavior of the day. Men could use profanity when they were around other men, but certainly not in mixed company.]* You see, I know the kind of stuff they use inside the bombs when they bomb Japan, and you just can't put out the fire it starts. Well, Japan is asking for it, and she'll get it. And if we start to use gas on Japan, you can consider the Jap race as plain human wreckage. Well, let's hope for the best.

I hope everyone out there is in the best of spirits. I hope Ma is feeling fine, and Pa [is] getting along good, and Tony [is] managing with the car and his job, and Francie [is] feeling fine and taking care of herself and Carlo [is] doing "perfect" in school and minding Ma, and I hope you are getting along good in everything. So-long and God bless you all.

Love To: Ma, Pa, Mary, Tony, Francie & Carlo
X X X X X X X X X X — Phil —

Wednesday June 6, 1945/Wendover, Utah

Dear Mary,

Today I received the letter you wrote me on Friday during your lunch hour. I was happy to hear that you are all feeling fine and especially Ma. I'm glad you and Ma went over to see my son on decoration day. Yep, he's growing everyday and if you miss seeing him, you get surprised. I guess I'll be in for a surprise myself, whenever I get to come home. I still picture the baby as helpless as when I left him, but I know by now he's nice and big and is beginning to understand.

I was glad to hear that Pa has started the crops growing in the backyard. I hope they come out okay. Darn it all, every year I've missed the peaches in the backyard. This year I'll see if I can make it okay.

Yes, I sent home a few silver dollars, about 10 I guess. My wife is supposed to give one to Pa, but I guess she's a little bashful to hand him just a silver dollar. I'm glad to hear Tony is still home and I hope he won't have to leave. Everything out here is going along pretty good, so don't worry. So-long and God bless you all.

Love To: Ma, Pa, Mary, Tony, Francie & Carlo
X X X X X X X X X X X — Phil —

Thursday June 7, 1945/Wendover, Utah

Dear Mary,
. . . I was glad to hear that Ma, and all of you, are feeling fine. You said you are sending Carmen, Frankie and Cousin Johnny a package each. That's swell. You asked me if there is something I want and you'll send me a package. Look, send one to Shadow and the rest, but honest, I don't want anything. The money you'll use for me, just use for yourselves for something. Honest, I don't need anything at all. Just knowing you'd send me a package is just as good as sending it, so forget it.

I'm sorry to hear that the weather out there is lousy, and I hope the weather gets better. Out here it's bad too. It's been raining and cold all week long, and there's a lot of snow up in the mountains. Well, hot weather will surely come.

Well so-long for now and God bless you all.

Love To: Ma, Pa, Mary, Tony, Francie & Carlo
X X X X X X X X X X — Phil

P.S. I'm glad Pa received the silver dollar from my wife and I'm glad he likes it. Tony, Here's 12 packs of cigarettes which I hope will get through to you. I sure hope you are still there to smoke them. So-long, Phil

Friday June 8, 1945/Wendover, Utah

Dear Mary,
. . . How do you like this ink? It's my own personal mixture. 1/2 bottle of blue ink mixed with ½ bottle of red ink. I still can't figure out if it's violet or brown.

Yesterday I received a letter from Cousin John. He's alright as far as I can tell.

Yes sir, I'd sure like to catch the peaches still on the tree and maybe I might even get there when they are still green, who knows? I hope Ma and the rest of you are feeling as well as possible today. I'm in pretty good shape and I can't kick about anything. Well, I guess I'll close again, but I'll be back tomorrow. So-long for now and God bless you all.

Love To: Ma, Pa, Mary, Tony, Francie & Carlo
X X X X X X X X X — Phil —

Saturday June 9, 1945/Wendover Field, Utah

[This letter is typed, which means he was writing while at work as explained in his letter of June 16, 1945. When he types a letter in his office, he always addresses it "Wendover Field" instead of just "Wendover."]

Dear Mary,

. . . It's been raining on and off all day long. I guess the only thing that keeps this land from being nice and fertile is the salt in the soil. Otherwise they get enough rain to raise crops and etc.

You said Pa went out to the farm to help plant some crops. It's okay for him to go, but still, he's getting old and can't take it so good either. But as I said it's okay if he wants, I hope he's feeling in good shape. Again I'll tell you not to send me a package. One thing it costs too much, and another thing if I was the only guy out here it wouldn't be so bad, but I'm not. Not that I don't want to share a package with these guys out here, but after all they are just plain strangers and it seems that they never get any packages so why should I always be the guy who's giving out the stuff? So don't forget, don't send anything. Besides if I'm still here it won't be too long and I'll get a furlough. So tell Ma not to feel hurt because I don't want her to send me a package. I've told my wife the same thing. Every time she sends me a package it costs more than $10, and I know it's about the same for you. If you've got money that's extra, just buy something for Ma, or [Shadow's boy] Little Ronny or my kid, better still save it, but don't go wasting it for a package on me. Well, I'll close for now, and no hard feelings or I'm liable to do some smashing when I come home. So-long for now and God bless you all and don't worry.

Love To: Ma, Pa, Mary, Tony, Francie & Carlo
X X X X X X X X X — Phil —

Sunday June 10, 1945/Wendover Field, Utah

Dear Mary,

Today is Sunday again out here. I know at this time you are probably out taking a ride out there if the weather is nice and I hope it is. I'm glad Ma enjoys those rides on Sundays. May as well take a ride now and then. You know, the furthest East I've ever been was to Almond, New York, when Tony and I took Shadow back to the CCC [Civilian Conservation Corps] camp. . . . It's about 80 miles East of Buffalo and it's very pretty country all the way. I wish Ma could see it.

Heck, it's so easy to travel. Even if you take the 7:00 A.M. train out of Buffalo, you'll be in Cleveland by noon, and Cleveland is a bigger city than Buffalo. If I was Tony and I had a couple of days to myself, I'd take a little ride to Cleveland and see how it is. Of course if he doesn't get off in Cleveland he'll find himself in the skyscraper city of Chicago by 6 o'clock that night. Yep, Chicago's buildings make Buffalo's buildings look pretty small. I know my wife wouldn't look at them, because they were too tall. [*This letter demonstrates how serving in the armed forces expanded the horizons of many Americans.*]

. . . I'll try to write Frankie, Carmen, and Cousin Johnny today if I find time. You'd be surprised how letter writing kills a lot of time. Sometimes I just can't find the time to write as much as I'd really like to. I'll close for now but I'll be back again tomorrow night. Till then so-long and God bless you all.

Love To: Ma, Pa, Mary, Tony, Francie & Carlo
X X X X X X X X X — Phil —

P.S. I haven't been able to buy any gum for quite a while, but when I do, I'll send you a few sticks each day.

Monday June 11, 1945/Wendover Field, Utah

Dear Mary,

Everything seems to be going along pretty good out here and there's nothing I can complain about except the usual small things, which don't amount to much. Some days I work, and some days I just plain loaf around all day accomplishing nothing. I hope this letter finds you all in the best of health and spirits.

Yesterday I wrote a letter to Frankie and Carmen and I enclosed a picture of myself to each of them. The pictures I sent are the same as I sent you in April. Carmen has a picture album, and he's always asking for my picture so I sent him one. I also sent him a little picture when I came back from furlough which I had taken with Shadow at Sattler's Department store. Of course, Frankie also got one. I know Carmen will place them in his album, but Frankie will just store them someplace. He better not throw them away or I'll smash him.

The weather isn't too bad out here. The sun is shining but it's not too hot. When you figure that I haven't had a cold since I got here 3 months ago, it really is a nice healthful climate. You should be having nice weather there also by now. I guess it's been a pretty bad year for Buffalo as far as weather is concerned because it started off with all that snow last January. But I expect it'll be mighty warm out there during July and August, I hope so any way. Well, I guess I haven't anything to gab about so I'll close for now but I'll be back again tomorrow. So-long for now and God bless you all.

> Love To: Ma, Pa, Mary, Tony, Francie & Carlo
> X X X X X X X X X X — Phil —

Tuesday June 12, 1945/Wendover Field, Utah

Dear Mary,

Last night I received the letter you wrote last Thursday while at work. You said that Ma went to the doctor and he said she was pretty good. Yes, I'm glad. Just so she has an appetite and eats, she'll be alright.

You said Carmen sends home his money. That's swell. $260 is okay and I'm sure it will grow larger. You said that Frankie has 678 dollars in the bank. He sure is getting up in the world. As for me, I've got 680 dollars all together. I've also got about 100 dollars in bonds all together. Of course that's counting all the bonds my wife and I have. We try to save as much as possible, but there are expenses. . . .

I was glad to hear that you were going down town with my wife last Thursday and I hope you both made out okay. Yes, my son is sure getting up in the world. 17 years from now he too will be in the army or navy. I hope not, but war is war. According to my wife he sure giggles out loud now and looks plenty smart. Well, I'll close for now but I'll be back again tomorrow. Till then so-long and God bless you all.

> Love To: Ma, Pa, Mary, Tony, Francie & Carlo
> X X X X X X X X X — Phil —

Wednesday June 13, 1945/Wendover, Utah

Dear Mary,

Just a few lines for today to let you know that everything out here is going along pretty good. I hope you can say the same for everyone out there. . . . Tomorrow I'll see if I can put in an application for a furlough. I know when I'll get it too. But I won't say any thing just yet. Don't expect me too soon, though. But also if I'm still here it won't be too long.

I hope Ma is feeling fine today. Just let her take it easy and tell her to forget about the farm. Well so-long for now and God bless you all.

> Love To: Ma, Pa, Mary, Tony, Francie & Carlo
> X X X X X X X X X X — Phil —

Thursday June 14, 1945/Wendover, Utah

Dear Mary,

. . . You said Ma and you paid a visit to Frankie's God Mother. That's fine. I was there when that lady and *Compare* Philip came to the hospital to see Ma and almost got kicked out. I'm glad to hear that the Plymouth is running good. Yes, I'll use it when I come home "sometime next month" if everything goes well out here. My wife knows in which 10 days I'll arrive. Ask her to tell you. I hate to take an old train for 3 days and nights to come home, but I'll go through any thing to get home. I know it'll have to be done. I know it'll be hard to leave my little son, but it'll have to be done. It's harder still to say good bye to my wife, Ma, and all of you, but that too must be done when a furlough ends. Well that's all for tonight, but I'll be back again tomorrow. So-long and God bless you all.

Love To: Ma, Pa, Mary, Tony, Francie & Carlo
X X X X X X X X X X X — Phil —

Friday June 15, 1945/Wendover, Utah

Dear Mary,

Half of June has gone by. Yep, I'm starting to sweat these days out again. Everything is going along okay though and the weather is very nice, although yesterday it was cold and cloudy and I thought it was going to snow. I hope you are having good weather too.

I received a letter from June yesterday and she is still sweating out her baby. I hope everything goes alright with her and I hope Shadow is able to come home like I did last February. You know if the baby was going to be born next month, there would've been a possibility that I'll see Shadow again.

Today my son sent me a package with 3 pairs of white sox and 3 hankies. Of course my wife did all the work, but it really seems as if my son sent them. It's for Father's Day.

Well, I hope you are all getting along fine out there and I hope Ma is feeling better as each day goes by. So-long and don't worry. God bless you all.

Love To: Ma, Pa, Mary, Tony, Francie & Carlo
X X X X X X X X — Phil.

Saturday June 16, 1945/Wendover Field, Utah

Dear Mary,

Again, I'm typing out a letter to you while I have time to write during my lunch hour. Everything out here is going along pretty good, and I can't kick. The weather out here is pretty good, also, and I hope it's the same for all of you out there.

How are the strawberries coming along this year? I know that you don't pick them [anymore] but maybe you do hear if they are growing pretty good. Of course, I'm not too interested in them, because it makes no difference to me if they are good or bad this year and I know the same goes for Ma.

Well, life out here goes on the same. Really only a coward would volunteer for overseas duty from out here [in Utah], because he'll be trying to get out of this place. It's really not too bad, though.

I don't get much news about the war these days because there aren't any radios in my barracks and also because it takes such a long time for the newspapers to get here from Salt Lake City, so the result is I don't buy any paper and I don't listen to any radio. There's no new developments or I'd have heard of them by now. But no doubt they are planning something big in the Pacific. I only wish they'd use gas against the Japs and I'm sure we'd get rid of more Japs and end the war sooner. But too many people are against using poison gas because they think it's too cruel. I guess it's not cruel when a guy gets blown to bits, but it is cruel to kill just by gassing the enemy. I guess, I'm just mad, because day in and day out I have to work at Chemical Warfare and practically all the work is wasted because they aren't even using it.

Well, I guess I'll close for now but I'll be back again tomorrow. Till then so-long and God bless you all.

Love To: Ma, Pa, Mary, Tony, Francie & Carlo

X X X X X X X X — Phil —

Sunday June 17, 1945/Wendover, Utah

Dear Mary,

. . . My wife told me that the weather there is nice and that she took the baby down to the house to see you all. She said he was crying all the time on [account] of his gums hurting him. I guess that's to be expected at this time.

Did I tell you that the army has rationed cigarettes to all the soldiers in the U.S. in every army camp? You see, this camp had a ration system of their own and they gave us 12 packs each week. Now, a complete army rationing system has stepped in and they are giving us only 6 packs each week. I think that when I get my furlough I'll have enough cigarettes for myself and also some for Tony. I've got 2½ cartons in reserve right now and I figure I'll come home with about 4 cartons.

I hope Ma is getting along nicely today and everyday and that goes for the rest of you. I was going to write to Carmen and Frankie today, but I forgot to buy some stamps yesterday so I'll wait till tomorrow to write to them. Well, I'll close for now, so take it easy and God bless you all.

Love To: Ma, Pa, Mary, Tony, Francie & Carlo

X X X X X X X X X X — Phil

Monday June 18, 1945/Wendover, Utah

Dear Mary,

Everything out here is going along alright and I hope it's the same for you out there. I hope Ma is also feeling fine in health and in spirits. It sure is pretty hot here today and I wrote part of my wife's letter while laying in the sun for an hour. I'll get some sun burn yet.

I hope the weather out there is okay. Today I received the letter Carmen wrote on May 31st, another one he wrote on June 4th, another one he wrote on June 7th, and one he wrote on June 10th. Just think he wrote it on June 10th and I got it June 18th. Only 8 days. For all we know he may be at Hawaii or some close place. I hope so. He's feeling okay, according to his letters.

Well, I guess that's all for now, but I'll be back tomorrow again. Till then so-long, don't worry, and God bless you all.

Love To: Ma, Pa, Mary, Tony, Francie & Carlo
X X X X X X X X X X X X — Phil —

Tuesday June 19, 1945/Wendover Field, Utah

Dear Mary,

Today I received the nice long letter you wrote last Thursday, I was very glad to hear from you. Don't worry about taking too long to write to me. I know how things are. I was glad to hear that my wife and son and Alice [his mother-in-law] were down to the house. You said my son had the evil eye. [*Many Italian immigrants believed that if a person had evil or jealous thoughts about you, you would develop a headache or worse. A folk cure for the "evil eye" was to pour water into a shallow bowl and hold it over the afflicted person's head. Then, someone would say a prayer and make the sign of the cross on the victim's forehead. A drop of olive oil would then be splashed into the water: if it dispersed, then the evil eye was cured and the person's headache went away; if it did not disperse, then the person did not have the evil eye. The diagnosis and cure were a typical southern Italian blend of Catholicism and older pagan superstitions.*]

Well, I don't believe in such things the way you and my wife and her family does. If the baby was crying when he was there, it's only because his gums were hurting him. Of course, he's a beautiful baby and people will admire him and also a lot of jealous people would wish he wasn't that cute, [but] they can't hurt him [with their thoughts]. However, you can go right on believing in that evil eye stuff if you want.

I was glad to hear that Joe was reclassified to 2B, and I hope they let him stay that way for the duration. As for Tony, I'm glad they are letting him stay a while longer.

Yesterday I wrote Carmen and Frankie a letter each. I try my best to write to them as much as I possibly can. I don't hear too much about Frankie, though. I guess his horse comes first. Anyway, I hope he'll be on his way home pretty soon. As for me, I'm sweating out the days. Pretty soon, it'll be only a matter of weeks for me and then I'll get to come home and see you all again. I'm glad to hear that Nick Mitri got himself another furlough. Yep, he should be in for a discharge pretty soon with all the points he should have.

I was glad to hear that the weather out there is nice now and I hope it stays that way for you. Out here it's rather hot, but not too bad like it was at Pratt, Kansas, last year.

Well, so-long for now and God bless you all.

Love To: Ma, Pa, Mary, Tony, Francie & Carlo
X X X X X X X X X — Phil.

Wednesday June 20, 1945/Wendover, Utah

Dear Mary,

. . . I hope Ma and the rest of you are feeling fine and in the best of health. My son is kind of sick and I sure hope he gets well. No telling what a little baby can take as far as sicknesses go. Well, it's up to God I guess and I sure hope he gets well soon. Well, not much more else to say, so I guess I'll close. God bless you all and don't worry.

Love To: Ma, Pa, Mary, Tony, Francie & Carlo
X X X X X X X X X — Phil.

[This entry is a Father's Day card that Phil sent his father. The front of the card reads: "A Wish for Father." Inside the verse says, "On Father's Day I send to Dad/ A wish sincere and true/ For all the goodly gifts of life/ Which surely are his due." Phil signed the card: "Love, Mary, Phil & Grandson Phil." That's the first time he wrote the baby's name. Previously, he just referred to him as the baby.]

Thursday June 21, 1945/Wendover, Utah

Dear Mary,

. . . I'm glad to hear that Pa liked the gift my wife got for him. It's not much, but maybe someday we can do more. And of course, I'm glad he liked the card I sent for him. It's too bad he lost his strawberry ticket and I hope the farmer makes it up to him. *[His father was picking strawberries out on the farm, and lost his card that indicated how many strawberries he had picked.]*

You said Tony has to report for a physical on June 22nd. I sure hope he doesn't have to go. You said Tony held my son and then when he put him in the crib my son started to cry because he wanted Tony to hold him some more. Of course he likes Tony and he'll like all of you too. See him all you want. In fact, I want you to see him always. The more Ma and the rest of you see him, the happier I feel. You are right when you said a baby needs a lot of sleep and rest. If Ronnie [Shadow and June's baby] isn't chubby, it means nothing at all, just so he's in good health. Also, you can't travel with a baby and let him put up with hardships and expect him to grow like you want. But then Ronnie may be taking after Shadow. Shadow never ate a lot, and still doesn't. Some day there'll be a reunion with all these kids. Has Ma ever stopped to think how big the family has grown? Of course when the rest get married, it'll still be bigger.

. . . Oh yes, I know how that farmer operates. He'll come down and talk to Ma about going to pick on Sundays or something. Well, she doesn't go anymore, no matter who says anything.

Tell Tony I may write him a letter soon. *[Whenever Phil thinks someone's morale is low, he writes them a letter.]* So-long for now and God bless you all.

Love To: Ma, Pa, Mary, Tony, Francie & Carlo
X X X X X X X X X X X — Phil.

[This next letter is addressed to Phil's older brother, who recently had to report for his induction physical.]

Friday June 22, 1945/Wendover Field, Utah

Hello Tony,

Yesterday I received a letter from our sister Mary and she said that you had received your GREETINGS, to report for a physical exam. If I'm not mistaken, this is it! I really hate to see you go, but I guess nothing can be done about it. The army isn't tough, it's just monotonous. At first it won't seem that way to you, because everything will be new to you. Of course you'll have a letter problem, but you can write whenever you please. As far as letters go, you need only worry about writing to Ma, because she always wants to know how we are making out, and also drop a letter to us guys when you get a chance.

I need not tell you what to expect, because there really isn't too much. However, if you have any questions about anything, just let me know and you can bet I'll answer you right away. Incidently, I don't think they give you any choice to pick out a branch of service you want in the army, but I don't have to tell you to stay out of the Infantry. Take anything but that. Another thing, if you ever get a chance to attend any schools at all, don't hesitate to take it, because after all you haven't a thing to lose. Try out your luck with anything beside just toting a rifle. *[This seems to have been Phil's basic approach. He went into the Air Cadets' Program and applied for Officer Candidate School, but later withdrew his application. To an extent, these may have been ploys to delay being sent overseas as an infantryman, but they also seem to be Phil's way of taking advantage of a bad situation. He believed he should try to improve himself as much as possible and make use of his talents.]* Of course, you'll have all the beer you want to drink, and you can always get liquor when you are out on a pass, so don't worry as far as liquor goes. You'll also find plenty of gambling, but in my opinion it doesn't pay. I figure if a guy can save at least 50% of his pay each month it'll add up in time and you'll have quite a sum saved up for when the war ends. But I guess that's up to you.

All in all I think you'll have a better time of it than you do now. You'll meet a lot more people for certain. And when you get to your permanent station, you can have someone send you your guitar, and you'll be popular with everybody before you know it, because everyone likes music and especially singing at the same time. *[Tony's favorite hobby was playing his guitar and writing songs.]*

As for traveling around, you'll get plenty of that in the states and of course you may get to see a great deal of the world. It would be a good deal if you were able to get into a European army of occupation, because you'd really see a lot of the modern world that way. Of course being in the army has its disadvantages, but no use worrying about that. One good thing though, you are getting in when the war is getting toward its end, at least I hope so. Well, Tony, I guess there's not much else I can say, except, after you get in and I can be of any help at all, just drop a little letter. So-long for now and God bless you, and I wish you a lot of luck.

Love, Your Brother and Pal, Phil

Friday June 22, 1945/Wendover, Utah

Dear Mary,

By the time you'll get this letter, I'll be home in less than a month, that is if everything goes along okay. I can't wait till these days go by I guess, because I keep counting them.

Today, I received a letter written by Carmen on June 13th. He's in good shape and is getting along okay.

I hope Ma and the rest of you are feeling fine. Out here, I'm getting along as usual. I wonder how Tony is making out. Today, according to you, he's taking his physical. I hope he's in good health, but still I wish he doesn't pass it. I'll be waiting for some news from you.

It sure is hot out here, but I figure it's not worse than Buffalo, except drier. We probably won't have anymore rain all summer long. Well, I'll close for today, but I'll be back again tomorrow. So-long and God bless you all.

Love To: Ma, Pa, Mary, Tony, Francie & Carlo
X X X X X X X — Phil —

Saturday June 23, 1945/Wendover Field, Utah

Dear Mary,

. . . I just got through writing a letter to Tony because I figure it will be my last chance to write to him in civilian life. However I do hope he still don't have to go in the service. . . .

Out here it's the same old story day in and day out. It gets monotonous but I can take it and still have a lot of patience. The days seem to go by very nicely and it won't be too long before I'll be running around Buffalo again. That will sure be swell and it can't come around too soon for me. I know I'll have a lot of fun with my kid. And another thing it's nice to come home and know that no one is in the hospital.

Well, I guess that's all for now but I'll be back again tomorrow. So-long and God bless you all.

Love To: Ma, Pa, Mary, Tony, Francie & Carlo
X X X X X X X X X X — Phil —

Sunday June 24, 1945/Wendover Field, Utah

Dear Mary,

Today I received the letter you wrote last Monday and the letter you wrote last Wednesday. I was especially glad to hear that June gave birth to a baby boy. Well that's not so bad. Having a girl for a daughter is a lot of bother anyway. Maybe Shadow can try again as soon as possible for a baby girl and who knows he may get one some day. I sure hope he comes home soon so that he can see his new son, and also his wife. I also hope that June is doing nicely, and also her new baby.

I guess every one in our family is getting used to being an aunt, uncle, grandmother, and grandfather by now. As for me getting a baby girl, so that you all can have a niece, I'm afraid I can't do anything about that. Before I even start to think of babies, I will have to get a job and have a home of my own. One baby is enough for a long time yet. If I have hard luck in the future, it'll only be tough on one baby and not two, see what I mean?

I also received the picture you sent of Frankie on his horse. . . . He even frightened me for a while until I faintly recognized him. He looks like Emperor Hirohito on his horse. I should write and tell him that after seeing his picture I ought to disown my brother, but don't worry I won't. Anyway he sure looks very comical with a bald head, and if you didn't tell me it was Frankie, I don't think I would've recognized him except for his horse. Of course, I'm sending it right back so that you can show it to Shadow. . . . Well so-long for now and God bless you all.

Love To: Ma, Pa, Mary, Tony, Francie & Carlo
X X X X X X X X X — Phil.

Fig. 2.8. Phil's brother, Frankie, on his horse in New Guinea in 1944. The photograph is discussed in Phil's letter of June 24, 1945. (Philip L. Aquila Collection)

Monday June 25, 1945/Wendover, Utah

Dear Mary,

I just got through calling you all up and it was swell to hear all your voices once again. Ma sounded real nice and so did the rest of you. I wish I could really stay a long time talking but it costs too much. I was very happy to hear that Tony wasn't drafted yet. You see, you told me he had gotten his "greetings" and had to report for a physical on the 22nd [of June]. I took it for granted that he would also be inducted on that date, because you said he got his greetings. But, now I'm glad it was just a physical and not his induction.

I also talked with my wife tonight. I couldn't hear the baby though. I was glad to hear that June is doing nicely. Yes, I received a letter from Shadow today and he said he couldn't get a leave, but in a couple weeks he'll get one. I hope so, because I know how it is to wait to get home. As for me I'll be home in less than a month and I hope I'm able to see Shadow and also catch Tony still home. So-long for now, and God bless you all.

Love To: Ma, Pa, Mary, Tony, Francie & Carlo
X X X X X X X X — Phil —

P.S. Tell Carlo he sounds like a girl on the phone, because he's got a real nice voice.

Tuesday June 26, 1945/Wendover Field, Utah

Dear Mary,

. . . I was going to surprise you all a little on my furlough by keeping away the exact date from you all, but now I've changed my mind. If everything goes along okay, I'll get my furlough by the 20th of July and I should be home by the 23rd or early on the 24th. That's all the information I have at this time. The only thing that can keep me from getting it is to be shipped from this base in the near future. Of course, I'll call up from Chicago on my way home, that is if I get a chance in between trains. Of course, I won't call up you, but I'll call my wife and she can tell you, okay? So till then just keep your fingers crossed.

Sunday I wrote letters to Frankie, Carmen, and cousin Johnny. Yesterday I wrote to cousin Angelo. I'd have written to Shadow, but I figured he'd be home, but yesterday I got his letter in which he said he wouldn't be home till July 5th or 6th, so I'll write to him as soon as I possibly can. You told me that June enjoys the letters I write to her. Well, I try my best to make every body smile once in awhile. . . .

The letter I sent to Tony should be torn up, because it's not time for him to get a letter like that yet. I only wrote it because you told me he had received his Presidential greetings and I thought he'd be leaving soon. Anyway I'm glad he's not. *[Phil is probably talking about the letter he wrote to Tony on June 22 in which he gives him information about what the army will be like.]* Well, I'll close for now so take it easy and God bless you all.

Love To: Ma, Pa, Mary, Tony, Francie & Carlo
X X X X X X X X X — Phil —

Wednesday June 27, 1945/Wendover Field, Utah

Dear Mary,

Just another little letter to let you know that everything out here seems to be going along pretty good. I hope you don't mind all these typewritten letters. You see, I get back from lunch a little early and I find time to write a letter and I prefer to use the typewriter.

According to you on the phone last Monday, you said that June's baby weighs 7¼ pounds. That's pretty good, I think.

Yesterday I told you that I'd get my furlough starting on July 20. Yes, I was going to surprise you all, but I just couldn't get my plans to work, because I was telling my wife everything a little at a time and finally I got tired of it and told her the exact date. Now I hope nothing comes up to spoil it because then we'll all be disappointed instead of only me if I had kept the date to myself from the beginning, like I wanted to. Oh well, there's not much difference.

The weather out here seems to be pretty nice and warm with a little strong wind blowing around. I really don't care how the weather out there is right now, just so it's nice towards the end of this month, because I'd hate to find bad weather there like I did last time. Anyway I'm sure it won't snow for July anymore, but then you never can tell. Well, I'll close for now, so God bless you all and don't worry.

Love To: Ma, Pa, Mary, Tony, Francie & Carlo
X X X X X X X X X — Phil.

P.S. I received a letter from Rae and Joe yesterday. It sure was a surprise. I may answer them right away or I may let them wait about 6 months the way they do. I also got a letter from you today. So-long.

Thursday June 28, 1945/Wendover, Utah

Dear Mary,

. . . Well, 22 more days and I should be on my way home. Of course, by the time you get this letter, it will be less than that. Do you know, that I'm set back a lot of money each time I get a furlough? Heck, if it wasn't for my furloughs, I'd be easily into my second thousand of dollars saved. But I want to get home as much as possible so expenses don't count one bit. So every time I can get a furlough I jump at it and that goes the same for the rest of the 12,000,000 men in the services. Well, I'll close for now, so take it easy and God bless you all.

Love To: Ma, Pa, Mary, Tony, Francie & Carlo
X X X X X X X X X X — Phil —

Friday June 29, 1945/Wendover Field, Utah

Dear Mary,

Just a little free time [here at work] and I figure I'd write a letter to you. Same old story out here with everything going along as well as possible. Today is Friday, or fish day, and I had a good piece of fish to eat this after noon.

Pretty soon July will be here, and if everything still keeps going along okay, I'll be home for sure. Here's hoping, anyway. It will sure be nice to see you all again. If I get this furlough I'll sure consider myself real lucky, because just think of all the nice long furloughs I've had since I've been in the army. I can say one thing for sure, that after this furlough, we won't be seeing each other for one solid year, and if I go overseas it'll be much more than that. It's not because I want it that way, it's because the army only gives the soldiers in the 2nd Air force one furlough each year, so if I take it in July, I won't get another one till next July. Oh well, I may as well take them when I can get them, and when they give them to me.

I hope Ma and the rest of you are getting along alright and also feeling in the best of health.

I guess my little son is getting along alright and I bet he's starting to recognize everybody. Little does he know that he has yet to meet the best guy and the most important guy in his life yet. Heck it won't take me much time to get acquainted with him. Yep, I wish June wouldn't put her kids on a strict schedule. In my opinion, if a little baby wants to eat a lot, then let him. Oh well, they are Shadow's and June's kids so let them raise them the way they want. One thing I know, when I'm home and my kid wants to eat, he'll eat just as much as he wants, and nobody better stop him either, doctors schedules or no doctors schedules.

Well, I'll close for now but I'll be back again tomorrow. Till then, so-long and God bless you all and don't worry.

Love To: Ma, Pa, Mary, Tony, Francie & Carlo
X X X X X X X X X X — Phil —

Saturday June 30, 1945/Wendover, Utah

Dear Mary,

Everything seems to be going along alright out here and I hope it continues that way just a little longer.

Today, I received a letter from Frankie. It's about time I heard from him. I finally found out where he is located. He is near the town called *Buna*. That's in the north east tip of New Guinea. He's pretty far away from the Japs. I remember though when there was some tough fighting at Buna. Tony should know where Buna is. It's a safe place now, or they wouldn't let those guys buy horses. So tell Ma not to worry about Frankie.

Well, I hope you are all feeling fine today. Don't forget, you just tell Ma to forget berry or bean picking this year or any other year. Sure, I know, her heart feels sad knowing she's losing money but you tell her that her life is more important.

I also got a letter from Shadow and June. They both feel bad because they can't see each other. I guess they will soon though. Well, so-long for now and God bless you all.

Love To: Ma, Pa, Mary, Tony, Francie & Carlo
X X X X X X X X X X — Phil —

Sunday July 1, 1945/Wendover, Utah

Dear Mary,

. . . As for the letter I wrote Tony [on June 22], I didn't tell him anything or give him any advice. I just wrote to him because I thought he was going to leave real soon. I was glad to hear that Shadow also called up on the 25th of June and glad we were able to make Ma and all of you happy.

Today is Sunday and the 1st of July. Everything is going along fine and if it continues that way, I should be home by 3 weeks on the 22nd or 23rd of July.

I was glad Joe drove Ma, Francie, Rae, Frankie [Joe and Rae's son] and Carlo to the farm last Sunday. My wife also took a ride out there, but I guess they missed her. I'm glad the farmer found Pa's ticket *[Phil's father had lost his card showing how many strawberries he had picked]*. Well, I guess that's all for today so take it easy and God bless you all.

Love To: Ma, Pa, Mary, Tony, Francie, & Carlo
X X X X X X X X X X X X — Phil —

[The next letter is addressed to Phil's older brother. It refers to the June 22 letter that Phil had written advising Tony about the military. Tony apparently had responded sarcastically to his younger brother's fatherly advice.]

Monday July 2, 1945/Wendover, Utah

Dear Anthony,

I received your letter written as of June 28th and I was very pleased to hear from you. I'm glad you took my previous letter with such fine spirit. I only wrote it, because I was certain you'd be leaving very soon, because according to Sister Mary, you had received your "Greetings."

However, I'm glad you didn't leave yet. About the only fault I can find with your letter is the compliment you pay me when you address me <u>Sir</u>. One of the army regulations is a sergeant, or any other soldier below the grade of Warrant Officer, is never addressed by <u>Sir</u>. I'm making a note of that at this time, because when you do become a soldier, you won't be flattering any enlisted man by saying Yes Sir or No Sir.

However all officers are addressed by <u>Sir</u>. For example, I make it a point to add "Sir" in every sentence when I'm talking to any officer. My opinion is that I'm better than most officers there are in this man's and woman's army, but to avoid trouble, I'll flatter even a WAC by saying <u>sir</u>. I'll tell anybody any thing, but as long as I add on "Sir" I figure I can't be accused of being rude.

I was delighted to learn that you have purchased a new 100′ hose. I didn't think there was so much rubber left. Remember the new saying that goes with the present lack of rubber: "Men who used to be called Dearie are now called Papa!" That's why I was surprised to hear you bought a hundred feet of hose. Am also glad to hear that the Plymouth is okay. No doubt though as soon as I come home July 22nd, something will go wrong with it as usual when I'm on furlough.

Well I reckon I'll be getting along now. You see, I want to make every one happy with my letters, therefore I'll have to close in order to lend my talents elsewhere. As usual, take it easy.

Your Brother Forever, Phil

P.S. I'm not trying to force myself upon you to keep writing, but if you find you aren't busy for awhile, you have my permission to write to me direct.

Monday July 2, 1945/Wendover, Utah

Dear Mary,

. . . I'm glad everything out there is going along fine. Out here, things are just the same as any other day and I hope it stays that way just a few more days. I'll let you know when to stop writing though.

You said Frankie sent you a letter with some pictures of the [New Guinea] natives. Yep, I've seen those kind of pictures and I know just what you mean. I'll close for now, so take it easy and God bless you all.

Love To: Ma, Pa, Mary, Tony, Francie & Carlo
X X X X X X X X X — Phil —

Tuesday July 3, 1945/Wendover Field, Utah

Dear Mary,

. . . I'm sorry you missed out on your vacation, but that's alright Ma comes first anyway. In one of your letters you said that Ma, Joe, Rae,

Francie, and Carlo went out to the farm and helped pick a while. I guess Ma just can't get it out of her blood. Can't she understand that she has only one life and must take it easy from now on? Oh well, I'll be there pretty soon and I'd just like to hear Ma mention the farm just once and hoping that she could be out there.

I was glad to hear that you bought a 100 foot hose. I thought Tony said he bought it? That's okay though, it makes no difference who bought it. I'll use it to give the car a good cleaning when I get home. I still like to ride in a nice shining car. This is the first time I'll be home when the summer is still going strong, and I'll show Tony how a car should be cleaned up.

. . . Today is July 3rd, and 16 more days I ought to grab a hold of that furlough paper in my hand and say good-bye to this place for about 20 days. Well, I guess that's all for now so take it easy and God bless you all.

Love To: Ma, Pa, Mary, Tony, Francie & Carlo
X X X X X X X X X — Phil —

Wednesday July 4, 1945/Wendover Field, Utah

Dear Mary,

Today is the Fourth of July once again, but it's not a holiday out here. Everything seems to be going along pretty good though, and I hope it's the same out there with all of you. . . .

Well 16 more days and I'll be on my way home, I hope. It sure is going to be tough riding those hot dirty trains for about three days and nights. You see, I'm practically on the West Coast out here and it's quite a long ride home. But that's the least of my worries, because I'd ride in anything to get home again. I can't promise that I'll have many cigarettes for Tony, but I'll have more than a carton for him and they'll be Camels. You see I only get six packs for seven days, so I can only save up a little bit. It should be easier to get cigarettes now anyway. Well, I guess I'll close for now so take it easy and God bless you all.

Love To: Ma, Pa, Mary, Tony, Francie & Carlo
X X X X X X X X X — Phil —

Thursday July 5, 1945/Wendover, Utah

Dear Mary,

. . . It's really nice [of you] to take Ma out for rides each Sunday. Show her a good time always.

The weather here is pretty hot and it makes me feel pretty lazy and drink a lot of water and relax at the same time. I guess it's real hot there also.

You said my son takes to people real nice and gets all excited when someone calls him. Yep, it shouldn't take you long to get acquainted with him. Well, about 2 more weeks now and I'll be on my way home. I'm sure cutting this time down day after day. So-long and God bless you all.

Love To: Ma, Pa, Mary, Tony, Francie & Carlo
X X X X X X X X X X — Phil.

Friday July 6, 1945/Wendover, Utah

Dear Mary,
. . . The days seem kind of long but they are going by pretty good. The weather is pretty hot out here. It hasn't rained for a long time and I hope when I'm in Buffalo, I can get caught in a nice thunderstorm with plenty of rain coming down.

I hope Ma is feeling fine today and I hope she sees my son a lot. Tell Ma to ask my wife to come and see you. Heck, once a week isn't so much. Well, I'll close for now, so take it easy and God bless you all.

Love To: Ma, Pa, Mary, Tony, Francie & Carlo
X X X X X X X X X — Phil.

Saturday July 7, 1945/Wendover, Utah

Dear Mary,
. . . The days are going by nicely and it won't be too long before I'll be there. Incidently, I'll tell you when to stop writing to me okay? Until then, though, you can continue to write as usual.

I hope Shadow got his furlough by now. If he didn't, I hope he stays just a while longer in Memphis, and when he comes to Buffalo, I'm bound to see him again. Here's hoping anyway. If he's there on the 22nd I'm bound to see him, because I figure I'll be pulling in at that time. My wife told me that you went with her to see June and her new baby. That was fine.

I hope Ma and the rest of you are all feeling fine. I'm in good shape out here myself. So-long and God bless you all.

Love To: Ma, Pa, Mary, Tony, Francie & Carlo
X X X X X X X X X X X X — Phil —

Sunday July 8, 1945/Wendover, Utah

Dear Mary,
. . . I was just laying outside my barracks. I got some nice sun tan on my back and legs. It looks like a rain storm and the sun is blocked so I came inside. Every time I want to get a complete tan, something happens [and] interferes. It's pretty hot out here though. Yesterday it was about 95 degrees and today it's about the same. I hope you took Ma for a ride today.

I read an article in today's Salt Lake City paper about some dope who is going down the Niagara Falls in a barrel today. You probably know about it. Well I guess I'll be closing for now so take it easy and God bless you all.

        Love To: Ma, Pa, Mary, Tony, Francie & Carlo
        X X X X X X X X X X X — Phil —

        Tuesday July 10, 1945/Wendover Field, Utah

Dear Mary,

   . . . It always seems that the few last days [before a furlough] seem the hardest. A lot of rumors are floating around of a lot of guys being shipped out [overseas], so naturally I'm kind of worried, a little. Oh well the days will go by and we'll soon see what will happen, so as of today, everything still seems to be going along pretty good so that only leaves about 10 more days to sweat out.

   The weather out here is fine, and I hope it's the same out there for you. I'm also feeling pretty good and I can't kick too much about anything at all. Well, I'll close for today but I'll write tomorrow again and let you know as usual how everything is proceeding. So-long for now and God bless you all.

        Love To: Ma, Pa, Mary, Tony, Francie & Carlo
        X X X X X X X X X X X X — Phil.

        Wednesday July 11, 1945/Wendover, Utah

Dear Mary,

   . . . Yesterday, I received a letter from Carmen dated June 30th and he also seems to be feeling alright. Monday July 9th I wrote a letter to Carmen and Frankie. I get along with Carmen pretty good, but with Frankie, he's always telling me something and I have to always put him straight on things. It's more than 2½ years since I've seen him last. I bet, physically, he's sure changed in that time. *[Frankie was closer in age to Phil, and now that he was in the army Frankie certainly didn't want to be bossed around anymore by the brother he used to refer to as "the Warden."]*

   I hate to think of Pa working all those long hours out [on] the farm. I know, I'm not used to that hard work anymore. I can't say I've been loafing but I certainly don't work too hard [physically]. Well, everything out here seems to be going along pretty good with me and I can't kick. Don't write me any more letters, don't even answer this one, because I'll be on my way home before I get them, if everything goes right. So-long and God bless you all.

        Love To: Ma, Pa, Mary, Tony, Francie & Carlo,
        X X X X X X X X X X X X — Phil

Thursday July 12, 1945/Wendover, Utah

Dear Mary,

. . . Today is a very hot day out here. Although I have only a little less than 8 more days to get the furlough, I still can't help but feel
a little worried that something may come up to prevent my getting it.
One of the reasons why I never want to tell anyone the date is because
it's so uncertain. Now that we all know it's on July 20th, here's hoping I can get it so that we won't be disappointed. Well, I hope Ma and
the rest of you are all feeling fine. So-long for now and God bless you
all.

Love To: Ma, Pa, Mary, Tony, Francie & Carlo
X X X X X X X X X — Phil —

Saturday July 14, 1945/Wendover, Utah

Dear Mary,

. . . If everything goes along okay, I should be home in a few days
after you get this letter (I'll be there on Sunday). My furlough has
already been approved and I'm to pick it up at 9 a.m. Thursday on the
19th of July. Yep, next Sunday I should be home at least by midnight
anyway. I sure hope Shadow will be able to get there during the time I'm
home. . . . Well, so-long for now and God bless you all.

Love To: Ma, Pa, Mary, Tony, Francie & Carlo
X X X X X X X X X — Phil —

Sunday July 15, 1945/Wendover, Utah

Dear Mary,

Everything out here is going along according to schedule. The
weather is nice. I took some more suntan today until some clouds
came over and now it looks like rain. But it hardly rains out here. I'm
feeling pretty good and I can't kick. Just a few more days now and if
nothing comes up then I'll come home. You know I used to be real
excited about coming home, but somehow, I don't feel too excited
anymore, although I want to come home as much as possible. Human
nature I guess. Besides I have been coming home too much in the past
1½ years. *[Phil is understating his excitement. After all he's been
counting off the days for the past few weeks. He probably feels
ambivalent because of the long train trip ahead of him. The last time
he rode that train, the constant motion made him ill. In addition, he
probably feels depressed because he is sick and tired of being in the
military.]*

Well so-long for now and God bless you all.

Love To: Ma, Pa, Mary, Tony, Francie & Carlo
X X X X X X X X — Phil —

Monday July 16, 1945/Wendover, Utah

Dear Mary,

Not much to say today except that everything out here seems to be going along pretty good and I can't kick. Just 2½ more days and I'll be on my way. When you get this letter, I should be near Denver, Colorado on my way home. I sure hope nothing comes up to spoil this furlough.

I hope you are all feeling well out there. I'm in pretty good shape. Today I got a V-Mail from Frankie. *[V-Mail, or victory mail, provided a quicker way for GI's overseas to receive and send mail. A letter was written on a special form, then photographed, along with other letters. The roll of film was shipped, developed, and delivered in at least half the time required to deliver other letters. The only drawbacks were that the photograph of the letter was smaller than a regular letter and therefore more difficult to read, and the format restricted the length of the letter.]* The kid's okay. At times he just doesn't feel like writing, so he doesn't write. I also heard from Carmen the other day and he too is doing pretty good. Well so-long for now and God bless you all.

Love To: Ma, Pa, Mary, Tony, Francie & Carlo
X X X X X X X X X — Phil —

Tuesday July 17, 1945/Wendover, Utah

Dear Mary,

. . . Well, the day after tomorrow is the great day. I sure hope nothing comes up, but if anything does, it just can't be helped so no use even worrying about it.

Tomorrow is Shadow's birthday and he'll be 26 years old. He's getting up in the world, isn't he? I'm right behind him though. The weather out here is pretty good. I'm getting quite a bit of suntan for myself and I guess when I come home, I'll get more. By the way, I'm pretty sure this is the last letter you'll get before I get there. If you get this on a Saturday, I may pull in the next day I guess or maybe a little earlier, depends on the connections I make. So-long for now and God bless you all.

Love To: Ma, Pa, Mary, Tony, Francie & Carlo
X X X X X X X X — Phil —

Wednesday July 18, 1945/Wendover, Utah

Dear Mary,

This is the last day I'll be here so it's the last letter I'll write to you. Tomorrow morning, I'll be on my way home and I hope I get there alright. It's like a big dream each time I come. . . . I should be home way before you get this letter. I know I'm writing it for nothing, but I'm used to writing every day.

I wrote Frankie and Carmen today and I told them I was coming home. So-long again and God bless you all.

> Love To: Ma, Pa, Mary, Tony, Francie & Carlo
> X X X X X X X — Phil.

[Phil Aquila received his furlough and left as scheduled on July 19, 1945, for a 20-day furlough at home with his wife, baby, and family in Buffalo, New York. He wouldn't return to Wendover Field, Utah, until August 10th at 10 p.m. While he was on furlough, the United States dropped an atomic bomb on Hiroshima on August 6th, killing nearly 80,000 people; two days later, the Soviet Union declared war on Japan; the following day, August 9th, the United States dropped another atomic bomb on Japan, this time on Nagasaki, killing another 60,000 people instantly. Phil didn't know it at the time, but he had helped train the crew of the Enola Gay *at Wendover Field in chemical warfare and his brother Carmen had been aboard a vessel that helped escort the first atomic bomb to the Pacific so it could be loaded onto the* Enola Gay.*]*

> Saturday August 11, 1945/Wendover, Utah

Dear Mary,

Last night at 10:00 p.m. (midnight Buffalo) I arrived here. I was on time okay, in fact I had 2 hours to spare. It's the same old place and I'll have to do the same old job. These first few days will be the hardest for me because I'll have to straighten out my work and also get used to being out of Buffalo again.

It was really swell to see all of you and I miss you all a great deal. That's to be expected I guess. I'll have to write to everyone again to get started all over with my correspondence. I found 4 letters from Carmen, 1 from Frankie, 1 from [cousin] Johnny, and 1 from [cousin] Angelo, and of course one from you and my wife that I hadn't received before I left for furlough. *[He felt as backed up on his correspondence as he was in his job managing the chemical warfare supplies.]*

Well, Russia is in the war against Japan, and Japan has asked for peace. It wouldn't surprise me if by the time you get this letter, the war will be over and I'll be sweating out my discharge.

My train trip here was as bad as always. I started from Buffalo at 8:00 Wednesday morning and arrived here at 10:00 Friday night. So you can see for yourself just how long it takes to get out here. I made a good connection in Chicago.

Well, I guess that's all for today, but I'll be back again tomorrow. Till then, so-long and God bless you all.

> Love To: Ma, Pa, Mary, Tony, Francie & Carlo
> X X X X X X X X X — Phil.

Sunday August 12, 1945/Wendover, Utah

Dear Mary,

. . . Right now I'm sweating out Japan's surrender and I guess everybody is wondering what Japan [will] choose to do. Boy, everyone will sure be happy if Japan does quit. Here's hoping anyway.

Well, I'm still trying to get used to being out here again, but I'll have to get used to it whether I like it or not. I just got through writing to Carmen and Frankie. Well, I guess that's all for today, but I'll be back again tomorrow. Till then so-long and God bless you all.

Love To: Ma, Pa, Mary, Tony, Francie & Carlo
X X X X X X X X X X X — Phil

Monday August 13, 1945/Wendover, Utah

Dear Mary,

. . . Those Japs still are stalling around before they surrender. They have no alternative. If they don't all their cities [will be destroyed] and millions of Japs will die. So don't worry even though they are stalling, peace has got to come sooner or later.

I bet you and the rest have been thinking that I had trouble with my wife [while home on furlough]. No, it wasn't trouble.

It's the usual thing, by my visiting everybody too much. Every body has their own personal troubles I guess. But don't worry about it. *[Phil's wife was upset because she felt he spent too much time visiting his relatives instead of being with her and the baby. Had he spent more time with her, then other family members would have been upset that he didn't visit them. Undoubtedly, numerous soldiers had to deal with similar problems. Psychologists have used the term "furlough syndrome" to describe the disillusionment and problems suffered by GI's when they went home on furlough.]* I hope you are all feeling fine. So-long for now and God bless you all.

Love To: Ma, Pa, Mary, Tony, Francie & Carlo
X X X X X X X X X — Phil —

* * * * * * * * * * * * * * *
Tuesday August 14, 1945
* * * * * * * * * * * * * * *

Dear Mary,

Peace is finally here, and I'm so happy. I'm happy for Ma, my wife, and all of you home, and all our brothers. After waiting so long, it seems like a dream that the war is finally over.

For a lot of people it will never be over. I know everyone out there is as happy as could be. I've been standing by a radio since Saturday night when this peace move first started. Boy, things have sure gone fast since the day I got my furlough [on July 19th]. Everybody is celebrating. I'd like to get drunk because I'm so glad I'm still alive, but I don't drink, so I'll take in a usual movie and then celebrate with an ice cream sundae for 15 cents.

Well, so-long for today and God bless you all.

Love To: Ma, Pa, Mary, Tony, Francie & Carlo
X X X X X X X X X X — Phil —

P.S. I'm sure glad for Tony. I'd have hated so much if he got drafted. The end of the war finds us 4 guys in uniform, exactly the same as when we left, so be mighty happy.

Wednesday August 15, 1945/Wendover, Utah

Dear Mary,

Just the day after Victory out here and everything seems to be going along pretty good out here. So far they haven't given us any day off or anything so everybody is still carrying on just as if the war hadn't ended just yet. I'm glad it's all over with though, but I still may be sent overseas. Nobody knows just yet.

Well, much as I'd hate to go I guess I'll have to if I'm told. No use worrying about it, though, because it won't do much good anyway. It sure is a laugh how everybody thinks he'll get out right away. Some day, though, I'll be able to come home again, so don't worry about it.

The weather out here has been pretty hot. It's much hotter here than it is out there. Oh well, I can take it I guess. I bet this war's end is a surprise to Frankie. He's the guy who always told me that Japan was ready to lose 10,000,000 men in this war and he said it wouldn't be over not even by 1947.

Well, I guess I'll close for now and I hope you are all feeling fine and happy out there. Out here I'm in pretty good shape and I can't kick too much. God bless you all.

Love To: Ma, Pa, Mary, Tony, Francie & Carlo
X X X X X X X X X X — Phil —

P.S. There's no more gasoline rationing. It's too bad I couldn't be home when I could get a lot of gas.

Thursday August 16, 1945/Wendover, Utah

Dear Mary,

. . . Today I got ½ day off to celebrate Japan's defeat. Not bad for a soldier. I guess a lot of soldiers out in the Pacific couldn't even celebrate. That's the way it goes. Soldiers win the wars and civilians do the celebrating with 2 days off. It doesn't bother me, though. I just can't wait to get out.

You know, I've been thinking a little. There's going to be a Depression pretty soon, and if I stayed in the army, I could be making more money than if I got out. But no, I won't stay in because I'm too sick of it. *[It didn't take him too long to change his mind on that one. Actually, Phil was not the only one worried about a possible depression following the end of the war. When President Roosevelt had cut back government spending in 1937, the economy plunged almost to its 1932 levels. Many people, including Phil apparently, feared that once the U.S. government stopped spending so much on the war effort, another serious economic depression would result.]*

I hope Ma and all of you are feeling fine and in good spirits. I don't think it'll be too long before Frankie comes to the U.S. Naturally, he'll get discharged way before I do [because of overseas duty].

Well, so-long for now and God bless you all.

Love To: Ma, Pa, Mary, Tony, Francie & Carlo

X X X X X X X X X X — Phil —

Friday August 17, 1945/Wendover, Utah

Dear Mary,

. . . I'm glad Ma went to see my son and I'm sorry my wife wasn't home. She had to go downtown. . . . Everything out here seems to be going along pretty good and I hope it's the same out there for all of you. Well, so-long for now and God bless you all.

Love To: Ma, Pa, Mary, Tony, Francie & Carlo

X X X X X X X X X — Phil

Saturday August 18, 1945/Wendover, Utah

Dear Mary,

. . . Nothing new out here. I do just about the same things day in and day out. There's rumors around that they'll be closing up this place in a few months, and that means that I'll be shipped out. Of course, I hope it's here in the states, but if I have to go across, I'll go, much as I hate it.

It's going on two weeks that I've left you in Buffalo, and it seems like two years already. Remember at the station, the train pulled in right on time? I really was surprised. It just goes to show that you've got to be at the station at the right time because you may miss the train. Well, I guess that's all for now, so till tomorrow so-long and God bless you all.

Love To: Ma, Pa, Mary, Tony, Francie, and Carlo

X X X X X X X X X X — Phil —

Sunday August 19, 1945/Wendover, Utah

Dear Mary,

. . . I've really spent a week of misery out here trying to get used to it all again. I can never tell you how much I really hate it, but I guess you can imagine it for yourselves. Today I wrote a letter to Carmen and to Frankie. Now that the war is over, I really don't see any reason to continue writing as much as I have. I'm really pretty tired of it after 2½ years of doing it. So don't worry if I only write a couple of letters each week to you later on.

No, nothing is wrong between my wife and me. Just misunderstandings at times. Normal things that cause quarrels between any couple. Don't worry about . . . the stories there are in the newspapers about unfaithful wives and all that stuff. My wife has been good, and I've got all the faith in the world in her, and I still think she'll be a better in-law than any of our in-laws. Well, so-long for now and God bless you all.

Love To: Ma, Pa, Mary, Tony, Francie & Carlo
X X X X X X X X X X — Phil —

Monday August 20, 1945/Wendover, Utah

Dear Mary,
. . . Life out here seems to be going on the same as usual and I can't kick. So far nothing has come up, but I expect things to change pretty soon. We are still operating on a war-time basis, but I don't see no reason for it anymore. It sure looks like a lot of guys will be out of work pretty soon all over. As yet, it's not my problem, but it will be in due time.

Well, I'll close for now, so God bless you all.

Love To: Ma, Pa, Mary, Tony, Francie & Carlo
X X X X X X X X X — Phil —

Monday August 20, 1945/Wendover, Utah

Dear Mary,
I just got the letter you wrote last Thursday. I did write one letter for today, but I thought I'd write again. Yep, I can imagine how happy you were, and Ma especially. Us guys are spared, and that's a lot to be thankful for. As for discharges, Frankie will be home first, and I may be second, but Carmen may even get out before I do. As far as that goes, Shadow may also get out before I do.

I'm sorry you didn't hear from me for such a long time, but I did write everyday. My wife never tells me to whom to write. I do my own writing. If she seemed happy when you told her you didn't get any mail, I'm sure she didn't mean it that way. I'm sure by now you've received my daily letters and I hope you get them regularly. *[So much for Phil's plan not to write to his family everyday anymore. See letter of August 19, 1945. He apparently realizes that he'd better keep writing, or else jealousy will result. Now that the war is over, family quarrels are looming on the horizon. His wife and his sister seem to be vying for Phil's attention and primary allegiance. These family problems first surfaced when he was home on furlough, and now that the war isn't life-threatening anymore everyone seems to be zeroing in on festering in-law problems.]*

As for my wife buying the furniture, she can, but she won't have no place to put it. I guess it's the thrill a girl wants in getting her furniture as soon as possible. When we set up our home, I'll give the word because nobody knows better than I when I'll be home and I won't be home for a long time yet.

I'm glad you like my son's proofs. I can't wait till I get a picture of him, myself. So-long for now and God bless you all.

Love To: Ma, Pa, Mary, Tony, Francie & Carlo
X X X X X X X X X X — Phil —

Tuesday August 21, 1945/Wendover, Utah

Dear Mary,

Not too much to say today. Everything is going along alright, but I'm kind of disgusted with the way things are going for me. I feel so helpless to do or say anything from out here. I hope you are all feeling fine out there. The weather out here is pretty good and I hope it's the same out there. So-long and excuse this real short letter, because I'm in no mood to write to anybody. God bless you all.

Love To: Ma, Pa, Mary, Tony, Francie & Carlo
X X X X X X X X — Phil —

[Apparently, Phil is still smarting from the letter his sister wrote that was negative toward his wife. He seems frustrated that the relationship between his wife and sister is deteriorating and he's too far away to straighten it out. Most likely, now that the war is over, his relatives at home feel they can discuss unpleasant things that might upset him. This suggests that after the war celebrations were over, disillusionment and feelings of emotional letdown set in. Very likely other soldiers and civilians were facing exactly the same types of emotional letdowns.]

Wednesday August 22, 1945/Wendover, Utah

Dear Mary,

Another day is slowly going by and everything seems to be going along pretty good out here, and I hope it's the same for all of you out there.

My wife told me that June left for Tennessee [to see Shadow] and she said June didn't say good-bye to her. You see, my wife holds it against June and Shadow not saying good-bye once when they came to Buffalo and then she also complains about Shadow not saying good-bye when he just left. So naturally, I got involved in the mess and I'm sick of it, so for my part I'll prefer if June don't call [my wife] Mary up and Mary don't call June up. I'm tired of trying to make peace so the best thing is to be enemies and then someday when we all come home and things are normal we can all make up. Right. So I'm not going to worry about any petty arguments. I have my own problems to worry about. Well, I guess I'll close for now so take it easy and God bless you all.

Love To: Ma, Pa, Mary, Tony, Francie & Carlo

X X X X X X X — Phil

[Phil seems extremely frustrated and angry, because he is caught in the middle of arguments between his wife and other relatives. The whole thing seems petty to him, and he simply wants everyone to back off until he can come home and straighten out the problem. Although this particular set of arguments was unique to the Aquilas, the same general pattern of bickering was probably affecting numerous GIs and their wives or sweethearts. Newlyweds have difficulties working out their relationships with each other and in-laws during the best of circumstances. During the World War II era, it was even more problematic, since couples were often separated by thousands of miles.]

Thursday August 23, 1945/Wendover, Utah

Dear Mary,

I just received the letter you wrote last Sunday and I'm glad to hear that you are all happy about everything during the past few weeks. I should be happy too, and I really am.

You told me about dropping June off at the station. I'm glad she and Shadow can get to see each other again. If I was a little closer to home, I'd also might let my wife come out here. It's too far for a girl to travel alone, though, and also it takes about $90 for her train fare so I just can't do it. I'm glad June's baby is feeling fine now. When I saw him he looked so small and helpless, but I know someday, he'll be nice and big, and Shadow, June, and all of us will be proud of him.

My son has a cold yet, and it bothers his eyes, but if I know my son, he'll be okay in no time. As for telling me that maybe it was my wife that told me not to write home [to you], don't worry about it. I know her actions seem odd, but some day she'll change and realize that you are all her friends. She probably thinks that you are all against her. Try talking to her about things and reassure her face-to-face that you haven't anything against her. I know when Ma says something she doesn't mean them. Just be real informal with her. If she comes down [to the house], let her help with the dishes. Make her feel like one of the family, catch on?

I'm sorry to hear that Ma still has those awful pains. I guess we'll just have to keep faith in God and hope that everything will go better.

As for us guys having more time on our hands, so far that hasn't happened. We are still on a war-time basis. Well, I guess that's all for now, but I'll be back again tomorrow. Till then so-long and God bless you all.

Love To: Ma, Pa, Mary, Tony, Francie & Carlo

X X X X X X X X — Phil —

Friday August 24, 1945/Wendover, Utah

Dear Mary,

I hope that Ma is feeling better these days? Pretty soon just as quickly as they get organized, us guys will be coming home, so she may as well start looking forward to it now. *[He's trying to give his mother something to look forward to in order to distract her from her pains.]*

Frankie, in my opinion, will be the first guy to come home. They may give him a discharge right away or give him a 30 day furlough first and then let him report for his discharge at some nearby camp around New York State some place. So I wouldn't be sending that guy anymore packages anymore, because I doubt if they'll get there in time for him to receive them. As for me, I'm not worried about a discharge, just so I don't go overseas anymore. They can't keep me in too long anyway. . . . Well, I guess that's all for now so take it easy and God bless you all.

Love To: Ma, Pa, Mary, Tony, Francie, and Carlo

X X X X X X X X X — Phil —

Saturday August 25, 1945/Wendover, Utah

Dear Mary,

Just a few more lines for today, hoping that this letter finds you all feeling fine and in the best of health out there. I hope, especially, that Ma is feeling fine and that the pains she has don't bother her too much.

Out here things are just about the same and I can't kick too much about anything, except that I think they're taking their time about discharging the men. Why in heck can't they give the guys a long furlough and let them go home? If there isn't any employment he'll have his army pay to [fall] back on, and then when he gets a job he can get his discharge. No, instead they keep him in the army and he doesn't accomplish anything. It's as if a guy has a thousand years to live on this earth when actually he has 40 or 50. It sure beats the hell out of me. Well so long for now and God bless you all. *[Phil is mirroring the feelings of most soldiers. The war is over, and now they desperately want out of the army.]*

Love To: Ma, Pa, Mary, Tony, Francie, and Carlo

X X X X X X X X X — Phil.

Sunday August 26, 1945/Wendover, Utah

Dear Mary,

Yesterday I received the letter you wrote last Tuesday and I was very glad to hear from you and especially that Ma is feeling as well as possible. I'm glad you've been receiving my mail regularly. The reason you had to wait so long at first was because it took me so long to get out here and then there was 2 days of holiday and I guess they stopped delivering mail. But now I see no reason why you shouldn't be getting the mail regularly from now on. *[He's emphasizing that he is writing regularly, and there is no truth to the belief that his wife told him not to write.]*

. . . I just got through finishing a letter to Frankie and a letter to Carmen. Really they weren't letters. I had some V-Mail left so I thought I'd finish it up before they came home.

Yes, June should be with Shadow right now and I bet they are both happy to be with each other again. After we all come home things will be alright again. When I'm on furlough I'm bound to make some people unhappy. It just can't be helped. My wife comes first and I just can't make her unhappy for somebody else even if she is wrong at times. So I guess if there are any complaints, they just can't be helped, and we'll have to wait to straighten them out.

I see in the papers where they won't draft anybody over 26 years old. So if they try to draft Tony, it will be only out of spite and jealousy, and I think he should fight his case in the highest board there is. Well, I guess that's all for now, so till tomorrow, so-long and God bless you all.

Love To: Ma, Pa, Mary, Tony, Francie & Carlo
X X X X X X X X X X — Phil.

Monday August 27, 1945/Wendover, Utah

Dear Mary,

Just another day going by out here. Nothing new happening and the days go by pretty slow, but I'll keep at it. I'm feeling pretty good here and I hope Ma and the rest of you are also feeling fine out there. The weather out here has been chilly at night and warm in the afternoons, so all in all it's pretty good. I know the nights out there should be cool by this time. It won't be long now and fall will be here and the cold weather and snow will start all over again. I wish I could say I could be there for Christmas, but no use kidding myself or all of you because I know very well that I won't be. There's a very good chance that Frankie will, though. It's too bad he hasn't got all the points guys get for being over 2 years and more. But Frankie hasn't seen no action so that accounts for it. It's better that way. Sooner or later a guy gets out and it makes no difference how many points he's got.

Well so long for now and God bless you all.

Love To: Ma, Pa, Mary, Tony, Francie & Carlo
X X X X X X X X X — Phil.

Tuesday August 28, 1945/Wendover, Utah

Dear Mary,

. . . It's too bad those awful pains keep bothering Ma, and I do hope they'd stop. Maybe someday she'll be well again. As for me drinking some beer when all four of us [brothers] are home, don't worry, I will. I'll break my promise for that time [i.e. he will toast on that occasion even though he doesn't drink].

Life out here is going on the same. It's pretty monotonous, but I don't expect it to be a picnic anyway, so I'll just make the most out of it. The weather is also cooling down, although I expect a lot more hot days. Well, I guess I'll close for now so take it easy and God bless you all.

Love To: Ma, Pa, Mary, Tony, Francie & Carlo
X X X X X X X X X X — Phil.

P.S. It's too bad about all the people losing their jobs out there. I guess they can live off the money they've saved without starving.

Wednesday August 29, 1945/Wendover, Utah

Dear Mary,

. . . I'm glad you went over to see my son and wife. Yep, my son has had a cold for a long while, but it's to be expected. When someone catches a cold in a house generally several other members get it too. I sure hope he gets rid of it. As for him playing the piano, he sure bangs it. I put him on the piano stool one day while I was home and I showed him how to bang it with his hands, and since then he likes it a lot, especially when people look at him. . . . I'll close for now so take it easy and God bless you all.

Love To: Ma, Pa, Mary, Tony, Francie & Carlo
X X X X X X X X X X X — Phil —

Thursday August 30, 1945/Wendover, Utah

Dear Mary,

. . . I just got a letter from June and she said that Carmen's ship was in the newspaper and that it's one of the warships in Tokyo Bay. Boy, Carmen sure is seeing the world. Tell Ma not to worry about him anymore, because he's more or less visiting the world now on a nice clean ship.

I just got through moving into another barracks. They're always moving around in this darn army. Oh well, some day it'll end, I hope. Well, I guess that's all for now, so take it easy and God bless you all.

Love To: Ma, Pa, Mary, Tony, Francie & Carlo,
X X X X X X X X X — Phil —

Friday August 31, 1945/Wendover, Utah

Dear Mary,

I received the letter you wrote last Monday and as always, I'm glad to hear from you. I'm glad you all are feeling as well as possible. Out here I'm just about the same. As for my writing too much, I don't. I just write you a short letter each day, and it's no bother at all. As for me calling up, I changed my mind, when I saw the telephone bills with my own eyes. Besides, the war has ended and there's nothing to worry about, tell Ma that. I promise, though, if anything new develops I'll call up right away, so meantime tell Ma not to worry. I'm not even calling up my wife. *[Phil is treading very carefully here. His sister, after complaining that he was not writing enough, is now telling him that he writes too much. Either she feels guilty or she is trying to make him feel guilty. Phil does not want to fall into the same trap regarding phone calls. He makes it clear that he is not going to be calling either his wife or his family.]*

Yep, Shadow must've sure been happy to see June and Ronnie. That's the way things go, I guess. Well, so-long for now and God bless you all.

Love To: Ma, Pa, Mary, Tony, Francie & Carlo,
X X X X X X X X X — Phil —

Saturday September 1, 1945/Wendover Field, Utah

Dear Mary,

. . . I hope by now you can easily get a lot of meat and other food. And also I hope that Tony can get his share of cigarettes again. Out here we are still on six packs of cigarettes each week, but I expect they'll do away with that too pretty soon. Also pretty soon we'll only work a half day on Saturdays and be off on Sundays, and we'll observe every holiday that comes along.

All in all this peacetime army life shouldn't be too bad after it starts going. Of course, I'm ready to come home anytime they give me the word to do so.

It's going to be quite a headache to get rid of all this war stuff they've got laying around but it must be done somehow or other.

I hope that Ma and the rest of you are all feeling as well as possible these days. I don't write too many letters [to other people] from out here. I'm really sick and tired of writing and by the time I get a discharge all I'll be writing to will be you and my wife. I wrote Carmen and Frankie last Sunday and I'll write to them again next Sunday. The war is over with so there's no use in monkeying around with a lot of letters anymore. *[He was writing frequently to his brothers to keep up their morale while the war was going on. And even though he complains about it and threatens to stop, he continues to write to everyone.]* Well, I guess that will be all for tonight. So till tomorrow, so long and God bless you all.

Love To: Ma, Pa, Mary, Tony, Francie & Carlo

X X X X X X X X X — Phil.

Sunday September 2, 1945/Wendover, Utah

Dear Mary,

Just another Sunday out here. I haven't written to no one except you and my wife, and then I didn't write much at that. I just feel too warm and restless, so the best thing to do is lay on my bunk and read a magazine and take life easy. . . .

Tomorrow is Labor Day and it's a holiday out here. I'm sure by next Labor Day we'll all be home for good. I bet Frankie and Carmen will have a lot of stories to talk about. Well that's all for now so take it easy and God bless you all.

Love To: Ma, Pa, Mary, Tony, Francie & Carlo

X X X X X X X X — Phil.

Monday September 3, 1945/Wendover, Utah

Dear Mary,

. . . I'm glad to hear that my wife is coming down [to the house] and I hope she did. Yep, Nicky [his wife's brother] came home again [on furlough]. I don't know how he did it, but in my opinion, I think he's headed for Japan so they let him come home for a little while. Don't tell anybody about it though.

Today is Labor Day and it's a holiday out here. Everything seems to be going along pretty good here and I hope you can say the same for yourselves out there. . . . Well, I haven't much to say so I'll close for now so take it easy and God bless you all.

Love To: Ma, Pa, Mary, Tony, Francie & Carlo

X X X X X X X X X X X X — Phil.

Tuesday September 4, 1945/Wendover, Utah

Dear Mary,

. . . Same old grind day in and day out and naturally I get sick of it but I guess I can last a while longer yet. I really don't have much to say because there are no new developments out here. I'm eating pretty good as usual and I sleep well at night so I guess that doesn't leave me much to complain about. I mostly write my wife all the extra time I get. Sometimes I write her at least 2 letters, sometimes 3 each day, sometimes 4 each day, and also at times I write her 5 or 6 letters each day. I've also written her 7, 8, and yesterday I even wrote her 10 letters and each one of them was long too. So you see I actually do nothing out here except see a show or get busy writing letters, 99% of them to my wife. She does a good job writing me too, but I doubt if there's anyone in the whole army who writes as many letters as I do. So it is that I'll be mighty glad when I get out of this army so that I won't have to write letters to nobody again. I like to keep everybody happy, but I really hate to write letters. *[He wasn't exaggerating about writing all those letters to his wife. Unfortunately, the letters were later destroyed, except for a handful. Phil complained about writing the letters, but apparently he derived great satisfaction from writing. It not only allowed him to assure people that he was okay, but it also enabled him to feel as if he had some stability in his own life. He remained close to loved ones at home and brothers and friends in the army through correspondence. He often claimed he did it to keep everyone's morale up. No doubt it did, but in the process he was also keeping his own morale up.]* Well, I guess I'll be closing for now so till tomorrow, so-long and God bless you all.

Love To: Ma, Pa, Mary, Tony, Francie & Carlo

X X X X X X X X X X — Phil —

Wednesday September 5, 1945/Wendover, Utah

Dear Mary,

Here I am again to write you a few lines to let you know that everything out here is still going along as well as possible and I hope it continues to be that way. I hope you all are feeling in the best possible health out there and that goes for Ma especially.

Yesterday I received a letter from Frankie dated August 20th. He's feeling pretty good and he's very happy about the war ending. He don't exactly know when he's coming home but it can be almost any day now. Yep, it'll sure be good when he does come home. It'll be like a dream to him, to Ma, and to all of you. So don't worry it will be a reality soon, so keep your chins up.

As for me, nothing is being said about my going overseas or not, so I'm not even worrying about it no more. I guess two years of sweating out my going across is enough for any guy. Yep, Frankie and even Carmen haven't even seen the new additions to the Aquila family. Frankie hasn't even seen Ronnie yet. I guess he sure is in for a lot of surprises.

The weather out here is hot as usual but I'm used to it by now. I hope it's okay out there. This is a fine exhibition of typewriting isn't it?

Don't tell Francie or she'll get sore, but I think I can type faster and better than she can. I'm even thinking about getting an office job when I get out of the army, because there's no sense in letting my talent go to waste. Well, I guess I'll be closing for now so take it easy and God bless you all.
                         Love To: Ma, Pa, Mary, Tony, Francie & Carlo
                         X X X X X X X X X X X — Phil

                         Thursday September 6, 1945/Wendover, Utah
Dear Mary,
    Everything out here seems to be going along pretty good again today so there's hardly anything I can talk about, but as usual I may as well say something anyway seeing that it doesn't cost anything. Yesterday I received the letter you wrote last Saturday and also the overseas edition of the BUFFALO EVENING NEWS. Thanks a lot for both of them. I was glad to hear that you are all feeling as well as possible out there and I hope as usual that it continues to be that way for all of you.
    We used to get six packs of cigarettes each week. But this week they raised it to ten packs per week. In the near future, they'll probably do away with rationing of cigarettes altogether.
    The weather out here has been sort of cold all day long. It rained all last night and I guess that kind of cooled things off quite a bit. I kind of like it this way, though. Well, as I said there's no new developments out here so that leaves me exactly nothing to write about. So take it easy and God bless you all and don't worry about anything.
                         Love To: Ma, Pa, Mary, Tony, Francie & Carlo
                         X X X X X X X X X X — Phil —

                         Friday September 7, 1945/Wendover Field, Utah
Dear Mary,
    Once again I'm back to write you a few more lines and let you know that everything out here is going along pretty good. I hope it's the same for you all out there. Yesterday I wrote you a letter about the situation between you and my wife and I hope you went down and had a talk with her. I'd like nothing better than to see you both getting along nicely. I think the only reason that there's been any kind of misunderstanding before is because both parties don't get together and talk things out face to face. Well, I hope that things will go better in the future. From where I am I can judge both our family and my wife and believe me there's nothing really wrong, but to satisfy my wife just go and have a talk with her and straighten out things once and for all. . . . Well, I'll close for now and tell Ma not to worry about anything. So-long and God bless you all.
                         Love To: Ma, Pa, Mary, Tony, Francie & Carlo
                         X X X X X X X X X — Phil

Saturday September 8, 1945/Wendover, Utah

Dear Mary,

This is just one of those slow days going by with nothing to do or say. . . . I suppose Carlo is back in school now. I guess he's in 6th grade this year, isn't he? The weather out here is nice and cool and rather cold in the morning. I suppose the leaves out there are falling off the trees. Out here I can't tell if it's spring, summer, autumn, or winter except by the heat and cold, outside of that it always looks the same.

Well, I hope Ma and all of you are feeling in top shape today. So-long for now and God bless you all.

Love To: Ma, Pa, Mary, Tony, Francie & Carlo

X X X X X X X X X — Phil —

Sunday September 9, 1945/Wendover, Utah

Dear Mary,

Just another Sunday going by out here and everything is dull and quiet as usual. . . . Incidently, this base is on Pacific Coast Time again, so now I'm three hours behind Buffalo time. So when it's 5:00 o'clock in the afternoon there, it's only 2 o'clock in the afternoon out here. It makes me feel pretty far away.

Well I hope Ma and all of you are feeling fine out there. Now that there's no gas rationing, you can take Ma for some nice long rides. So-long for now and God bless you all.

Love To: Ma, Pa, Mary, Tony, Francie & Carlo

X X X X X X X X X — Phil.

Monday September 10, 1945/Wendover Field, Utah

Dear Mary,

Today I received the letter you wrote on Labor Day and I was glad to hear that you are all getting along fine. Yep, I remember two years ago when I spent Labor Day at home there. Maybe by next year on Labor Day, I might be home for good, at least I hope so anyway. I'm sorry I forgot to send Carlo a card for his birthday on August 26th. I know it is his birthday at that time, but believe me, I really had a lot of problems to solve last month and it slipped by me completely. You tell Carlo that next year I won't forget that easily.

I was glad to hear that my wife and son came down to our house for a while on Labor Day, and I'm glad she ate some sausage while she was there. Yep, my son was 7 months old and each day he grows bigger and bigger. He'll be walking for sure by the time I get to come home.

It sure was nice of Pa to make $14.65 in three days work out in the

Fig. 2.9. Photograph of Phil's wife, Mary, holding "Little Phil" in September 1945. (Philip L. Aquila Collection)

farm. Everything out here seems to be going along pretty good today. . . . So take it easy and God bless you all.

Love To: Ma, Pa, Mary, Tony, Francie & Carlo

X X X X X X X X X X — Phil

Tuesday September 11, 1945/Wendover Field, Utah

Dear Mary,

. . . I hope you don't mind these little typewritten letters, but between you and me I'm kind of tired writing with a pen. I'm glad you finally heard from Frankie. Tell Ma not to worry about him when you don't get mail from him for a few weeks. The kid told me that he's just plain tired of writing letters and that he'll write only when he's got something to say, so again tell Ma not to worry about him. *[All the brothers seem to be sick of writing letters now that the war is over and there is less concern about their safety.]* He should be coming home mighty soon and if I'm right he won't say anything until he lands in California and then he'll call up from there. So if I was you people I'd be kind of expecting Frankie or Carmen any one of these nights.

One of the reasons I'm not calling up these days is because I know that if one of our brothers lands in California they are going to call up and you'll have a mighty big telephone bill to pay, so just tell Ma that the war is over with now and that I'm still out here and not to worry about me because everything out here with me is going along okay. Besides, I've been home so many times that she saw for herself that there's not any need to ever worry about me. I sure wish I could hear the same radio programs you people hear concerning the discharging of men from the army. The only thing I heard about it was last night and they said that by September 1st, 1946, most men with 2 years service regardless if they are married or not will get discharged. I expect a man with a wife and kid will be out a little sooner though. Well, I guess that's all for now so take it easy and God bless you all.

Love To: Ma, Pa, Mary, Tony, Francie & Carlo

X X X X X X X X X X — Phil.

Wednesday September 12, 1945/Wendover Field, Utah

Dear Mary,

It's all quiet on this Western Front today, and I hope as usual that it continues to be that way. . . . There's nothing new about discharges as yet, but I expect, as soon as Congress starts working things will happen kind of fast as far as getting out of the army goes. Things out here are going on a war-time basis as usual, and it kind of burns me up because there's no point in it anymore unless they are preparing for another war or something. I'm telling you, they can find more ways of wasting money needlessly. If only they'd give the money to somebody who really needs it instead of building things for war the way they are doing. It beats the Hell out of me, because I'll never be able to understand these Army big shots, at least they think they're big anyway.

By now June should be home from Memphis. In her last letter to me she said that she was leaving Monday morning of September 10th. Well, at least they had some time together anyway.

Well, I guess that's all for now so take it easy and God bless you all and till tomorrow so-long.

Love To: Ma, Pa, Mary, Tony, Francie & Carlo
X X X X X X X X X X X — Phil —

Thursday September 13, 1945/Wendover, Utah

Dear Mary,

It's a bright sunny day out here not too hot or too cold. Everything seems to be going along pretty good as usual and I can't complain too much about anything. I'm in top shape, and I guess that helps my morale quite a bit also. I hope Ma and all the rest of you can say the same for yourselves out there.

Last night I heard an announcement on the radio, which said that six million men would be discharged by next July 1, 1946. Naturally, I'll be included in that. We can only hope for the best I guess. I personally believe that Frankie will be out long before that time is here. I guess we'll have our problems when we do get out. I know I will, but somehow or other I know I can manage what ever comes up be it hard or easy.

It is nice that Frank M. is coming home, but I'm not concerned with him or nobody else. All I can say he's lucky to be alive and that goes the same for anybody coming home. Take it from me, if a guy is no darn good when he got drafted he'll be more of a bum when he gets back, because this army is really the place to get all the [bad] habits there are in life.

Well, I guess that's all for now, so till tomorrow, take it easy and God bless you all.

Love To: Ma, Pa, Mary, Tony, Francie & Carlo
X X X X X X X X X X — Phil

Friday September 14, 1945/Wendover, Utah

Dear Mary,

Just little ole me so there's nothing to get excited about. . . . The latest radio announcement states that 2,000,000 men will be discharged by this Christmas. Well, I won't be in that 2,000,000 men. I might be in the later groups that they'll discharge in the first half of next year. Yep, I guess I'm sweating it out in my own way out here. It sure is getting monotonous out here. Things go along pretty slow, but okay. I guess I'll just have to have some patience.

My son's two front teeth are coming out. Pretty soon he'll be looking real cute. No matter what, he's an Aquila baby so don't worry about it. The only thing he'll know about the Cavarella name is that it used to be his mother's name. Outside of that he'll be strictly an Aquila. *[Much of the tension between Phil's family and his wife's family involves the baby. The Aquilas are concerned that Phil's wife and her family are monopolizing the baby.]*

I hope that Ma is feeling fine these days. As for her recognizing Frankie's voice when he calls up, why of course she can. His voice hasn't changed a bit so don't worry about it. People think that just because a guy's been away for a long time that he'll be all changed. Look at me, you've seen me once in a while and you can never find anything that has changed me. Even if I was away for three years, it would still be the same.

Well, I guess that's all for now so till tomorrow, so-long and God bless you all.

Love To: Ma, Pa, Mary, Tony, Francie & Carlo

X X X X — Phil — X X X X

Saturday September 15, 1945/Wendover, Utah

Dear Mary,

I just got the letter Tony wrote last Tuesday telling me about Ma [being back in the hospital]. I feel so bad that I don't know just what to say. When I think of Ma suffering with those great pains, I can't help but feel worse than I ever did in my life. I can't understand why God wants things to be this way. I guess we can only pray that Ma will feel better again. I know how she dreads the hospital and doctors.

I feel like any guy feels when the mother he loves is sick. But tell Ma not to worry about me and that goes for all our other brothers. I know how you all have suffered out there. It's so very much harder for you out there to take than us guys who are away from home. We can only worry and imagine things but we actually don't feel the pain. All I know is that I want to be with Ma at this time, more than ever. Tonight, I'm going to call you up to find out how Ma is. One thing, don't spare the money where Ma is concerned. I've got a little money and I'm sure my wife will agree to let you have it if you need it. And if you think I should be home, don't hesitate to send for me. You'll have to send a telegram through to me telling me that I'm needed home for Ma and also the doctor will have to send a telegram through the Red Cross to this Red Cross requesting me home. But let's pray that she'll feel better. I wish Ma could be well and safe and that I could be suffering on some battlefield in her place. I know you all feel the same out there. No matter what, though, just keep your chin up, and let me be the least of all the worries because of all our family, I think I'm stronger than all of you when it comes to taking such news.

I'll close for now, but I hope when I call up tonight that you can tell me that Ma is actually getting better.

So-long for now, don't worry and God bless you all.

Love To: Ma, Pa, Mary, Tony, Francie & Carlo
X X X X X X X X X X X — Phil —

P.S. I'd suggest that you do try to get Frankie and Carmen home. Now that the war is over with, they may give them an Emergency Furlough. Try it anyway. If you can get Frankie home, he'll be the best medicine that Ma can have to make her recover. *[Phil realizes that the worrying and stress of having four of her sons in the war has taken a toll on his mother.]*

Sunday September 16, 1945/Wendover, Utah

Dear Mary,

Late last night—2:40 A.M. Buffalo time—I called you up. I'm sorry I scared you all. You see, I wanted to call when Tony would get back from work, but I couldn't make it. I called up because I had to know how Ma was feeling. The letter Tony wrote was on Tuesday and yesterday was Saturday. So I was curious to know how Ma had made out on Wednesday, Thursday, and Friday. Gee, I was so glad to hear that she'd be out of the hospital in a few days and I just can't wait till she's home. I tried to make the phone call as short as possible, because I know it would take a day's work for any one of you to pay for it. I was shouting in the phone, but you still couldn't hear me. I couldn't hear you either. That is I couldn't hear the words right. I guess some thing was wrong with the connection. I'll call up next month again when Ma is home, okay?

Is Ma in the same hospital [as last time]? If so, how close is she to the room where she was? I sure hope she'll get out real soon because I know she don't like it in a hospital. *[Phil wants all the details. Not only will they help him understand what's going on back in Buffalo, but they will make him feel like he is taking part in the ordeal. He feels desperate and frustrated being so far away from home at a time like this.]*

Naturally I'll always worry and things like that will shock me, but I always want to know the truth about everything as soon as possible when Ma is well and when she isn't. I hate to be thinking that last Tuesday I may have been in a show laughing, while Ma was suffering in pain, so please tell me everything and trust to God. Well, I'll close for now but tell Ma to get well because we are all thinking of her so very much. We want to come home and find her well in the house. Just tell her she's got to be brave and can't let us down now that the war has ended and we are all coming home. God bless you all.

Love To: Ma, Pa, Mary, Tony, Francie & Carlo
X X X X X X X X X — Phil —

Monday September 17, 1945/Wendover, Utah

Dear Mary,

. . . I'm glad [to hear] they treated Ma nicely at the hospital, and that she was starting to feel better and I hope to hear soon that she's out of the hospital. When she comes out this time, watch her more closely than ever. I'll be mighty relieved when I can come home to stay and the same goes for our other brothers.

As for my wife and that trouble, don't worry about it or her. I'm getting mighty sick of fighting over something that's stupid and silly. When I come home to stay it's going to be completely different. Nobody better ever dare think that I'm the one who's being bossed [around] because I'm not. I'm the boss in my family and what I say goes. I know only too well that my son is getting to be a Cavarella, but I'll be damned if he'll continue that way after I come home. Right now I'm stuck and Mary has to live where she's living, but if she ever has to take any baloney from anybody, she can easily move. Either our family and my wife are friends or I'm going to take Mary and Little Phil away to some other city where she and my son can't see her family either. I want to be fair and square about everything.

You've got a good excuse for not stopping at her house that Sunday. If they don't appreciate you even stopping to bring them the beans, then don't do them anymore favors. I'm sick and tired of it all. It's so stupid and silly. Right now I'm helpless because I'm away, but someday I'll be back again and straighten things out once and for all. I'll be damned, if it's not one thing it's something else, all the time. You tell my wife to tell you whatever grudges she holds against you and Ma. I've bawled her out plenty. I don't want to hurt her, but I can't help it. But I'll be damned if I'm going to make anybody tell me anything that's stupid. So-long for now but I'll be back tomorrow when I've cooled down a little. God bless you all and I hope Ma gets real well soon.

Love To: Ma, Pa, Mary, Tony, Francie & Carlo
X X X X X X X X X X — Phil —

[Obviously, Phil is under a tremendous amount of stress. First he hears that his mother is again in the hospital with tremendous pains; then he gets a letter complaining about the bickering between his wife and sister, and perhaps his mother, too. Yet he's a long way from home and

unable to deal directly with any of it. Undoubtedly everyone was under a considerable amount of stress because Phil's mother was in the hospital, perhaps in critical condition. That situation probably exacerbated, if not sparked, the in-law problems. What was happening to the Aquilas was probably very similar to what was playing out for hundreds of thousands, if not millions, of other American families who were also worn down by the anxieties caused by four long years of war. Now that the war was finally over, all their suppressed fears and emotions were bubbling to the surface. Subconsciously, the Aquilas and other families had probably believed that once the war was over their problems would disappear. Obviously that was not the case, and the continued separation of loved ones made those problems that much more difficult to deal with.]

Tuesday September 18, 1945/Wendover, Utah

Dear Mary,

Yesterday I was kind of angry, but today I feel pretty good. Whatever you do, don't tell Ma anything I say, because I know she'll feel bad about it. Really it's all silly and don't amount to anything at all. I don't worry about it at all, except that it burns me up at times.

I hope today finds Ma in better shape than usual. I know that you do a lot of work and worrying, but you don't have to. There's no need whatsoever any more for Ma to do a bit of hard work around the house. Keep watching her and bawl her out if necessary. As for washing clothes, there's you and Francie. I only wish that I could be there and if I was single I'd really wash those clothes for Ma. And as far as keeping that house clean, there's nothing to it. I sure hope not, but if my wife was sick, I know that I wouldn't let her do anything hard around the house. Well, when Ma comes home you just bawl her out when she tries and insists on working. Meantime, you can all pitch in and do the heavy work around the house. Carlo is big and can do a lot of work to develop his muscle. When Carmen comes back, I'm sure he'll be glad to help out home. I know that whenever I drop by the house and there's something hard to be done, I'll do it for you. Now that winter is coming again, don't even let Ma lift a bucket of coal. Well, right now it's up to all of you that are home. Us guys out here can only worry about you out there.

So-long for now and God bless you all.

Love To: Ma, Pa, Mary, Tony, Francie & Carlo

X X X X X X X X X X — Phil

Wednesday September 19, 1945/Wendover, Utah

Dear Mary,

. . . I can hardly wait to see what you say in your letters, especially now that Ma is sick. I know how she must suffer and how lonely she feels in that hospital with nothing to do but stare at the ceiling till parts of our family visit her during visiting hours. She does too much worrying and thinking to do her much good. If only you could find some thing to occupy her mind if she is still in the hospital. Get her a nice puzzle to work out. Show her how to do it and get her interested in it. Maybe she can knit or sew something. Teach her how to write. Hand her one of my letters or something and give her some paper and a pencil to write with and let her see if she can copy it. There must be something to occupy her mind with. When I saw her in the hospital [last time], tears came to my eyes, because I'd walk in and find her all alone just staring at the walls and thinking. It just won't help any to let her stay that way. I know you must be reading our letters to her, so I want you to read mine to her personally:

> Dear Ma,
>   I can't ever explain to you how I feel knowing that you are suffering out there while us boys out here are in fine health and spirits. If you are worrying about Frankie, Carmen, Shadow, or even me, you shouldn't because we are all feeling fine. Sure, we want to come home, but we want you well when we do. Don't ever give up hope of not seeing any of us, because you will. I know if I ever had gotten hurt and I was sick I wouldn't give up hope, even a little bit of coming home to see you, my wife, and son. So, be a little happy, because even now Frankie and maybe even Carmen are on their way home again. Don't ever be afraid, because there's nothing to be afraid about. It's up to God to do the things He wants to do, and I know that God is on our side and he'll help us out.
>   You may be sure that we are all thinking of you at this moment and hoping that you'll be feeling well real quickly. Now don't forget, don't be discouraged. I got a picture of my son that my wife had taken at the studio and I think by now you should have one too. Any way he looks real nice, and I can easily see that his face is just like yours and mine. Another thing, I don't want you to worry or think about the times I came home on furlough and didn't call you up. Next time it will be different, so don't worry about it anymore. [*This is an important admission that might help explain some of the family squabbling. Apparently when Phil came home on furlough he didn't visit his family as much as they had hoped. He was, after all, living with his wife at his wife's parents' house. But, apparently he didn't even call as much as his family wanted.*] Just because I'm married doesn't make me different. I'm just the same as always. When you see Shadow and me climbing all over the house and fixing it, you'll think that we aren't even married. Heck, you haven't even started to live and be happy yet. Just wait till we all come home and get settled down again. Well, Ma, that's all for now, but if you want to tell me anything at all, just tell Mary and she'll tell me just as if you were writing yourself. So long for now and God bless you always and don't feel discouraged or worried, because I know that you are going to be alright again.

Well, Mary, I hope by the time you get this letter that Ma will be out of the hospital, and feeling better. I think that inside of 7 or 8 months I'll be home for good and that goes the same for Frankie. As for Carmen and Shadow I don't know, but it shouldn't be much longer than that. Keep your chins up and don't none of you worry too much. You can bet that I'll say a lot of extra prayers for Ma. So-long for now and God bless you all.

Love To: Ma, Pa, Mary, Tony, Francie & Carlo
X X X X X X X X X — Phil —

Thursday September 20, 1945/Wendover, Utah

Dear Mary,

. . . I hope by now that Ma is out of the hospital. As yet I didn't get any mail for today, but later on I will.

Yesterday I wrote a letter to Carmen. I also received one from him. You know I was listening to the news this morning on the radio and I was on the far end of my barracks when the announcer named some warships that are headed for the U.S. When he came to Light Cruisers he mentioned a name that had "Burg" on the end. I couldn't hear it too plainly but I'm almost positive that he said it was the Vicksburg. If so, Carmen is now on his way home. It may take a couple weeks because those ships stop at Hawaii to re-fuel but any way I figure Carmen should be in the U.S. before long. I'm not telling you this just to pep Ma up. I heard it personally on the radio. Another thing, I think all of us will be out sooner than I expected, because a lot of big things are going to happen in Congress to get all the men back to civilian life again. So tell Ma to keep her chin up, and not to worry about anything silly.

Well, I guess that's all for now, but if I get a letter from you later on today, I may write again later.

So-long for now and God bless you all.

Love To: Ma, Pa, Mary, Tony, Francie & Carlo
X X X X X X X X X X X — Phil —

Friday September 21, 1945/Wendover Field, Utah

Dear Mary,

Yesterday I received the letter you wrote last Sunday and today I received the letter you wrote last Monday. I was especially happy to hear that Ma is now back home again. As for me calling up, I won't just yet. I know you have a lot of expenses now, so one [long-distance] phone bill for one month is enough. However, I'll call up early next month sometime. I'll let you know when, ahead of time. So tell Ma not to worry about me. You see, I expect Carmen and Frankie both to call up from the West coast inside of 3 weeks or so. As for Carmen, well, I told you that the radio said his ship was headed for the U.S. At least I'm pretty sure it was his ship. As for Frankie, I just got a letter from him, which I'll send there tomorrow so that you too can see it. Frankie closed by saying: "By the way this is going to be my _____ _____ in a long time." The two blanks were words that were cut out by the censor. He could only mean one thing and that was that he meant to say it was his "last letter" for a long time. Well, that means only one thing and he's moving out of New Guinea, and I think he's on his way home even now. Another thing, he sold his horse and he wouldn't sell it if he wasn't coming home. All in all, he wrote this letter on September 6th and right now it's the 21st, so as I said you can be expecting calls from both Carmen and Frankie, so tell Ma not to be too surprised. I wrote to Frankie yesterday and I also received a letter from Carmen yesterday. He's getting along fine. Well, I guess that's all for now, but I'll be back again later on tomorrow. So long and God bless you all, and tell Ma to be happy because it won't be long before we are all together again.

Love To: Ma, Pa, Mary, Tony, Francie & Carlo
X X X X X X X X X X — Phil —

P.S. I'm sure mighty happy that Ma is feeling better and is home again. It sure takes a lot of worries from a guy's mind.

Saturday September 22, 1945/Wendover, Utah
Dear Mary,

. . . It sure is nice to know that Ma is home now. When a member of a guy's family is sick, a guy doesn't even feel like taking in a show or anything. Now at least I can laugh a little. Have Ma go through a check up every little while. Heck, Ma is still young. Look at all the people who live for a long time and are real sick. Look at President Roosevelt who got infantile paralysis when he was a young man, but still he lived the happiest years of his life as he got older. I could rattle off the names of a lot of people who are real sick and yet are enjoying life. So tell Ma not to become discouraged or anything like that. She'll just have to have courage and patience with herself.

It's pretty cold out here today. Yesterday, the wind was blowing harder than I ever saw it, with a lot of dark clouds overhead. This morning there was a lot of snow in the mountains. I guess that's the way it will be from now on, so we'll just have to light the fires again.

As for my wife giving a picture of my son to Shadow, I believe she [already] did. Yep, they sure were expensive. I guess they cost us $20, that's including the large ones also. Well, some good pictures had to be taken sooner or later of him.

Enclosed is the letter that Frankie wrote me. . . . According to the radio, they will do away with the point system in a couple months and then they'll start letting guys out who've been in 2 or more years. Yep, I feel that this is my last stretch of army life. They will try to bribe the guys into re-enlisting by making them some good propositions. They may as well forget about me because I wouldn't re-enlist for $25,000 cash. Anyway that's how I feel about it. Well, I guess that's all I have to say, but give my personal love to Ma. God bless you all.

Love To: Ma, Pa, Mary, Tony, Francie & Carlo

X X X X X X X X X — Phil.

Sunday September 23, 1945/Wendover, Utah

Dear Mary,

. . . I hope Ma is feeling alright today, and I hope you took her out for a nice long ride, to some place. When I was there and I was going to Angola to pick up Joe [out at the farm], Ma wanted to come along. I was going all alone though and I was going to drive too fast, so I was afraid to take her with me. Why don't you take a ride to Angola some Sunday and show her the place? Also take her to some show. They show a lot of colored cartoons with no talking in them that Ma can watch and understand as well as anybody *[Although Calogera does not speak or understand English, Phil realizes that would not be a handicap if she were watching cartoons. Phil's idea was not new. In the early 1900s, immigrants who could not speak English commonly attended movie the-aters where they could watch and understand silent movies.]* Just keep her occupied and let her look forward to things. Well, so-long for now and God bless you all.

Love To: Ma, Pa, Mary, Tony, Francie & Carlo

X X X X X X X X X — Phil.

P.S. I think Carmen's ship stopped at Okinawa and should be on its way to Hawaii before reaching the U.S.A.

Monday September 24, 1945/Wendover, Utah

Dear Mary,

. . . I'm glad that Ma is up and around the same as usual. Only don't let her stay on her feet too much. I know that she wants to do a lot of work, but explain to her that she just can't if she wants to stay well. As for Shadow being sore because you didn't get him home don't pay any attention to him. I know that each time I come home it costs me close to $200. I don't know how much it costs Shadow but I imagine it costs him quite a sum. However, I'm not worried about the cost. If anything does come up in the future always try to get me home. You can use your own judgement if I should be there or not. Like this last time when Ma was in the hospital for so short a period it wouldn't be good to get me home, because she wasn't in much danger outside of the terrific pain. I know she must have suffered a great deal though. Let's hope that we'll never have to have an emergency furlough.

I'm glad my wife came down there last Wednesday with the baby. I hope she can come down whenever she gets the chance. Everything out here seems to be going along pretty good. Incidently, I think that any man with 36 points or more doesn't have to go overseas, and that includes me. Well, I guess that's all for now so take it easy and God bless you all.

Love To: Ma, Pa, Mary, Tony, Francie & Carlo
X X X X X X X X X — Phil.

Tuesday September 25, 1945/Wendover, Utah

Dear Mary,

I just received the swell long letter you wrote last Friday, and I'm glad that Ma is feeling as well as possible. I think if she doesn't exert herself and if she gets a check up once in a while, she'll be okay. So, no matter how much she insists upon working, just don't let her. As for the stationery I forgot there that June gave me, well, you just go ahead and use it.

I'm glad to hear that Tony hasn't got that expensive insurance on the car anymore. He should have written to Albany long ago. As for Frankie coming home, I don't know any more about it than you do. I just got 2 letters from Carmen and he's okay. I think those guys are both on their way home.

Well so-long for now and God bless you all.

Love To: Ma, Pa, Mary, Tony, Francie & Carlo
X X X X X X X X X X X X — Phil

Wednesday September 26, 1945/Wendover Field, Utah

Dear Mary,

. . . I hope that Ma is still feeling as well as possible, and also the rest of you. I just got through writing a letter to both Carmen and Frankie, although I doubt if they'll be getting them. The letters will follow them to the U.S., I guess.

I just sent my wife a nice little gold locket. Go up and see it when you get the time. I sure can't get over how cute my son came in those pictures. Each time I look at his picture I get a big kick out of him. I'd sure like to see the big picture of him.

I guess a lot of guys must be in Buffalo by this time with discharges. Our turn must come in time and all us guys will be home too. Just have to have a little more patience. I think Shadow will be getting a break pretty soon. He's got two children, so I figure when it comes to letting guys out in a hurry he should be one of them.

I hope you are back to work again. No doubt you probably missed all the days that Ma was in the hospital. That's the way things go so there's no use in worrying about them. Well, I guess that's just about all for today, but I'll be back again tomorrow. Take it easy and God bless you all.

Love To: Ma, Pa, Mary, Tony, Francie & Carlo

X X X X X X X X X X X X — <u>Phil</u>

Thursday September 27, 1945/Wendover Field, Utah

Dear Mary,

. . . I received the edition of the BUFFALO EVENING NEWS you sent me and thanks a lot for it. I like to glance over it once in a while, although I know there's no change at all as far as Buffalo is concerned. It's always the same each time I come home.

There's nothing new going on out here, so I really haven't got much to say. I'm eating, and sleeping as well as always. It's a little cool this time of the year but that's to be expected. But we keep the fires going in the stoves in our barracks so it's nice and warm. Besides, at night I've got 3 army blankets on they keep a guy real warm. There's really nothing to do out here. I'm tired of writing letters I guess. I generally take in a show or get a book to read from the library. All in all I'm passing the time away while waiting for my discharge which I hope won't be too far away. Honestly, I just don't know how a lot of these guys get out of the army the way they do. Why, I've seen guys half dead out here and still they can't get out. It just beats the heck out of me. Oh well some day us guys will be home too, so there's no use in worrying about it. Well I guess I'll be closing for now so take it easy and God bless you all.

Love To: Ma, Pa, Mary, Tony, Francie & Carlo

X X X X X X X X X — <u>Phil</u>

Friday September 28, 1945/Wendover Field, Utah

Dear Mary,

. . . You sent me the clipping from the newspaper that I was right about hearing that Carmen's ship is on its way to the United States. Well, now we know for sure that he's coming. Naturally, they'll give him a nice long leave after they get through celebrating their naval victories. But you can be sure that he'll be in the U.S. in about a week or two and he'll be able to call up regularly till he gets his leave which should be a nice long leave. As for Frankie, I'm pretty sure he'll be on his way home [soon], if he isn't on his way home this very minute. All in all I see better days ahead for us.

I was sure surprised and very glad to hear that Shadow came home, even if it was for just a few hours. I bet he sure surprised everybody there. That guy sure gets around and I've got to give him credit. Just [as] everybody likes him in civilian life, I bet everyone likes him in the Navy.

I hope that Ma is feeling as well as possible at this time. Don't let her work too hard but let her keep busy at something so that she won't have too much time to think of anything that'll worry her. . . . About discharges, you know about as much as I do at this time, but if anything special comes up I'll let you know about it right away. So long for now and God bless you all.

Love To: Ma, Pa, Mary, Tony, Francie & Carlo
X X X X X X X X X — Phil —

P.S. I'm sending that clipping about Carmen's ship back to you. You may want to keep it.

Saturday September 29, 1945/Wendover, Utah
Dear Mary,

Not so much to say for myself out here today. Everything seems to be going along alright and I can't complain. Naturally I get disgusted with things but as usual I figure I'm mighty lucky the way things turned out for me in this war. I hope that Ma is continuing to feel as well as possible. Just make sure she gets examined every so often by a doctor, and tell her not to worry about the cost.

I hope by now you've had time to have a heart-to-heart talk with my wife. There's no reason on earth why there should be a misunderstanding between you on anything at all.

So-long and God bless you all.

Love To: Ma, Pa, Mary, Tony, Francie & Carlo
X X X X X X X X — Phil —

Sunday September 30, 1945/Wendover, Utah
Dear Mary,

. . . Tomorrow, October starts and I've got a hunch both Frankie and Carmen will be in the U.S. by the end of the month. Let's hope so anyway. I'm sorry that my wife didn't give Shadow a picture of Little Phil. She's waiting for him to write her and so far he hasn't. Oh well, I'm getting sick of those silly things and I can't wait till I come home for keeps and straighten things out. Well, I'll close for today because I haven't much to say so take it easy and God bless you all.

Love To: Ma, Pa, Mary, Tony, Francie & Carlo
X X X X X X X — Phil —

Monday October 1, 1945/Wendover, Utah

Dear Mary,

Same old stuff out here and I can't kick. I just got a letter from Shadow and he told me that he was in Buffalo from 9:00 p.m. Saturday to 10:00 a.m. Monday. It's pretty good. Now he knows how Buffalo looks from the air. He said my son is getting too fat. I guess he's used to seeing his kids put on a food schedule and not getting fat. Besides food doesn't make babies fat. How can my son be fat? My wife is skinny and I'm just husky. He's just chubby that's all.

I also got a letter from Carmen and he said that he'll be starting towards the states on September 20th and be on the West Coast around October 5th. So by the time you get this letter, he may be in the states again. Well, I hope Ma is feeling in great shape and tell her not to worry. So-long and God bless you all.

Love To: Ma, Pa, Mary, Tony, Francie & Carlo
X X X X X X X X X — Phil.

Tuesday October 2, 1945/Wendover Field, Utah

Dear Mary,

Same old thing also today. Just writing this letter though because I'm used to writing a daily letter to you and I know Ma is used to getting a daily letter from me. The weather out here has been pretty good lately. I haven't worked any too hard either. Now that the war is all over with there's no sense to working anymore unless we are out to start another war. At times I get disgusted but it means nothing at all. I guess I'm very impatient to get out of the army. I know fully well that it won't be any picnic once I do get out but I'm willing to take my chances at anything.

I hope Ma is feeling as well as possible these days. I guess we were all worried there for a while. Just let her go for a check up every once in a while. Maybe the doctor can tell about when she'll have those awful pains and can prevent them for her. Well you just do what you think is best and I'm sure everything is going to turn out alright for all of us.

Well, I guess that's all for now but I'll be back again tomorrow so take it easy and God bless you all.

Love To: Ma, Pa, Mary, Tony, Francie & Carlo
X X X X X X X X X — Phil —

Wednesday October 3, 1945/Wendover, Utah

Dear Mary,

It's quite a while since I've received a letter from you, but I understand so don't worry about it. I'm mainly interested to know if Ma is okay, so I guess just so I don't get a letter from you I know she's alright.

Then again this darn mail gets delayed along the road to Utah some place. . . . Incidently, Carlo is in the 6th grade right now, isn't he? About Tony and Pa, they still working on the same jobs? Well, I guess that's all for now so take it easy and God bless you all.

Love To: Ma, Pa, Mary, Tony, Francie & Carlo

X X X X X X X X X X — Phil —

P.S. I'd call up home, but you know it's hard to hear over the line. There's no use in wasting $6.50. [$6.50 was a lot of money to the Aquilas. That was about 1½ day's work picking beans out on the farms. Even Phil's army take-home pay was only about $40 per month.] Tell Ma not to worry about it, because it can't be too long before I come home for good.

Thursday October 4, 1945/Wendover, Utah

Dear Mary,

. . . I was glad to hear that Ma is feeling as well as possible, and I hope she continues like that. I'm glad to hear that you canned some tomatoes. My wife also canned some tomatoes and ½ bushel of peaches for us. I don't know when we'll use them but I hope real soon anyway. . . . You mentioned that Frankie was going to Manila. Well, in that case he won't be home for a while yet. But you can never tell.

It sure must've been a great thrill for Ma and the rest of you to see Shadow take off in an airplane from the airport. There's really nothing to be afraid of. Just think of all the people who die by automobile. When you take into consideration that there's thousands of planes flying around each day there really are few accidents.

I was glad to hear that you, my wife and Josephine Mitri went down to see June. I'm glad she liked the gift my wife bought for her son [evidently, the rift among the sisters-in-law has healed somewhat]. . . . Take it easy for now and God bless you all.

Love To: Ma, Pa, Mary, Tony, Francie & Carlo

X X X X X X X X X — Phil —

Friday October 5, 1945/Wendover Field, Utah

Dear Mary,

. . . I received the letter you wrote last Sunday and as usual I was very glad to hear from you, and glad that Ma is feeling as well as possible under the circumstances. . . .

I'm glad you spent 2 hours at my wife's house. I hope you had a chance to talk with her upon different subjects and straighten out any little misunderstanding. Yes, my son is sure growing and is a lot of fun to be with. Does he recognize any of our family yet? If he doesn't, he will in time. You see, as soon as I get back for keeps, I'll have my own home, and he'll see our family just as much as he sees my wife's family. So don't worry about things the way they are right now. *[The baby seems to be the crux of the problems between the in-laws. Naturally, Phil's wife feels more comfortable living with her parents while he's in the army. So the Aquila baby is for the present being raised in the Cavarella household. The Aquilas seem to resent that. No doubt this type of situation was quite common throughout the country during the war years. Perhaps it is heightened by the fact that Phil's wife, sister, and mother typified Italian American women who insisted upon powerful, active roles in family matters.]*

I guess by now the farming season is over with out there. Where did Pa sleep and how did he eat when he used to go to the farm on weekends? Well, I guess that's all for now but I'll be back again tomorrow to give you the latest from out here. Till then, so long and God bless you all.

Love To: Ma, Pa, Mary, Tony, Francie & Carlo

X X X X X X — Phil

P.S. There's no use in my writing to Carmen and Frankie any more for awhile, because of the fact that they are on their way home or will be shortly. So, when you write them just tell them that and send them my love, okay?

Saturday October 6, 1945/Wendover, Utah

Dear Mary,

. . . Today being Saturday, we only work a half day. The weather is pretty good out here, not too cold or too warm. All in all it's pretty good and I can't complain too much. Well, by today Carmen should have reached the West Coast. According to him, he'll stay there for a little while and then sail to the East Coast. It depends upon his luck, when he'll get home. He said that half of his crew will be sent home for Thanksgiving and the other half for Christmas. Starting the first of next month, the points will be lowered to 60. It's too bad that Frankie has about 55 points only, at least that's what I think he has. If he had a battle star or something that was worth 5 points, I think he'd be getting a discharge. I really believe that he might be a civilian by Christmas, at least I hope so. Well, I guess that's all for today so take it easy and God bless you all.

Love To: Ma, Pa, Mary, Tony, Francie, & Carlo

X X X X X X X X X — Phil.

Sunday October 7, 1945/Wendover, Utah

Dear Mary,

. . . Yesterday I received the letter you wrote last Tuesday and also the letter Carlo wrote last Monday. I'm glad Ma looks well and I sure hope she stays that way. As for putting up a Christmas Tree this year, by all means do. The war is over and we've got a lot to be grateful for. It's about time you get some gay happy spirit in that house. *[Apparently, business did not go on as usual in this Italian American household while the boys were away at war. The Aquilas have not had a Christmas tree since the boys were drafted in 1943.]*

I also received the picture you sent of Carlo and I think it came out pretty good. There's nothing new out here to talk about so I guess I'll close for now. So-long and God bless you all.

Love To: Ma, Pa, Mary, Tony, Francie & Carlo
X X X X X X X X X X X X — Phil —

[The next entry is written and addressed to Phil's youngest brother, Carlo, who is in the 6th grade.]

Sunday October 7, 1945/Wendover, Utah

Hello Carlo,

I just got the letter you wrote last Monday and I was very surprised to get it, because I thought for sure that you had forgotten about me by this time. As for the world ending, don't worry about it. Nobody knows when it will. If you believed in God you wouldn't even worry a little bit about what some guys predict. *[Evidently the use of atomic bombs and the vast destruction caused by the war brought prophets of doom out of the woodwork. The fact that young children are worried about the end of the world anticipates the fear of nuclear holocaust that will be common during the Cold War era of the late 1940s and 1950s.]*

No, I didn't hear no thunder in Utah when Buffalo had the big rain storm. I'm glad to hear that you are taking trumpet and drum lessons. Just stick to it and you'll be a musician some day. As for 6th grade being tough, you are wrong. It's real easy. All you have to do is study hard while you are in school.

So-long Carlo and God bless you, Love, Phil.

P.S. Learn these words real good because you misspelled them in your letter:

Right Way		you spelled them this way
concerned	——————	consirns
until	——————	untill
assure	——————	issure

[Phil is obviously trying to help his young brother, but he is taking a hard-line approach. That is how Phil reacted in all these situations— you always had to be tough and keep your chin up. He believed you had to confront problems head on.]

Monday October 8, 1945/Wendover, Utah

Dear Mary,

. . . Everything seems to be going along pretty good so far. I hope you can say the same for Ma and all of you there. . . . Nothing new about discharges as far as I'm concerned. They are letting men out this month who have 70 or more points, and next month they'll let out the men with 60 or more points. I've got 43 points so you can figure it out for yourselves. It's only a matter of months and not years anymore. So actually, I don't expect to come home on furlough anymore. Next time I come home it'll be for good. I will get another furlough in February but if I get a discharge in March there's just no sense in wasting any money to come home on furlough when I can wait a month or two more and come home for good. Well, anyway that's the way things stand as they are right now and if anything new comes up, I'll let you know right away.

Life out here goes on the same day in and day out and I can't complain about anything at all. Eat, sleep, work, and wait is all I can do at this time. By now, Carmen should be on the West coast, or maybe he already called up home. I hope so. As for Frankie, you said he is going to Manila so maybe he may catch a ship from there, you can never tell anyway. Well, I guess that's all for now, so take it easy and God bless you all.

Love To: Ma, Pa, Mary, Tony, Francie & Carlo
X X X X X X X X X X — Phil —

Tuesday October 9, 1945/Wendover Field, Utah

Dear Mary,

. . . I just got a letter from Carmen dated September 26, just before he started off from Okinawa to go to Pearl Harbor. According to him, he should be on the West Coast today, but I think he'll be getting there around the 15th of the month or a few days sooner. He also should be on furlough before Christmas. It takes a little longer time in the Navy to get a furlough than it does in the army. You see half the crew has to remain aboard ship all the time while the other half goes on leave. Whereby in Frankie's case, about a week after he gets home to the U.S. he'll be given a 30 day furlough or even 45 days right now, I think. . . . Don't forget when you write to Carmen and Frankie, just mention that I'll write to them after they get to the United States.

October 13 is your birthday, so I'm sending you a birthday card. It's a 10 cents card but I was overcharged and it cost me 15 cents, but it's worth it.

I also made a nice frame for my son's picture out of plexi-glass. It sure looks nice. I've got my son's picture in it now and it's on my desk,

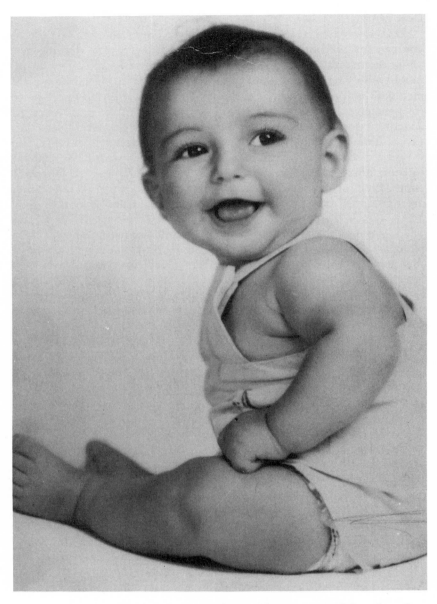

Fig. 2.10. Baby picture of Philip L. Aquila Jr., taken in 1945. Phil made a plex-iglass frame for this picture, which he discusses in his letter of October 9, 1945. (Philip L. Aquila Collection)

where everyone can admire my son and everybody does. Well, I guess that's all for now, but I'll be back again tomorrow. Till then so long and God bless you all.

Love To: Ma, Pa, Mary, Tony, Francie & Carlo
X X X X X X X X X — Phil.

P.S. I hope that Ma is feeling pretty good these days.

Wednesday October 10, 1945/Wendover Field, Utah

Dear Mary,

Today I received the letter you wrote last Friday . . . I also received a letter from Carmen and one from Frankie. They're both getting along pretty good. Carmen was at Pearl Harbor at the time he wrote his letter and should be in the U.S. mighty soon. As for Frankie, he's sure having the time of his life in Manila, but doesn't say when he'll be getting home yet. Oh well, we can look forward to them coming home some day any way.

I'm glad that Ma is feeling pretty good and I hope she continues that way. How often does she get those pains now? Well, let's hope for the best, but tell her to have a lot of faith in herself. She's got no reason to be thinking as much as she does. Tell her to let the politicians in Washington do the thinking. The war is over with now and there's nothing to worry about.

Everything out here seems to be under control today and I can't kick about anything. The weather has been fine and I hope it continues to be that way. Of course it doesn't make any difference to me whether it's warm or cold. The food is also pretty good. All in all everything except my getting a discharge is okay. Well, I guess that's about all I have to say for today, so take it easy and God bless you all.

Love To: Ma, Pa, Mary, Tony, Francie & Carlo
X X X X — Phil — X X X X X

Thursday October 11, 1945/Wendover Field, Utah

Dear Mary,

. . . Last night I made a very beautiful glass frame for my wedding picture. That is the small wedding picture I have with me. The frame is all plexiglass and has glass bolts at each corner. It really makes a swell frame which would cost quite a bit if someone tried to buy one. Now I have a little frame with my son's picture in, and a larger frame with my wedding picture in.

. . . I wrote a letter to Frankie and Carmen but I forgot to get some stamps, so I'll have to wait till tomorrow to mail them. I know I said I wouldn't write to them for a while, but I'll start again and write regularly, to Frankie anyway. Now that Carmen will be home for a while, I'll just drop him a FREE letter every so often.

It gets a little monotonous out here every day, but I rather like it this way than to have a lot of things happening.

I hope Ma is feeling better as each day goes on. Tell her not to worry about anything. All the problems are out there in Buffalo, and not with us guys in the service. I don't know about the rest of the guys but once in a while I think of Tony having a flat tire; of Pa, who is an old man going to and from work; of Francie walking down some dark street; and even June living all alone [while Shadow is away]. Heck, compared to us guys, it's you people with all the problems right now. So tell Ma she has no reason to worry about anybody away from home. The only thing that bothers us is wanting to get home as soon as possible.

Well, I guess that's all for now so take it easy and God bless you all.
Love To: Ma, Pa, Mary, Tony, Francie, & Carlo.
X X X X X X X X X X X — Phil —

[The next entry is written to his brother Tony.]

Thursday October 11, 1945/Wendover Field, Utah
Hello Tony,

Last month I received the letter you wrote telling me about Ma going to the hospital. I was glad to hear from you even though the news wasn't too good. I take news like that and also flat tires on the chin. I understand your viewpoint about taking a drink to make things seem unimportant afterwards. I guess it's different with me. I measure the importance of a thing and then either worry about it or get mad at it accordingly.

Life goes on just about the same day in and day out here at Wendover, Utah. I'm just sweating out my discharge, which I should get some time next spring, if everything goes alright.

I guess you are still working the second shift out there. As for me whenever I get back I doubt if I will ever work a second shift again. It's alright when a guy's single but not when he's married. I'll either find a job or make myself a job one way or another.

One good thing, I consider myself pretty lucky to go through a major war like this without getting banged up any, and without even going overseas. It's just plain luck I guess because I know I don't have no connections from keeping me from going across.

Well, I guess I'll be closing now. It's almost 5 p.m. here and I'll go wrap my insides around some of their stew and cockroaches. A guy has to eat regardless of the insects around. One thing about being home and that is you can at least see what's being cooked. Well take it easy and I'll write you a few more lines whenever I get the ambition. Love, Phil

Friday October 12, 1945/Wendover, Utah

Dear Mary,

    . . . I just mailed Frankie and Carmen each a letter. *[He had said several times he no longer was going to write to them, but, evidently, he just can't stop writing letters to his brothers and family.]* Yep, Frankie is sure having a big time for himself in Manila. That's a lot of money you are sending him, and he's going to spend it stupidly. If he asks for more money after he's got only $500 left, don't send him anymore. Let him get sore, but when he gets back, he'll thank you. For something he can buy in Buffalo for 10 cents, he's spending 50 cents out there. It's up to you, but I know I wouldn't send him anymore money besides that what you already sent him. It's his money, but somebody better think for him. *[Frankie is his younger brother, and Phil was accustomed to thinking for him and telling him what to do. Despite the war and the fact that Frankie is now a soldier, Phil is still paternalistic toward him.]*

    I'm glad Ma is feeling pretty good and I hope she continues that way. Everything out here is alright, so make me the least of your worries. So-long and God bless you all.

Love To: Ma, Pa, Mary, Tony, Francie & Carlo

X X X X X X X — Phil —

Saturday October 13, 1945/Wendover Field, Utah

Dear Mary,

    It's a dark, gloomy day out here and everything is kind of damp. It's not too cold though. According to you Shadow must be either winning quite a bit of money or saving it up. Well, it's up to him to think about the things he'll need when he gets out of the navy. As for me I know I'll need $1000 when I get out to buy all the furniture. Somehow I'll get it, I guess.

    Yep, [our neighbor] is back on furlough. It beats me how those guys get all that furlough time. I'm in the worst outfit a guy can be in. They raised the furlough time to 20 days, whereby other army outfits get about 30 to 45 days. The discharges out here are very slow. Guys who are 39 years old are still here, and guys with 85 to 100 points are still here. Their excuse for keeping them is that there aren't any separation centers open for this Second Air Force. Other outfits get their men out quick, but not this one.

    I'm glad you liked the locket I sent to my wife. It's pretty. Everything out here seems to be going along alright today. I hope Ma and all of you are also fine. Well, I guess I'll be closing for today, but I'll be back again tomorrow, till then so long and God bless you all.

Love To: Ma, Pa, Mary, Tony, Francie & Carlo

X X X X X X X X X — Phil

Sunday October 14, 1945/Wendover, Utah

Dear Mary,

Another dull Sunday going by today with nothing to do but read and loaf on my bed. The weather is real nice though. I'd rather loaf around than do something that's useless anyway.

There's a lot of men shipping out of this place. I'm pretty lucky I've got a son, because right now I'd be on my way to Europe and I'm not kidding. Little Phil's 12 points sure helped me. It's a joke how they are still doing things at this late stage of the war. It burns me up at times. Oh well, I guess I'll have to take all this baloney for just a while longer.

Well, I'll close for today and I hope Ma and all of you are getting along fine. So-long and God bless you all.

Love To: Ma, Pa, Mary, Tony, Francie & Carlo
X X X X X X X X X — Phil —

Monday October 15, 1945/Wendover, Utah

Dear Mary,

. . . I'm glad [to hear] that Ma is feeling pretty good and I hope she continues to be that way. According to the Salt Lake City newspaper this morning, the Third Fleet has already come into San Francisco. By now you should have received a phone call from [Carmen]. I think he'll get a leave before they pull out to sea again, so don't worry about it.

Everything out here is going along just about the same. The way I see it, in a few weeks the only guys who'll be left at this field are the guys like myself who have between 36 and 60 points. Oh well, I need something to break up this monotony out here just so I don't go across, which I doubt at this time. As long as I'm to be in this army a little while longer, I may as well do some more traveling around the country, don't you think? We'll soon see what's going to happen around here, anyway. . . . As for anymore phone calls from me, please forget them. I don't like to call up unless I can pay for it, and I can't pay for it at this time. Even if I called you up and reversed the charges, I'd have to call my wife up or else she'd feel bad about it, and that would cost us $6.50. So tell Ma to understand that the war is over with and there's no sense in wasting money any more. You can tell our other brothers to call up if you wish, but I won't. At the end of the month when I don't call up you have saved $6.50, and so have I with my wife. I don't call up my wife either, so tell Ma not to feel badly about it. Well, I guess that's all for now so take it easy and God bless you all.

Love To: Ma, Pa, Mary, Tony, Francie & Carlo
X X X X X X X X X X — Phil —

[This letter makes it clear that Phil is trying to treat his mother and his wife equally. Pressure from the two strong-willed women must have

made him feel like he was trapped between the proverbial rock and hard place. He had to make sure that neither thought the other was getting privileged treatment.]

Tuesday October 16, 1945/Wendover, Utah

Dear Mary,

Just another day going by with the same old routine out here. . . . I didn't get any mail from anybody today, so that really leaves me very little to write about. I hope Ma and the rest of you are feeling fine out there, and I hope you all continue to stay that way. It's still a hustle and a bustle out here with guys shipping out or getting a discharge. I suppose my turn will be coming around some day. Maybe by now you've heard from Carmen, or else he's on his way to the East Coast.

I was working on the picture frame for my small wedding picture. I spoiled the frame a little but it sure looks beautiful with all red hearts in a blue background. I don't think anyone could buy a frame that beautiful.

Now that the time is getting close to the end of my army career, I'm trying to save up as much money as possible because I know it'll cost quite a bit when I come home. I've always been trying to save, but now I'm trying a little harder. Well, I guess that's all for now so take it easy and God bless you all.

Love To: Ma, Pa, Mary, Tony, Francie & Carlo

X X X X X X X X X — Phil

Wednesday October 17, 1945/Wendover, Utah

Dear Mary,

I received some mail from Frankie and my wife today, but not from you. In Frankie's letter, he sent me 5 pictures of himself on his horse. I think you already received them. All in all he's getting along pretty good. He feels a little bad that he still isn't on his way home, but that's to be expected.

Everything out here seems to be going along as well as usual and I can't complain about anything. Same old grind and same old routine day in and day out. I hope Ma and the rest of you are feeling alright today. I'm in as good as health as I've always been and I guess I'll be staying that way for a while yet, so there's no need to worry about me in any way. . . . A lot of guys are getting out of the army from out here, but they have 70 points or more. Next month it will be those with 60 points or more. Then for the month of December, I don't know what they are cooking up, but I expect they will let the guys out according to how long they've been in the service. I'll have to wait patiently, but my time, Frankie's time, Carmen and Shadow's time will be coming around some time in the near future, so just keep your chins up a little while longer. Well, I guess that's all for now, so take it easy and God bless you all.

Love To: Ma, Pa, Mary, Tony, Francie & Carlo
X X X X X X X X X X X X — Phil.

Thursday October 18, 1945/Wendover Field, Utah

Dear Mary,

Not much to say for today, except that everything out here seems to be going along pretty good.

I heard over the radio that they might lower the points down to 50 for December 1st. That won't be too bad. By January and February at that rate they ought to be getting around to me. I think Frankie should be getting out around Christmas sometime. I hope so anyway. That's why I hate to see him spending a lot of money when he goes to places like Manila, because he'll soon be out of the army and he'll need his money more than ever. Of course he'll be getting 20 or 25 dollars each week from this GI Bill of Rights.

The weather out here is still holding up pretty good. That's about the only good thing that can be said about this place out here. It's still nice and warm, but cool in the mornings and at night, and that is to be expected at this time of the year.

I'm sure that you've heard from Carmen by this time. If not, he must be on his way to the East Coast, through the Panama Canal, because his ship must be on the East Coast by October 27th I believe. I just mailed a letter to Frankie. Well, I guess that's all for now, so take it easy and God bless you all.

Love To: Ma, Pa, Mary, Tony, Francie & Carlo
X X X X X X X X X X X X X — Phil.

Friday October 19, 1945/Wendover, Utah

Dear Mary,

I received the letter you wrote last Sunday and I was glad to hear from you. You said that Ma doesn't have to go to the doctor any more, because there's no use. I know just what you mean and I can't believe it's true. It's a good idea, though, to go to another doctor and see what his opinion is. If Ma has got cancer then we may as well be brave about it and face the fact. Sure, that gives us a lot to worry about, but don't forget a lot of people with that sickness keep living for a long time. No telling how long Ma's had it. Now that we know about it, let's not keep thinking the worse of it. In other words no matter what the doctors say let's never lose faith. You can say what you want about the medical world and even science, but there's a lot of times where God Himself does the curing. It's a bad disease because they can't fight it any too good, so actually I don't think any doctor knows too much about it. So let's keep the faith and be brave about it. Meantime, try and let Ma forget that she's sick.

Everything out here seems to be going along pretty good out here and I can't complain about anything. I'm glad to hear that you visited Lackawanna. Incidently, the points were lowered yesterday to 60. So anybody with 60 points can now apply for a discharge and will be getting out any day now. You said Frankie has 61 points. I don't see how he has that much because I figured his to about 57 or 58 unless he's got a battle star or something. Anyway if he has 61 points he'll get his discharge as soon as he gets to the states. I think he'll be home in November some time and discharged easily by Christmas, although he says they are keeping his outfit in the Orient for a while longer. But he don't exactly know when he'll actually start for home. As for me, the way things are going, I may even be home in January some time and be a civilian again. Well, I guess that's all for now, so take it easy and God bless you all and tell Ma not to worry.

Love To: Ma, Pa, Mary, Tony, Francie & Carlo
X X X X X X X X X X X — Phil —

Saturday October 20, 1945/Wendover, Utah

Dear Mary,

I just got the letter you wrote last Wednesday and as always, I was glad to hear from you. Especially about Carmen coming home. According to you, he'll get a 30 or more days leave. If so, that'll be swell and will pep up Ma quite a bit.

Please don't ask me to call up, cause I won't. I'd like nothing better than to hear Ma's voice and the rest of you, but each time I call, it costs you $6.50 for your phone call bill and $6.50 for my phone call bill when I call my wife, so I'm not calling up anybody. It's too close to the end of our being apart to keep calling. So tell Ma and Carmen to understand. I hope Carmen is home by this time and I bet he's got a lot to talk about.

I'm glad my wife was down there with my son and I'm especially glad to hear that Ma held him while he drank 8 oz. of milk. Tell Ma never to be shy or afraid to hold him because I want her to feel real close to him. Because he lives with the Cavarella's temporarily doesn't make him one. He's an Aquila just as much as any of us are, and don't you forget that.

I hope Ma is feeling nice these days. I just can't say as much as I'd like to about Ma getting well and getting rid of those pains of hers. I can only keep hoping just the way you do.

Today it's real cloudy and chilly out here with a few snow flurries.

First time this year I've seen snow falling and you really have to strain your eyes to see it. Well, I'll be closing for now, so till tomorrow, so-long and God bless you all.

Love To: Ma, Pa, Mary, Tony, Francie, Carlo, & Carmen
[For the first time, he has added his brother Carmen's name to his closing.]

X X X X X X X X X X X X — Phil —

Sunday October 21, 1945/Wendover, Utah

Dear Mary,

. . . Everything out here is going along pretty good and I hope you can say the same for Ma and yourselves out there. I hope by now Carmen's home on his furlough. I bet he'll sure be surprised when he sees his two new nephews. All I'm doing today out here is just loafing around laying on my bunk reading a long novel to pass the time away. Well, I guess that's all for now, so take it easy and God bless you all.

Love To: Ma, Pa, Mary, Tony, Francie, Carlo & Carmen
X X X X X X X X X — Phil.

Monday October 22, 1945/Wendover, Utah

Dear Mary,

. . . The weather isn't too bad. It's a little windy, cool, and cloudy. Typical fall weather I'd say. I received a letter from Frankie. Yep, he's eligible for a discharge, but he doubts if he'll get sent home for a while yet. I think differently though. I believe he'll be a civilian by Christmas, whether he thinks so or not. I hope that Carmen is home by now.

Incidently, I've quit smoking cigarettes and I'm smoking a pipe now. I'll never touch another cigarette again. It's going on two weeks since I quit cigarettes. In time, I may even stop smoking, although it only costs me 20 to 30 cents a week now for tobacco and that's not too expensive, is it?

I hope Ma is feeling fine today and that goes for the rest of you. Well, so-long for now and God bless you all.

Love To: Ma, Pa, Mary, Tony, Francie, Carlo & Carmen
X X X X X X X X X X X X — Phil —

Tuesday October 23, 1945/Wendover, Utah

Dear Mary,

. . . Guys are leaving this base everyday and everybody has to pitch in and do extra little duties. Well, I'll keep working I guess till I get my discharge. As for that, it's the same old story. I'll have to just wait and see what's going to happen. It won't be too long though and it's just a matter of a few more months at the most.

I hope Ma is feeling fine today. We'll just have to pray and hope for the best. Just don't let her get discouraged. We've come through the biggest war in the history of the world and our family is intact and in one piece.

Yep, I'm still smoking my pipe. I've quit cigarettes for good and someday I'll even quit this pipe. Well, I guess that's all for now, so take it easy and God bless you all.

Love To: Ma, Pa, Mary, Tony, Francie, Carlo & Carmen
X X X X X X X X X X X — Phil.

Wednesday October 24, 1945/Wendover Field, Utah

Dear Mary,

Same old thing today with hardly nothing new to say, except that everything out here seems to be going along pretty good as usual. Physically, I've got a little cold and a slight headache, but it's nothing to be worried about, because it will be gone in a day or two. I rubbed some of that mentholatum or something that you sent me about two and a half years ago. It's a sample, I guess. Anyway I put some on my nose and forehead before going to bed each night. This is the first cold I've had since I came out here last March. That's a pretty good record, I think.

I hope Carmen is there by this time. I won't write to him anymore until he goes back to his ship after his leave. There's no need for him to waste his time and write to me either, until he gets back to his ship. Of course, let me know once in a while how he's getting along out there.

I hope Ma is still feeling fine and I wish she'd stay that way. Of course that goes the same for the rest of you out there.

Yesterday on the 23rd I remembered it was Joe and Rae's wedding anniversary. I guess I should of sent them a card, but then again I got very few cards on my wedding anniversary, so why should I always be the one to take the initiative, right? *[Phil seems resentful that his family doesn't seem to be acknowledging his marriage as much as he thinks they should be. This attitude suggests the tensions between his wife and his family.]*

Well, there's nothing new concerning discharges. If Frankie was in the states, he'd be on his way home as a civilian by now. It won't be long though, cause remember I said he'd be a civilian before Christmas. I really think he'll be a civilian in November sometime no matter what he says in his letters right now. He doesn't know what happens out there no more than we do out here.

Well, I guess that's all for now so take it easy and God bless you all.

Love To: Ma, Pa, Mary, Tony, Francie, Carlo & Carmen
X X X X X X X X X X X — Phil.

Thursday October 25, 1945/Wendover Field, Utah

Dear Mary,

. . . According to you, Carmen would be home in a few days. I hope so. As for him re-enlisting just to get that 30 day leave, I hardly think so. He'd be crazy if he did.

Everything out here seems to be going along about the same as usual. I'm feeling about the same as yesterday. I can't understand my catching a cold when we are having some real nice weather out here every day. Oh well, I'll just have to make the most of it I guess, so I won't let it worry me any. Nothing new about discharges as yet. There's a lot of rumors though, and pretty soon they'll be coming out with something that will affect me some.

As for the way Frankie is carrying on, I know all about it [how he's partying in Manila]. At least he's frank about it anyway. I only did as much as I could by writing him a little nasty letter. No doubt if I was with him I'd beat him up too, but then he's 21 years old and if he hasn't got the brains and sense to take care of himself, then there's no use in my getting angry with him and trying to tell him right from wrong. [Even though Phil is in the army, he still tries to provide advice to family members, as evidenced by his "nasty letter" to Frankie, as well as the comments to his sister. Apparently, "the warden," as Frankie used to call him, still wants to keep a close watch over his younger brother.]

Some of these guys think they've been through Hell or something. Not only Frankie, but every one else that is overseas. They forget that they are still alive and some poor guys are dead. Yep, things can be worse than they are. I get mad when somebody tries to tell me that because I haven't been over I don't know anything about it. Hell, if I couldn't take it better than some of these guys, I'd hang up. Well, I guess that's all for now, but I'll be back again tomorrow. So-long and God bless you all.

Love To: Ma, Pa, Mary, Tony, Francie, Carlo and Carmen

X X X X X X X X X X X X — Phil.

P.S. I'm sorry this paper ripped as I was taking it out of the typewriter.

Friday October 26, 1945/Wendover, Utah

Dear Mary,

. . . My cold is sure much better and by tomorrow I shouldn't even notice it anymore. I'm sure glad of that. I received a letter from Frankie today which he wrote on October 17. Just 9 days from the day he wrote it for the letter to get here. He's feeling alright as far as I can see.

I hope Ma and everybody there is feeling alright and I hope things continue that way always. By now Carmen should be there. Honest there's no use in wasting any money to call up. Your bill is big enough as it is. Well, I guess that's all for now so take it easy and God bless you all.

Love To: Ma, Pa, Mary, Tony, Francie, Carlo, and Carmen
X X X X X X X X X X X — Phil —

Saturday October 27, 1945/Wendover Field, Utah
Dear Mary,

. . . My cold is almost gone and doesn't bother me anymore. It sure is a relief to get rid of it. So now I'm in top shape again. I hope that Ma isn't feeling too many pains these days. I know she must be suffering quite a bit with those pains. Let's hope that some day they will be over with.

Well, how are things there at home? My wife tells me that my son does a lot of walking all over the house when he is held by one hand. He also crawls around the floor quite a bit. As for me, I can't even start to realize that I'm a father with a son who is about to talk and walk. I'll get used to it when I come home, I guess. What I don't understand is why my son weighs 22 lbs. and Ronnie [who is a year older] weighs little more than 30 pounds. I always said that when a baby wants to eat, then let him eat. If my son has no manners right now when it comes to food, it's only that he's so small yet, but don't you worry, when I get home he'll do just as I say, for example, washing his hands before he eats, and eating with his mouth closed, and etc. You know how I am when it comes to things like that. In time everything will be alright. Of course, right now my wife is doing a good job of bringing him up and I can't complain.

Well, I guess that's all for now, so take it easy and God bless you all.

Love To: Ma, Pa, Mary, Tony, Francie, Carlo & Carmen
X X X X X X X X X X X X — Phil —

Sunday October 28, 1945/Wendover, Utah
Dear Mary,

Just another Sunday going by out here. The weather is very nice out here and my cold is all gone. Yesterday I received the letter you wrote last Monday and I'm glad to hear that everything there is going along okay. According to you, Carmen was going to be home that night sometime. Yep, Ma will sure be happy. You said you were taking my son's picture to your shop so that the girls who know my wife can see it. May as well show them all.

Today this base changed time again. Now we are on Mountain Time, so we are now 2 hours behind Buffalo Time. This base sure does a lot of changing. We don't have too much spare time out here. In fact, I'm doing more work than when the war was going on. *[As soldiers were discharged or shipped overseas, the few remaining ones had to pick up the slack.]* Well, I guess that's all for now, so take it easy and God bless you all.

Love To: Ma, Pa, Mary, Tony, Francie & Carlo & Carmen
X X X X X X X X X X X — Phil —

Monday October 29, 1945/Wendover, Utah

Dear Mary,

. . . I was glad to hear Carmen pulled into Buffalo. Thirty days is a nice long furlough. I hope he'll be stationed in the U.S. Well, anyway, now that there is no war going on, even travelling is safe. I hope Carmen has a good time while at home. Don't worry about Frankie. I just got a letter today from him dated October 21st. Less than 9 days to get here and that's pretty good. He doesn't say anything definite, but I know he'll be a civilian before Christmas regardless. If men with 60 points are getting discharged now, and Frankie has 61, I believe he'll be rushed to the states as soon as possible.

I'm glad to hear that Ma and the rest of you are getting along pretty good and I hope it continues to be that way. You said our aunt was surprised when she saw the picture of my son. She could've walked two blocks to see him in person I think. Oh well, that's alright. Well, I guess that's all for now, so take it easy and God bless you all.

Love To: Ma, Pa, Mary, Tony, Francie, Carlo & Carmen
X X X X X X X X X X X X — Phil.

P.S. As you know I quit smoking cigarettes. I had 1 carton left so I'm sending them to Tony. I mailed them today and you'll get them either this Saturday or Monday sometime.

Tuesday October 30, 1945/Wendover, Utah

Dear Mary,

. . . I'm working about twice as hard as ever. All brain work, though, and no physical work. May as well work till I get my discharge. Then when I come home I'll still have to work. That's how it goes I guess. One never stops working in this world. Incidently, ask Carmen which way he came home from San Francisco. Most of the trains from San Francisco pass through Wendover, Utah, on their way to Salt Lake City and Chicago. Wendover is half in Utah and half in Nevada.

I hope Ma is feeling happy and also well and that goes the same for the rest of you. Well not much to say so take it easy and God bless you all.

Love To: Ma, Pa, Mary, Tony, Francie, & Carlo & Carmen
X X X X X X X X X X X X — Phil.

Wednesday October 31, 1945/Wendover Field, Utah

Dear Mary:

I received the letter you wrote last Friday and as always I was glad to hear from you. As for Carmen becoming engaged it didn't surprise me at all. It's his life and I guess he should know what he's doing. Helen is a very nice girl as far as I know, and I know how Carmen must feel about the situation. A lot of luck to him anyway, although he shouldn't be getting married till after his discharge and he gets himself a job. As for me I knew my problems that would face me when I got married, so now I'm ready to face them when I come home.

I'm sorry to hear that Ma isn't feeling as well as she should. It's as you said, we can only hope for the best. I hope she feels better by now. The same goes for the rest of you. Incidently, Carmen's birthday is November 4th I believe, so tell him happy birthday for me.

I got paid today. I've been saving almost every possible cent since I came back from my furlough in August. So with pay for July, August, September, and October, I managed to save up a little money, and I'm sending my wife $135 to boost up our furniture needs and other little things. Well, I guess that's all for now so take it easy and God bless you all.

Love To: Ma, Pa, Mary, Tony, Francie, Carlo, & Carmen
X X X X X X X X X X — Phil —

Thursday November 1, 1945/Wendover Field, Utah

Dear Mary,

. . . The snow is on the mountain tops now and seems to be creeping lower and lower. It doesn't snow around here too much according to the guys who were out here last year.

I'm sending Carmen a birthday card. I think he did a fine job of remembering every one's birthday out there, so I'll remember his.

I hope Ma is feeling alright these days. Now when the war has ended and our family has grown up to take its place in this world, Ma has to get sick. We can only hope for the best. I hope that everything out there is going along fine for you. It's too bad you can't go to work yet, and I know that you are losing out on a lot of money, but Ma comes first.

Life out here is going along just about the same for me. Nothing new about discharges. I figured that something new would come up by November 1st, but I guess I was wrong. The army thinks that they are letting the men out too fast as it is. Just so these Generals can be with their families and get a lot of glory and still hold their rank, that's all they worry about. In time I'll be out, so don't worry about it. Well, I guess that's all for now so take it easy and God bless you all.

Love To: Ma, Pa, Mary, Tony, Francie, Carlo & Carmen
X X X X X X X X X — Phil.

*[The following birthday card was enclosed for Carmen: The front of
the card pictured three guys standing in a soup line. It read: "Ain't
'Handing Out' good wishes that last for just a day . . ." And then inside,
it shows one of the guys receiving a briefcase filled with money. The
card read: "Cause Here's a million bucks worth to bring you joys that
stay. Happy Birthday." It is signed "Love, Mary, Philip I, & Philip II."
A toothpick was enclosed in the card and Phil wrote: "Use the toothpick on Saturday for your steak."]*

Friday November 2, 1945/Wendover, Utah

Dear Mary,

I received the letter you wrote last Sunday and I was glad to hear
that you are all feeling as well as possible. As for the pain Ma is feeling,
I'm very sorry. I know she tries to be brave about it and doesn't say a
word about it. About the pills she is taking, I know they don't do her
heart any good, so tell her to take as few as possible of them. I hope she
feels better by now.

Yesterday, the points were lowered to 50. In other words, a man has
to have 50 points and 2 years service. The next step, whenever it comes,
will be to lower the points to 40 and that will take me in. Provided of
course they don't say 40 points and 3 years service, because I've only got
2 years and 9 months in. Well, I can only hope for the best.

I'm glad to hear that my wife was down to see Ma and all of you
last Sunday. I bet my son is really getting big by now. . . . Well, I guess
that's all for now so take it easy and God bless you all.

Love To: Ma, Pa, Mary, Tony, Francie, Carlo & Carmen,
X X X X X X X X X X X — Phil —

Saturday November 3, 1945/Wendover, Utah

Dear Mary,

. . . Right now it's 1:00 p.m. (Buffalo Time is 3:00 p.m.). I have
nothing to do till Monday morning except eat, sleep, read, and rest
on my bunk. It's a big joke how they still hang on to these men and
let them just waste their lives like this. I'll let you know as soon as
anything comes up concerning my discharge. If they lower it to 40
points plus 2 years, I'll be home in 4 or 5 weeks or so, but if they
lower it to 40 points plus 3 years service then I'll have to sweat it out
till February.

I hope Ma is getting along swell. We can't expect no miracle, but we
can always hope for the best. Well, I guess that's all for now, so take it
easy and God bless you all.

Love To: Ma, Pa, Mary, Tony, Francie, Carlo & Carmen
X X X X X X X X X X X — Phil —

Sunday November 4, 1945/Wendover, Utah

Dear Mary,

Just another day out here and I'm resting, reading, and loafing around with a stomach full of fried chicken. The meals are getting better each day that goes by, because less and less men are on this base. All in all, I'm feeling pretty good. I'm in my last round of my military career. No doubt Frankie will be discharged before I do. As I said he'll be a civilian way before Christmas. In fact, I won't be surprised if he gets home by Thanksgiving although don't count on that too much.

I hope Ma is feeling better than usual these days. Try to make her forget her illness and give her a lot of things to look forward to. Well, I'll close for now. So take it easy and God bless you all.

Love To: Ma, Pa, Mary, Tony, Francie, Carlo & Carmen

X X X X X X X X X X X X X — Phil —

Monday November 5, 1945/Wendover, Utah

Dear Mary,

. . . I'm glad to hear that my wife and son went with you to June's house. I guess June and [my wife] Mary are getting used to each other again. . . . As yet there's nothing new concerning my discharge. The place is full of rumors which I don't pay any attention to. The only time I believe something is when I see it in black and white.

Well, I hope Ma is feeling better. Let me know how she makes out at the Cancer Clinic. Of course Carmen will be there to take you and Ma up there and back. Well take it easy and God bless you all.

Love To: Ma, Pa, Mary, Tony, Francie, Carlo, & Carmen

X X X X X X X X X X X X X — Phil —

Tuesday November 6, 1945/Wendover, Utah

Dear Mary,

It's a gloomy night out here. It's raining and kind of chilly. I guess winter is settling in out here. Everything seems to be going along alright though and I can't kick. Time is going by as well as can be expected. Slowly but surely December will be around. I'm almost positive in saying that either Frankie or me will be a civilian in December. If they lower the points in my direction, I may even get out before Frankie because I'm here in the states and can proceed right to a Separation Center. It can't be too long now though and we'll all be home again.

I hope Ma is feeling better. Keep her cheered up all the time. It's pretty hard to get a person down when she's happy, so tell Ma not to worry. Well, I have hardly nothing to say, so take it easy and God bless you all.

Love To: Ma, Pa, Mary, Tony, Francie & Carlo & Carmen

X X X X X X X X X X X X — Phil —

Wednesday November 7, 1945/Wendover, Utah

Dear Mary,

. . . I'm glad to hear that Carmen has Shadow's car running. Shadow is crazy to even suggest trying to ship it. As for him coming to Buffalo and driving it back, it's still a bad idea. Well, if he's got the money to spend it's alright I guess. As for the automobile situation when the boys come home to stay, don't even worry about it.

No doubt Frankie will get himself some kind of car and so will Carmen. I don't know where I'll be living yet, but I won't need any car. After I get myself situated, I'll buy a car, but first I'll buy a house and etc. Big plans aren't they? But if I can get a decent job, that's what will happen. A nice modern cottage comes before any car in my head and I'm sure my wife thinks the same.

Well, I hope Ma and the rest of you are alright. I'm okay out here. It snowed last night but it's all melted now except on the mountains. So-long for now and God bless you all.

Love To: Ma, Pa, Mary, Tony, Francie & Carlo & Carmen

X X X X X X X X X X — Phil.

Thursday November 8, 1945/Wendover Field, Utah

Dear Mary,

Everything out here seems to be going along alright, and I can't complain. It's been a little cold though. In fact yesterday and today were the coldest days yet.

I hope Ma is feeling alright these days. Don't forget to tell me how she makes out at that [cancer] clinic you are supposed to take her to on the 9th of November.

So Victor Antonelli moved upstairs of Ferraro's house. That's alright, I guess. As for me, I won't be having any of my old friends back again. I just won't have time for them.

There's nothing new about discharges as yet. All the guys with 50 points plus two years of service will be leaving any day now as soon as they get their orders. The next step should be to 40 points, but I think it's too good to be true, and somehow or other they'll change some regulation, just before it gets to me.

I'm glad to hear that my wife calls up regularly. Well, I guess that's all I have to say for today so take it easy and God bless you all.

Love To: Ma, Pa, Mary, Tony, Francie, Carlo & Carmen

X X X X X X X X X X — Phil —

Friday November 9, 1945/Wendover Field, Utah

Dear Mary,

. . . Yep, you sure must've had a nice little gathering for Carmen's birthday last Sunday. It sure must've made Ma feel happy.

It's too bad Shadow's car's clutch broke down so that he couldn't take it to Tennessee with him. It's for the best, I guess. If he stood without a car till now, I'm sure he can stay a little while longer till he gets his discharge.

My wife told me that she was down there last Sunday for Carmen's birthday. She said she only got him some socks and handkerchiefs. That's pretty good, don't you think?

You said you were taking Ma to the Hospital on Friday the 9th. That's today, and I sure hope she makes out good. To think we all came through this war alright, except Ma. Well, we can only face the facts and hope for the best.

I'm sorry you didn't receive any mail from me last Friday and Saturday. My wife didn't either, so I guess the mail was delayed someplace along the line. I'm sure though that you received it all by last Monday. Heck, don't ever worry about me when something like that happens. If I can't take care of myself, then nobody can take care of themselves in this world. . . . I'll close for now, and I hope Ma's cold is better. So long for now, and God bless you all.

Love To: Ma, Pa, Mary, Tony, Francie, Carlo, & Carmen
X X X X X X X X X X X — Phil.

Saturday November 10, 1945/Wendover, Utah

Dear Mary,

Today I received a letter from Tony and I was glad to hear from him and that he also received the carton of cigarettes. I'll write to him one of these days whenever possible. I also received a letter from Frankie dated the 31st of October. As far as I can tell he's getting along alright. I'll write him tomorrow, I guess.

Everything out here is going along pretty good and I can't kick. I'm doing a lot of work. It's all brain work, though, so I don't exert my body at all. Just as soon as I hear anything about my discharge, I'll call up my wife and she'll tell you. In other words, I'll let you know, even before you can find out by newspapers or radio.

I hope Ma is feeling better today. Keep her hopes high and don't let her lose faith in nothing. Well, take it easy for now and God bless you all.

Love To: Ma, Pa, Mary, Tony, Francie, & Carlo & Carmen
X X X X X X X X X X — Phil.

Sunday November 11, 1945/Wendover, Utah

Dear Mary,

Just another Sunday going by out here. The weather is cold and damp with half rain and half snow falling. Everything seems to be alright though. Yesterday I forgot a 6 cent airmail stamp in either the letter I wrote to you or the letter I wrote to my wife. I hope you didn't throw [away] yesterday's letter and envelope I sent you. I was supposed to write Frankie a letter today, but I haven't any stamp, so I'll wait till Tuesday when the post office opens. Tomorrow, which is Monday, Armistice Day is being celebrated.

I hope Ma and the rest of you are feeling as well as possible and I hope everything there is going along alright. Tony said that Shadow was there for one day [from his base in Memphis]. He's a hard-headed guy, and I guess the Navy doesn't remedy that. Well take it easy and God bless you all.

Love To: Ma, Pa, Mary, Tony, Francie, Carlo, & Carmen
X X X X X X X X X X X X — Phil —

Monday November 12, 1945/Wendover, Utah

Dear Mary,

. . . I'm glad you are all feeling fine and that Ma's getting along as fine as possible. I think you, Ma, and June worried too much about Shadow trying to take his car to Tennessee. He's no kid and he knows what he's doing. Actually there's more danger in leaving the car running in Buffalo. At every base I've been at there's hundreds of guys with cars from every state. They drive all over with them. I know if I had a car, I'd rather drive home in it than take a train. If Shadow is stubborn at times, he might have his reasons.

Everything out here seems to be going along alright. The weather is cool but it's warming up a little. Well, I guess that's all for now so take it easy and God bless you all.

Love To: Ma, Pa, Mary, Tony, Francie, Carlo, & Carmen
X X X X X X X X X X X X — Phil —

Tuesday November 13, 1945/Wendover, Utah

Dear Mary,

I'm glad [to hear] Ma is getting along as well as possible and I hope she does okay at the Cancer Clinic.

They lowered the points to 45. Also anyone with 42 months of service as of September 2nd can get out of the army. I've got 43 points, so you can see my situation for yourself. I may and I may not be home for Christmas, it all depends upon the method they use. I'll keep you posted as to how things turn out for me.

I'm glad to hear that Tony fixed the car clutch on the Plymouth.

Yep, a lot of guys get discharges and I just can't see how they do it. Well some guys got a lot of guts though, while the guys who go according to the rules get stuck. Oh well in time we'll all get out, so nobody gains anything. Well, I guess that's all for now so take it easy and God bless you all.

Love To: Ma, Pa, Mary, Tony, Francie, Carlo & Carmen
X X X X X X X X X X — Phil —

P.S. Glad to hear that Carmen's having a good time.

Wednesday November 14, 1945/Wendover Field, Utah

Dear Mary,

. . . There's nothing new concerning discharges yet. Any man with 45 points and 2 years of service, or any man with 42 months of service can get out. My only hope is that they will lower the points to 40 with 2 years service. I hope you've got some idea of the system by now. I hope Ma is feeling fine these days and I hope she can continue that way.

I just wrote Frankie a letter, and I told him that we'll see each other for sure inside the next month and a half or two, as civilians. In other words, I haven't seen Frankie as a soldier in this war, and I haven't seen him at all since February 1, 1943 [when Phil was inducted]. That's longer than any of you, right?

. . . I'm glad to hear that Carmen is having a good time for himself. It's only natural I guess. As for Cousin Angelo trying to get a discharge, well, I wish him luck, although I know some of those guys are no sicker than I am. Look at poor Shadow with all his headaches, and yet he don't kick. I guess we are the type of people who never complain even if we are dying. Well, I guess that's all for now so take it easy and God bless you all.

Love To: Ma, Pa, Mary, Tony, Francie, Carlo, & Carmen

X X X X X X X X X X — Phil —

P.S. Another bulletin just came out. Any man who will have 42 months of service by 15th of December can sign up for a discharge right now. Slowly but surely it's getting down to me.

[The next letter is addressed to Phil's brother Tony.]

Wednesday November 14, 1945/Wendover, Utah

Hello Tony,

Just figured I'd drop you a few lines. I'm glad you received the cigarettes I sent you. I've been smoking a pipe for quite a while now, about a month I guess. I doubt if I'll go back to cigarettes. I find a pipe quite a bother, but I'm smoking less and it's more economical. I guess I'll have to be pretty thrifty in the future, cause I've got some big ideas in mind.

I'm glad to hear about the new clutch you had placed in the car. I noticed when I was home last time that it didn't work too good.

I can understand my kid crying when you look at him. You probably are too stern with him. But, he won't be afraid too long, until he'll get used to everybody and starts to recognize them.

Yep, Shadow's a bossy guy. It looks as if the Navy didn't teach him discipline. He's okay though and really means to be sensible at times.

Fig. 2.11. Phil Aquila home on furlough, holding the pipe he mentions in his letter of November 14, 1945. (Philip L. Aquila Collection)

He's only narrow minded and thinks he's right all the time. It's only because he hasn't been near me for 3 years. Well, I guess that's all for now. I hope you are getting along with your job. Love, Phil —

Thursday November 15, 1945/Wendover Field, Utah

Dear Mary,

. . . You told me about Ma taking a stiff examination at the Cancer hospital. I'm glad to hear about that. I didn't know Buffalo had a cancer clinic until you told me. I knew there were a few around the country. I guess we are lucky to have one at home. I'm sure they can help Ma out a great deal more than the regular hospital can. You were talking about [biopsies]. That don't mean anything at all. But I'm glad you didn't sign anything. I sure hope they can do something for Ma. You just tell her not to lose faith in anything. Yes, there are a lot of people with Cancer, and most of them keep living a normal life even though they feel ill at times, so tell Ma that she has a lot to live for and we don't want any more of that silly talk that she hasn't much longer to live.

I was glad to hear that my wife went for a ride to Niagara Falls with Carmen, June, Francie, and his shipmate. That shipmate of his has spent quite a long time there. I don't understand how a guy gets a long leave and doesn't spend it in his own home. Oh well that's his business I guess.

I just sent my wife a clipping about Wendover Field, which I found in the Salt Lake Paper. I'd like you to read it. You see, I haven't said anything about this field, but I knew way back in May or June that as soon as one of these Wendover outfits went across the war would end real quickly. In other words, I'm talking about the Atomic Bomb, and this is the field that trained the men who dropped it on Japan twice. I can't say I did much except keep the field going and help these outfits as much as possible.

In other words, this field is or was the most important in the world, and did the most to win the war. I'm sure if you look in the newspapers there, you may see it mentioned sometime.

Well, so long for now and God bless you all.

Love To: Ma, Pa, Mary, Tony, Francie, Carlo & Carmen
X X X X X X X X — Phil —

Saturday November 17, 1945/Wendover, Utah

Dear Mary,

I put in a grueling day out here and I haven't much of anything to say. I'm feeling fine and all that, and everything is going along so I can't complain.

I hope Ma is feeling good and I hope that [cancer] hospital can do wonders for her.

I wrote a letter to Frankie. He's a good kid. For a while when he hit the Philippines I thought he'd change, but he had his fun and quit. He'll be the same guy when he comes home, so don't worry about him.

Say good-bye to Carmen for me. Next time he comes home he'll find me as a civilian. That won't be too long from now I think. I hope everything out there is going along alright. So-long for now and God bless you all.

Love To: Ma, Pa, Mary, Tony, Francie, Carlo & Carmen
X X X X X X X X X X — Phil.

Sunday November 18, 1945/Wendover, Utah

Dear Mary,

Just another Sunday out here. I don't know how many more Sundays I'll be away, but I think we can count them on maybe just the fingers of one hand or so. . . . I hope Ma is feeling as well as possible and in the best of spirits.

Thursday is Thanksgiving day. As usual we'll have turkey to eat. I hope you have a nice meal out there. Let me know if Carmen left or if they let him stay for Thanksgiving. I haven't spent a Thanksgiving there since 1941. In 1942 I had to go to work in the afternoon and in 1943 I was in the army. 1944 and 1945 is the same. Next year I'll be there for sure.

Well, so-long for now, and God bless you all.

Love To: Ma, Pa, Mary, Tony, Francie, Carlo & Carmen
X X X X X X X X X — Phil —

Monday November 19, 1945/Wendover, Utah

Dear Mary,

Everything out here is going along alright. The weather is cloudy, cool, and rainy and windy. Nothing new going on out here and nothing else has been said about discharges. I just know some darn thing will be said in the regulation whenever they lower the points again and I'll be stuck as usual. I may be lucky to be alive, but I've sure had my unlucky times in the army.

I hope Ma is feeling in good health and fine spirits today, and I hope everything there is going along fine. There's not much for me to say so I guess I'll close for now and God bless you all.

Love To: Ma, Pa, Mary, Tony, Francie, & Carlo
[Carmen's furlough is over, so he doesn't mention him in the closing.]
X X X X X X X X — Phil —

Tuesday November 20, 1945/Wendover, Utah

Dear Mary,

. . . There's still nothing new concerning my discharge and I'm sure getting impatient about it, because it seems that every time I get something, I always get it the hard way. Oh well, I'll just have to wait and see what happens. It wouldn't be so bad if all I had to do was sit and wait, but I keep getting the jobs the other guys had. I'm practically running the jobs 3 or 4 men used to work on. I'm sure getting mighty disgusted because everything was left in a mess [when the other soldiers left].

I hope you are all feeling fine and that goes for Ma. I'm feeling alright out here. Well, so-long for now and God bless you all.

Love To: Ma, Pa, Mary, Tony, Francie & Carlo
X X X X X X X X — Phil —

[The November 20, 1945 letter to his family was the last letter in the collection that was saved by his sister Mary. Fortunately, one last letter has survived. Fittingly, this one was saved by Phil himself, and was addressed to the person for whom he cared most. He wrote this letter to his wife on his baby's first birthday. It contains the announcement that they all had been anxiously waiting for—Phil is finally being discharged from the Army Air Force, and he is returning home:]

Monday, February 4, 1946/Wendover, Utah

(** Happy Birthday to Little Phil. I love you truly **)

My Very Dearest Beloved Wife,

I love you as never before. I'll always love you as long as I live. You are by far the most wonderful and beautiful girl on earth. Please believe me, darling. If I was lying, then, it would be flattery, but I'm telling the truth and therefore it is not flattery. You are sweet and kind and considerate, even if at times you are a little spitfire and won't listen to reason. Darling, I love you and only you. You come first, second, third, etc. with me and that's the way it's always been, believe me.

Now darling . . . I'll give you some good news. Today, I signed up for a *DISCHARGE*. I really had them where I wanted. I was eligible because I'll have three years in, and I was eligible because our dependency discharge was approved. In other words, I am eligible in two ways. Yes, darling, the letters you had notarized were successful. I'm getting a discharge on the Dependency deal. I've got my choice. I picked the Dependency because it has first priority at the Separation Center. Today they reported to me to the Separation Center. I may be here [at Wendover] for 2 or 2½ [more] weeks. You see the Separation Center wires back here, to tell them to send me. Then by the time I clear the field and get my orders, a couple weeks will go by. I still think I'll be [home] by the 20th of February.

Honey, they closed down all Air Corp[s] separation centers so now the Air Force gets their discharges through the ground forces separation centers. I'm scheduled to go to Fort Dix, New Jersey. If they route me with the New York Central Railroad, which I doubt, I'll be able to get off at Buffalo maybe for a day. But, honey, don't count on it, because I'm pretty sure they'll put me on the Pennsylvania Railroad from Chicago to New Jersey. Either way, I'll call you up from Chicago. It should be around the 17th of the month or thereabouts. Also, I'll send you a telegram as soon as I know the date I'm leaving Wendover, okay? So, don't be afraid if the telephone rings and you get a telegram read to you.

Right now I'm sweating out to clear the field. In other words I'm waiting for the Separation Center to wire back here [to Wendover Field] stating they have a vacancy for me at Ft. Dix.

Honey, are you excited by this news? I know I am and I just can't wait to be with you again. When I'm with you I love you with all my heart. When I'm far away like now, I realize the greatness of our love and I miss you more than words can ever explain. Honey, about the dates I gave you, please don't bank on them. For certain I can only say that I'll be home for *sure* by the end of the month. Keep your chin up and remember, I love you truly.

Honey, I received the two swell letters you wrote last Wednesday and thank you very much for them. . . . I know you miss me very much, but just keep your chin up and soon I'll be there <u>for keeps</u> and no more will I ever leave you for <u>anything</u>. You and Little Phil are all I want in this world. I've got me the most perfect little family in the world, and I can't ever stop thanking God for that. . . . I want to tell you over and over again how much you mean to me, but I just can't. I love the way you act, talk, smile, sing, cook, take care of Little Phil, and <u>everything</u>. Please don't doubt me in any way at all. I've always said I'm going to make you the most <u>satisfied</u> woman on earth, and by God I will, just you wait and see. . . .

Honey, I'm enclosing one dollar for Little Phil's bank. I made 68 cents on K.P. yesterday, so I want to send one dollar to you. Yesterday, I also sent 50 cents in Little Phil's valentine. Let me know if you received it alright.

Darling, right now I'm going down to the gym for a workout, okay? You told me I should take in a show. Okay, honey, I'll go either tomorrow or Wednesday. I'll let you know when and what I see. Today, I also worked full blast. It's a mess out here, and I doubt if I can straighten it out. It really takes a genius.

Well, honey, I'll close for now, but I'll be back tomorrow again. Till then, I love you for keeps and give Little Phil my love. God bless you and him always for me.

<u>Your Loving Husband</u>, Phil

P.S. Little Phil is one year old today. Give him a nice big kiss and hug for me, and I owe him a gift. <u>I love you truly! For Keeps!</u>

[Shortly after writing the above letter, Sgt. Philip L. Aquila received his orders to leave Wendover Field for the Separation Center at Fort Dix, New Jersey. On February 22, 1946, he was discharged from the Army Air Force, and returned immediately to his wife and family in Buffalo, New York.]

PART 3

Epilogue: "So Long and God Bless You All"

Approximately one month after Phil Aquila got out of the Army Air Force, he sat down in his favorite chair in his rented home at 526 South Division Street, Buffalo, New York, and he wrote his last commentary about his World War II experience:

Unfailing America

America, we've worked for thee
With sweat upon our brow.
We've died to keep you free
and liberate a world afoul.
From Washington to Roosevelt,
From Tokyo to Berlin,
Tyranny our might has felt
As we rid the world of sin.
Across the greatness of our land
We're shouting loud and strong
For nations all to form a band
To crush forever every wrong.
America, we'll work for thee
With sweat upon our brow.
We'll die again to keep you free
And liberate a world afoul.[1]

Although certainly not a polished poem by professional standards, "Unfailing America" reverberates with historical significance. The poem reflects the patriotic attitude that permeated American society and culture of the postwar period. Americans were convinced that their nation

261

had emerged from World War II as the undisputed leader of the Free World. *Time-Life* publisher Henry Luce captured the nation's sense of mission by predicting that the last half of the twentieth century would be known as "the American Century."[2]

Americans had every reason to feel optimistic about the future. Their nation had defeated the Axis powers in World War II and stood at the pinnacle of its military power. When President Truman remarked one month after the end of the war, "[Our nation possesses] the greatest strength and power which man has ever reached," it was no idle boast. The United States had the world's largest army with 12,000,000 troops. The military benefited from America's leadership in science, technology, and industry. The sole proprietor of atomic weapons, the United States was, indeed, the most powerful nation in the history of the world.[3]

America's military strength was matched by its economic clout. World War II had brought the nation out of the Depression. By 1947, the United States was producing over 50 percent of the world's manufactured goods, including 57 percent of the steel and 80 percent of the cars. The United States also produced 62 percent of the world's oil. American dominance was greatest in fields such as aviation, engineering, and electronics. Two statistics spotlight Americans' enviable economic position: in 1945 the average American consumed 3,500 calories per day, as compared to 1,500 for Europeans; four years later, the income of the average American was fifteen times greater than that of the average foreigner. Following the war, a "liberal consensus" emerged among Americans, according to historian and journalist Godfrey Hodgson, that presupposed American capitalism and democracy were the finest economic and political systems available in the world.[4]

While Phil Aquila and his family shared the general public's optimism and dreams for the future, personal problems soon brought them back to reality. The Aquila family had come through the war intact only to suffer a devastating loss in peacetime. In September 1946—only months after her sons returned from military duty—Ma passed away. Calogera had been in and out of the hospital during 1944 and 1945, suffering from a painful stomach ailment eventually diagnosed as cancer. But always, she had managed to hold on. But once her boys were safely home from the war, her body lost its personal struggle with the deadly disease.

An Italian proverb maintains: "If the father should die, the family would suffer; if the mother should die, the family ceases to exist."[5] Those words proved prophetic for the Aquilas, for they never bounced back completely from the loss of Calogera. She was the glue that had held the family together.

The once close family slowly began drifting apart. Although their father lived until 1965, he remained on the fringes of his children's lives. The oldest son, Joe, got a job at Bethlehem Steel in nearby Lackawanna where he worked for the next thirty years to support his wife, Rae, and their son. Tony moved thirty miles away to Angola with his wife, Marion, and her two children from a previous marriage. He worked at a series of blue-collar jobs and continued to enjoy playing his guitar and arguing with his brother Phil about politics until the day he died in 1986. Sister Mary got married after the war to Nick Pardi, a mailman, and raised two children in Cheektowaga, New York. Shadow, along with his wife, June, and their three sons, moved out to a farm in Alden, New York, where he eventually opened up a gas station. Frankie got a job after the war with Chevrolet, and he and his wife, Evelyn, raised two boys. Frankie died in 1997. Carmen, after getting out of the Navy, also got a job at Chevrolet. He and his wife, Helen, had eight children. Carmen passed away in 1988. Francie married Art Ross and had seven children. She died in 1986. The youngest member of the Aquila family, Carlo, found employment in the grocery and food business. He and his wife, Audrey, raised three children.

Calogera Aquila's death in 1946 undoubtedly had a tremendous impact on all her children, but no one took it harder than Phil. Always devoted to his mother, he had a particularly rough time coping with her passing. "Phil was extremely religious until his mother died," recalls his wife, Mary, "then he didn't believe anymore. He thought God had forsaken them."[6] Throughout the rest of his life, Phil very seldom even mentioned his mother. Apparently the pain was just too great.

True to form, though, Phil tried "to take it on the chin" and keep going. One month after his mother's death, his wife gave birth to Phil's second son, whom they named Richard. Phil transferred his devotion and all his attention and energy to his new family.

After the war family obligations once again prevented him from going to college. By then Phil was determined to get the best-paying job available so that he could take care of his wife and two young sons. Although he could have returned to a promising career as a head machinist at Bell Aircraft, his wife balked because it would have meant moving thirty miles away to Bell's new location in Niagara Falls, New York.

Phil's superb war record, excellent high school grades, and determination to succeed eventually helped him land a position as an apprentice bricklayer at Bethlehem Steel Company in nearby Lackawanna. For the next thirty years, Phil earned an extremely high salary doing a highly skilled job that was both dangerous and physically exhausting. He and his fellow bricklayers formed an elite corps within the steel plant known as the "Hot Dog Gang," because they were the ones who had to go into the fire and heat everyday to reline blast furnaces with brick.

When *The Buffalo Evening News* polled its readers in 1984 for a special issue about the city's "hottest jobs," Phil wrote about his work:

> It made no difference what the climate was outside, we would find ourselves up against 2900 degrees of raw heat. I could use adjectives such as sweltering, seething, scalding, blazing, broiling, and scorching, but getting down to the nitty-gritty, I'd only be putting it mildly. . . . Yes, we had some protective equipment, but the hot winds generated by the infernos we were up against created havoc with it. Big bulky asbestos gloves were useless and dangerous, because they made one's hands feel like they were in an oven of 1000 degrees. The bulky gloves also made it impossible to use the tools needed on jobs. . . .
>
> Heatstroke and exhaustion? I've been there and back. Yes, it did put food on the table, although many were the times when I couldn't grip my fork and spoon to eat with, due to the severe heat cramps still with me in my hands at night, after a hard day's work. During my career I've had literally thousands of burns and blisters. . . .
>
> The plant's safety man constantly told us to go to the dispensary when hurt. Had I followed those instructions, though, I'd have been there almost every day. I generally cared for my own medical needs, unless it was a smashed finger or steel chip in the eye. In that case it was a two-man job, and I needed aid. Every day was like a state of war. Being a veteran of World War II, I think I can say that.
>
> The job was hell, in the pure sense of the word. Being somewhat on the religious side, I sort of humored myself by reflecting on the thought that if I didn't wind up in Heaven, I'd be already trained to go the other way.[7]

Despite the dangers, Phil never quit. One of his World War II letters offers a clue as to why Phil remained at Bethlehem Steel for thirty years: "I never quit any job . . . just because I don't like it."[8] His background reinforced his determination to stick it out at Bethlehem. Growing up in an extremely poor immigrant family during the Great Depression taught Phil family responsibility and caused him to value whatever work he had. He often quoted the Aesop's fable about the dog and his meat bone:

> A dog was crossing a plank bridge over a stream with a piece of meat in his mouth, when he happened to see his own reflection in the water. He thought it was another dog with a piece of meat twice as big; so he let go his own, and flew at the other dog to get the large piece. But, of course, all that happened was that he got neither: for one was only a shadow, and the other was carried away by the current.[9]

No matter how bad Phil's job was, he did not want to risk losing the good salary he earned at Bethlehem. "I had a family to support," he explained, and the Hot Dog Gang "was one of the steadiest and highest-paying jobs around. I kept hoping I'd get something better, but the years went by. It was like spending thirty years before the mast."[10]

By the mid-1950s, Phil Aquila was earning as much some lawyers and judges. The money allowed him to buy all the things that he had always dreamed of for his wife and children: new houses, new cars, toys for the kids, good clothes for everyone. Most important, the high salary guaranteed his wife and kids the security and opportunities he never had. After 1960, Mary contributed to the family income by becoming one of Buffalo's most successful dress store managers and buyers. As their economic success grew, the couple thought often about how far they had come since their days picking beans on the farms in North Collins.

Though Phil was never able to go to college, he instilled in his sons the importance of an education. From the time they were in elementary school, he drummed into their heads the belief that they were going to college when they grew up. "I never ever want to see you boys working at the steel plant," he would say in a way that was more a threat than advice. He was proud when both sons went off to college in the late 1960s.

Phil Aquila retired as a bricklayer from Bethlehem Steel in 1977 and spent the last seventeen years of his life keeping up with history and geography, tinkering with inventions and home improvements, arguing about politics, and writing essays and letters to the editors of Buffalo's two newspapers. He was particularly proud of an op-ed piece that *The Courier-Express* published in 1982. Searching for a way that could help his hometown reverse its rust-belt image and inspired by Buffalo's "Big Blizzard of '77," Phil wrote a humorous essay suggesting that the city should put to good use its negative image as the nation's snow capital. "The core of my concept," he explained, "would be a structure both in size and scope of the Statue of Liberty, only made to resemble a snowman, and billed as the world's largest snowman." Like the St. Louis arch or Toronto's CN Tower, this structure, along with its accompanying businesses and winter sports facilities, would attract thousands of tourists, pumping new life into Buffalo's economy. "Buffalo's skyline would [become] unique and identifiable world-wide."[11]

Phil Aquila's interest in politics and history was eclipsed only by his love for his family. Not surprisingly one of the things he enjoyed most in his remaining years was playing with and talking to his two grand-children, Stephen (born in 1980) and Valerie (1982). His close relationship to his grandchildren is evident in the following essay, which he submitted to *Reader's Digest*:

One Sunday afternoon while our family was relaxing in the parlor of my son's house, I suggested to Stephen, our two-year-old grandson, that he should imitate his dad and make believe he was going to work.

Barely able to carry his father's brief case with two hands, he sadly kissed everybody goodbye, and slowly hid behind the couch. Stephen was determined to put in a good day's work, because no amount of coaxing could persuade him to leave his hiding place and create a "return-home" scene.

Moments later, a transit bus happened to go past the house. A tricky grandfatherly thought entered my mind, and I instantly shouted, "I hear a bus. I think it's stopping. I don't believe it! That's Stephen getting off the bus. He's back from work!"

In a flash Stephen darted from behind the couch to look through the window to see if he was really returning from work.[12]

* * * *

On March 25, 1994, Phil and Mary Aquila celebrated their 50th wedding anniversary. Later that December just before going to bed, Phil died—with Mary at his side.

* * * *

Phil Aquila was in his early twenties when he wrote his letters to his family during World War II. The correspondence reveals a bright, caring, determined, and ambitious young man who would not quit until the task at hand was completed. The letters also show a wife and family who stood by him providing encouragement and support. Phil Aquila and his loved ones personify millions of GIs and their families during World War II. The Aquilas' story is the story of America at war during the 1940s.

In 1945, Phil wrote a very personal message to his newborn son, Philip L. Aquila Jr. The letter offers insights into Phil's personality, basic values, and close family ties. But in a larger sense, it also demonstrates what Americans were fighting for in World War II. Like their forefathers, they dreamed of life, liberty, and the pursuit of happiness for themselves and their families. As Phil addressed his little son, he was also writing for posterity:

Sunday, April 22, 1945/Wendover, Utah
My Darling Little Son,
I'm writing you the first letter you've received so far in your life. I did write you one before when you were about 22, but I tore it up because I thought [your] Mama would laugh at me. But now you are 77 and I've picked up enough courage to write to you. Of course, when I say you are 77, I mean 77 days old.

Fig. 3.1. Picture of a proud dad and his son taken in March 1946, shortly after Phil was discharged from the army. (Philip L. Aquila Collection)

Beyond any doubt in my mind, you are by far the best little baby I've ever seen. You are intelligent, beautiful, and have one of the finest physiques I ever saw for a baby. If you don't grow up to be a real man, then I'll be very disappointed. Everything I have is at your disposal, if you make wise use of them. Indeed you are a very lucky baby in having the most wonderful, sweetest and most understanding mother on Earth. As for me, right now I have to be away from you, but my thoughts are always with Mama and you, and they'll always stay that way. No doubt before you learn to read, I shall be there to stay, never to leave again.

I hardly know you right now, but from the little I've seen of you, you've carved a section of my heart for yourself. I know when we meet again, we'll take to each other in a very natural way. You will be the best son any father ever had and I shall be proud of you. And you can be very sure that I'll try with all the power I possess to be the grandest Dad any boy ever had.

I know you are too small as yet, but from the day you can understand, I want you to defend your mother whether right or wrong from all hardships and evil, with your very life if necessary.

So-long my son and God bless you and keep you well and safe always for Mama and me.

Always, your loving Dad,
Philip L. Aquila, Senior

P.S. Let Mama give you the one dollar that I sent . . . as soon as you can read this.

* * * *

In the last paragraph of the letter to his baby, Phil says "So-long my son and God bless you. . . ." That phrase was a variation on the closing that he used in almost every letter that he wrote to his wife and family during the war. The expression functions on several levels: it expresses Phil's deep love for his family; it affirms his faith in God and the future; and it shows that he understood the power of repetition. He jotted down and mailed off those words each day like a literary talisman designed to protect those he loved. Today, over fifty years later, the carefully chosen words still retain their power and meaning. The expression is, therefore, an appropriate ending for this book. Phil Aquila is telling his family one last time: "So long and God bless you all."

NOTES

PART 1. INTRODUCTION

1. Interview with Mary (Aquila) Pardi, September 14, 1995.

2. Sgt. Philip L. Aquila to his sister Mary, November 3, 1944.

3. Sgt. Philip L. Aquila to his sister Mary, November 9, 1944.

4. Phil Aquila kept many of his homework assignments from grammar school through high school. After his death, I went through his box of papers and found samples of letter writing that followed the same form as the letters he wrote while in the Army Air Force.

5. Sgt. Philip L. Aquila to his sister Mary, October 7, 1944; October 10, 1944.

6. Lee Kennett, *GI: The American Soldier in World War II* (New York: Scribner's Sons, 1987), 73.

7. Ibid., 75.

8. Ibid., 76.

9. The significance of the Italian family is discussed in Virginia Yans-McLaughlin, *Family and Community: Italian Immigrants in Buffalo, 1880–1930* (Ithaca, N.Y.: Cornell University Press, 1977), 61, 109–11, 177–78, and Jere Mangione and Ben Morreale, *La Storia: Five Centuries of the Italian American Experience* (New York: HarperCollins, 1992), 232–37. See also P. Balancio and D. Fusaro, "The Italian American Clan," in *American Italian Historical Association* 13, Annual Conference, 1980; Donna Gabaccia, *From Sicily to Elizabeth Street* (Albany, N.Y.: State University of New York Press, 1984).

10. For examples, see the following letters of Sgt. Philip L. Aquila to his sister Mary: September 26, 1945; September 19, 1945.

11. For information about "family honor," see Virginia Yans-McLaughlin, *Family and Community*, 61, 83; for additional information, see Leonard Covello, "The Social Background of the Italo-American School Child: A Study of the Southern Italian Family Mores and Their Effect on the School Situation in Italy and America" (Ph.D. Dissertation, New York University, 1944), 242–43, and Leonard W. Moss and Walter H. Thomson, "The South Italian Family: Literature and Observation," *Human Organization* 18 (Spring 1959). Sgt. Aquila's letters about the money owed by the farmer are dated September 24, 1944, and September 25, 1944. Aquila's letter about the person threatening him and his wife was written shortly after he received the police officer's letter of September 6, 1944.

12. Jere Mangione and Ben Morreale, *La Storia*, 233; Constance Cronin, *The Sting of Change* (Chicago: University of Chicago Press, 1970). Additional

information about the role of women in Italian American families can be found in Gabaccia, *From Sicily to Elizabeth Street*, and Andrew Rolle, *The American Italians: Their History and Culture* (Belmont, Calif.: Wadsworth, 1972).

13. A generation ago, scholars led by Oscar Handlin argued that "uprooted" immigrant families became disorganized as a result of their abrupt move from folk to urban societies. See Handlin's *The Uprooted* (Boston: Little, Brown, 1951). Later experts argued that cultural continuity occurred, helping immigrants deal with the problems they encountered in America. See Rudolph Vecoli, "Contadini in Chicago: A Critique of *The Uprooted*," *Journal of American History* 51 (1964): 404–17. Still others, such as Talcott Parsons, theorized that new "functional" family forms emerged that allowed Italian American immigrants to cope with America's industrial economy. See his "Kinship System of the Contemporary United States," *American Anthropologist* 45 (1943): 22–38. Historian Virginia Yans-McLaughlin rejects all three approaches, because they fail to take into account social change: "In order to understand fully the family changes among the Italians in Buffalo or any other group, past traditions, historical context, and particular situations . . . all require examination." See Yans-McLaughlin, *Family and Community*, 18–20. Sgt. Aquila's letters support Yans-McLaughlin's thesis by providing detailed evidence of how one Italian American family responded to the social and cultural crises related to the Great Depression and World War II.

14. *Paesani* originally referred to people who came from the same village in Italy, but later in America the term was often extended to include people from the same province, or, in some cases, even someone from Italy in general. *Compari* were children's godparents, chosen at the time of baptism. Sometimes they were relatives, other times close friends of the family.

15. I would like to thank one of the anonymous readers from the State University of New York Press for calling this to my attention.

16. Letter from Sgt. Philip L. Aquila to brother Tony, May 14, 1945; letter from Sgt. Philip L. Aquila to sister Mary, January 18, 1945.

17. Sgt. Philip L. Aquila to his sister Mary, March 30, 1945.

18. Kennett, *GI*, 26, 98.

19. Sgt. Philip L. Aquila to his sister Mary, November 12, 1945.

20. Sgt. Philip L. Aquila to his sister Mary, August 19, 1945; September 11, 1945.

21. Information about the Aquila family has come from a variety of sources, primarily from stories my father, Phil, told me and my brother as we were growing up. This information was then checked for accuracy against similar stories told by his brothers and sisters, particularly recent interviews I conducted with Mary and Frank. Whenever possible I used information from passports, naturalization papers, and other official documents.

22. Proverb quoted in Virginia Yans-McLaughlin, *Family and Community*, 82.

23. Jere Mangione and Ben Morreale, *La Storia*, 103. For a more detailed account of the trip across the ocean, see Michael La Sorte, *La Merica: Images of Italian Greenhorn Experiences* (Philadelphia: Temple University Press, 1985), 18–27.

24. Mangione and Morreale, *La Storia*, 104–25.

25. Mangione and Morreale, *La Storia*, 111, 115. See also La Sorte, *La Merica*, 42; Barbara Benton, *Ellis Island: A Pictorial History* (New York: Facts on File, 1985); and Willard A. Heaps, *The Story of Ellis Island* (New York: Seabury Press, 1967).

26. Yans-McLaughlin, *Family and Community*, 96.

27. I first came across the song in Mangione and Morreale's *La Storia*, 267. When I asked my parents about it, they smiled as they recalled the lyrics. My mother said her father used to sing it to her when she was just a child, and as he was singing he would pretend that he was pushing a broom. My father, who lived a few blocks away, remembered that the song was very popular in his Italian neighborhood when he was a boy.

28. The immigrant quoted was Thomas Angelico. His comments about how difficult it was to find work in Buffalo can be found in Virginia Yans-McLaughlin, *Family and Community*, 40.

29. Ibid., 85, 105, 106.

30. Ibid., 161–62.

31. Information about life on the farms comes primarily from an interview with Mary (Cavarella) Aquila, the wife of Phil Aquila, on November 28, 1995. Additional information came from an interview with Frank Aquila on December 27, 1995.

32. Interview with Mary (Cavarella) Aquila, November 28, 1995.

33. Ibid.

34. Ibid. My commentary appears throughout in italic and within square brackets.

35. Interview with Mrs. Mary (Aquila) Pardi, September 14, 1995.

36. I can remember my father, Phil Aquila, telling the story about the grapes and how he got lost. When I was going through his school papers after his death, I came upon this essay, "How I Was Lost," which he wrote for a sophomore English class at Buffalo's Technical High School, September 1937.

37. Interview with Frank(ie) Aquila, December 27, 1995.

38. Welcome Hall, *Annual Report*, 1916, p. 19, quoted in Yans-McLaughlin, *Family and Community*, 158.

39. Yans-McLaughlin, *Family and Community*, 158; for additional information about Italian attitudes toward charity, crime, and employment, see Gabaccia, *From Sicily to Elizabeth Street*; Mangione and Morreale, *La Storia*; and Luciano Iorizzo and Salvatore Mondello, *The Italian Americans* (New York: Twayne, 1971).

40. Detailed information about the Aquilas' farm earnings can be found in Sgt. Philip L. Aquila's letter to his sister Mary, September 24, 1944. Estimates of Francesco's income are based on statistics found in Yans-McLaughlin, *Family and Community*, 162.

41. Yans-McLaughlin, *Family and Community*, 26, 27, 28, 30.

42. U.S. Congress. Senate, 61st Congress, 2nd session. *Reports of the Immigration Commission, Recent Immigrants in Agriculture*, II, Washington, D.C., 1911, p. 491.

43. Sgt. Philip L. Aquila to his sister Mary, May 4, 1945.

44. Mangione and Morreale, *La Storia*, 32; Yans-McLaughlin, *Family and Community*, 186.

45. Interview with Mary (Cavarella) Aquila and Frank Aquila, December 27, 1995.

46. Kennett, *GI*, 11, 12.

47. Induction notice, quoted in Ralph G. Martin, *The GI War, 1941–45* (Boston: Little, Brown, 1967), 2.

48. Kennett, *GI*, 34–35.

49. William L. O'Neill, *A Democracy at War: America's Fight at Home and Abroad in World War II* (Cambridge, Mass.: Harvard University Press, 1993), 321; Kennett, *GI*, 35, 38.

50. William Graebner, *Coming of Age in Buffalo: Youth and Authority in the Postwar Era* (Philadelphia: Temple University Press, 1990), 103.

51. Philip L. Aquila, "What I Am Going To Be," report written for his high school English class, November 7, 1938.

52. Interview with Frank Aquila, December 27, 1995.

53. Letter from Corporal Philip Aquila at McChord Field, Washington, to his brother, Carlo, June 14, 1943.

54. Sgt. Philip L. Aquila to his sister Mary, April 18, 1945.

55. Sgt. Philip L. Aquila to his sister Mary, April 8, 1945.

56. Philip L. Aquila, "Letter to the Editor," published in *The Buffalo Evening News*, 1940.

57. A. Pappalardo, editorial in *Il Corriere Italiano*, Buffalo, New York, November 9, 1907.

58. Yans-McLaughlin, *Family and Community*, 85.

59. Letter written by Philip Aquila as a school assignment, November 17, 1938.

60. Information about Phil Aquila's earnings comes from check stubs that were found in his private papers after his death. Other information comes from interviews conducted with Mary (Cavarella) Aquila and Frank(ie) Aquila on December 27, 1995.

61. Yans-McLaughlin, *Family and Community*, 47.

62. Interview with Mary (Cavarella) Aquila, November 28, 1995.

63. Henry Wadsworth Longfellow, poem published in *The Buffalo Evening News*, 1942.

64. Kennett, *GI*, 36.

65. Information was obtained from Sgt. Philip L. Aquila's separation papers, February 22, 1946.

66. Lecture notes hand-written in 1943 by Pvt. Philip L. Aquila found in his copy of *The Basic Field Manual, Soldier's Handbook* (Washington, D.C.: U.S. Government Printing Office, 1941).

67. This story was told to me numerous times by my father as I was growing up. Recently, my mother, Mary (Cavarella) Aquila, corroborated it in an interview, November 28, 1995.

68. Letter of Recommendation on behalf of Sgt. Philip L. Aquila for Air Cadet Training, written by William C. Magnuson, 2nd Lt. C.E., July 9, 1943.

69. Letter from Frankie Aquila to Phil Aquila, August 26, 1943.

70. Letter from Frankie Aquila to Phil Aquila, September 1, 1943.

71. Grades are from official transcripts obtained in 1995 from the National Personnel Records Center (Military Personnel Records), 9700 Page Avenue, St. Louis, Missouri. The original diploma was obtained from Mary (Cavarella) Aquila in December, 1995.

72. Letter from P.F.C. Frankie Aquila to Sgt. Philip Aquila, September 11, 1943.

73. My father told me and my brother this story on numerous occasions. The last time he mentioned it was when we were having a discussion about his military record on December 26, 1993.

74. Yans-McLaughlin, *Family and Community*, 43, 112–14, 116; Mangione and Morreale, *La Storia*, 341–42; For firsthand accounts of discrimination against Italian Americans, see Wayne Moquin, ed., *A Documentary History of the Italian Americans* (New York: Praeger, 1974).

75. Interview with Philip L. Aquila, December 26, 1993.

76. Job description found in "Separation Papers," February 22, 1946.

77. Interview with Mary (Cavarella) Aquila, November 28, 1995.

78. Ibid.

79. Ibid.

80. In Phil Aquila's papers, I found three scoresheets that had been filled out by officers at Pratt Air Base. They gave him extremely high marks in each of the categories on the form: leadership qualities, education, general characteristics, dependability, devotion to duty, initiative, military knowledge, and personal conduct.

81. Leonard J. Arrington and Thomas G. Alexander, "World's Largest Military Reserve: Wendover Air Force Base, 1941–63." *Utah Historical Quarterly* 31 (Fall 1963): 324.

82. Ibid., 329.

83. Ibid., 329.

84. Sgt. Phil Aquila to his sister Mary, March 9, 1945.

85. Sgt. Philip Aquila to his sister Mary, November 15, 1945.

86. President Harry Truman, the White House, 1946.

87. Phil Aquila's comments about a George Will column, "Enola Gay to Take Honored Place at New Museum," in *Buffalo News*, 1994.

PART 3. EPILOGUE

1. Philip L. Aquila, "Unfailing America," March 27, 1946.

2. Henry Luce's comments are noted in Douglas T. Miller and Marion Nowak, *The Fifties: The Way We Really Were* (Garden City, N.Y.: Doubleday, 1975), 398, n. 1.

3. President Truman quoted in Godfrey Hodgson, *America in Our Time: From World War II to Nixon, What Happened and Why* (New York: Vintage Books, 1976), 18, 19.

4. Hodgson, *America in Our Time*, 18, 19. The "ideology of the Liberal Consensus" is explained on pages 67–98.

5. Leonard W. Moss and Walter H. Thomson, "The South Italian Family: Literature and Observation," *Human Organization* 18 (Spring 1959): 38.

6. Interview with Mrs. Mary (Cavarella) Aquila, November 28, 1995.

7. Philip L. Aquila, unpublished essay entitled "Hot Job." Submitted to *The Buffalo Evening News*, July 31, 1984.

8. Letter from Sgt. Philip Aquila to his sister, April 8, 1945.

9. "The Dog and the Shadow," in *Aesop's Fables: A New Translation*, by V. S. Vernon Jones, with an introduction by G. K. Chesterton and illustrations by Arthur Rackham (New York: Gramercy Books), 75.

10. Philip L. Aquila, unpublished essay entitled "Hot Job." Submitted to *The Buffalo Evening News*, July 31, 1984.

11. Philip L. Aquila, "Really Putting Buffalo on the Map," *Buffalo Courier-Express*, January 8, 1982, p. A-7.

12. Philip L. Aquila, unpublished essay. Submitted to *Reader's Digest*, December 11, 1986.

INDEX